M000018472

Plan of Chicago

One thousand six hundred and fifty copies of this edition were print-ed in June, nineteen hundred and nine, of which this is numbered

984

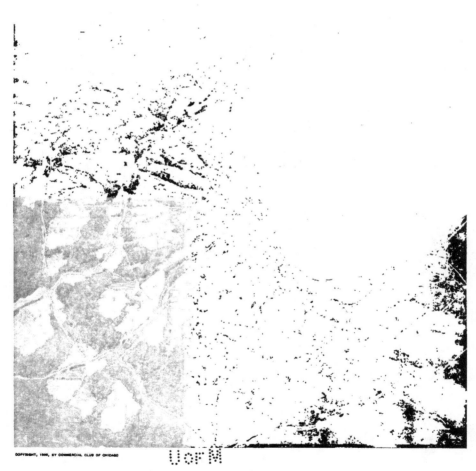

COPYRIGHT, 1909, BY COMMERCIAL CLUB OF CHICAGO

I. CHICAGO. BIRD'S-EYE VIEW, SHOWING THE LOCATION OF THE CITY ON THE SHORES OF LAKE MICHIGAN, TOGETHER
WITH THE SMALLER SURROUNDING TOWNS CONNECTED WITH CHICAGO BY RADIATING ARTERIES.
Painted for the Commercial Club by Jules Guerin.

PLAN OF
CHICAGO

PREPARED UNDER THE DIRECTION OF

THE COMMERCIAL CLUB

DURING THE YEARS MCMVI, MCMVII, AND MCMVIII

BY

DANIEL H. BURNHAM

AND

EDWARD H. BENNETT

ARCHITECTS

EDITED BY

CHARLES MOORE

CORRESPONDING MEMBER AMERICAN INSTITUTE OF ARCHITECTS

CHICAGO
THE COMMERCIAL CLUB
MCMIX

Architectural
Library

NA
9127
.C4
C734
C.2

Copyright, 1908
BY
COMMERCIAL CLUB OF CHICAGO

CONTENTS

CHAPTER I

ORIGIN OF THE PLAN OF CHICAGO

The tendency towards city life 1
Problems of the great city 1
Necessity for city-planning 2
Economy and efficiency promoted by a city-plan 2
Elements of a comprehensive plan 4
Influence of the World's Columbian Exposition on city-planning in the United States . . . 4
The success of the Exposition due to competent direction and loyalty to Chicago 4
Improvement of the Lake front proposed by the South Park Commissioners 6
Expansion of the South Parks system 7
The Commercial Club undertakes a plan of Chicago 7
Progress of the work 7
Scope of the undertaking 8
An ideal arrangement proposed 8
The Spirit of Chicago 8

CHAPTER II

CITY PLANNING IN ANCIENT AND MODERN TIMES

Commerce, the leading motive in the building of cities 9
Semiramis, the first city-builder 10
The building of Babylon 10
The pyramids and temples of Egypt 10
The work of Pericles at Athens 11
The development of Rome 12
City-building during the Middle Ages 13
Rise of the city during the Renaissance 13
Origin and growth of Paris 14
Paris built according to a definite plan 14
Louis XIV. and his city-builders 15
Napoleon Bonaparte begins the transformation of Paris 15
Haussmann completes the transformation of Paris 17
City-planning in Europe since 1872 19
The influence of European peace on city-building 19
City-planning in Germany 20
The creation of new thoroughfares in London 21
Town-planning in England 22
The L'Enfant plan of Washington 23
The United States Senate Park Commission plan for Washington 25

vii

The Cleveland group-plan . . . . , ... 27
The Boston park system 27
City-planning in Baltimore, St. Louis and San Francisco 28
Plans for Manila, and for a summer-capital at Baguio 28
Improvements in various American cities 28

CHAPTER III

CHICAGO, THE METROPOLIS OF THE MIDDLE WEST

The Old North-West Territory 31
Reasons for expecting continuous growth in the Middle West 31
Increase in the population of Chicago 32
Recovery after the great fire of 1871 32
Chicago's population fifty years hence 33
Attractions of city life 33
The suburbs of Chicago 34
Real-estate speculation subversive of good planning 35
The development of the suburb 36
Dependence of the suburb on the municipality 37
Highways along Lake Michigan 38
A system of highways for the territory within sixty miles of Chicago 39
Suburban transit facilities 39
The advantages of good roads 39
Four sets of encircling highways proposed 40
Highways parallel to railroads 41
Suburban travel needs more comfortable conditions 41
The influence of the electric-railway and the automobile on suburban life 42

CHAPTER IV

THE CHICAGO PARK SYSTEM

The motto of Chicago 43
Beginnings of the Chicago Park system 43
The Chicago boulevards 44
Park legislation 44
The small parks of Chicago 44
A metropolitan park system proposed 44
The Special Park Commission 44
London's larger parks 48
The pleasures of Henley 48
The great parks of Paris and Vienna 49
Boston park reservations 49
The park system of the District of Columbia 49
The possibility of a comprehensive park system for Chicago 49
Treatment of the Chicago Lake front 50
A system of lagoons and lake parkways proposed 50
The acquisition and improvements of forest spaces . . . . 53·
Physical characteristics of the country surrounding Chicago 55
An encircling system of forest parks 57

CHAPTER V
TRANSPORTATION

Chicago the creation of its railroads 61
Present problems in transportation 61
Congestion of railway traffic in 1906–07 62
The necessity for improved terminals 63
A freight center proposed for Chicago 63
Advantages of such an arrangement 63
Railroad and water traffic compared 64
A loop-system for handling freight traffic 66
Harbor freight and passenger connections 68
The location of passenger stations on Twelfth and Canal streets . . . 70
Terminal stations 70
The traction systems 73
Comfort an object in passenger transportation 74
A perfect passenger and freight handling machine 76
The handling of the mails 76
The suburban station 78
The necessity for, and advantages of, harmonious action among the Chicago railroads . . . 78

CHAPTER VI
STREETS WITHIN THE CITY

The dominant natural features of Chicago 79
The need of new and enlarged channels of circulation 80
Causes of the growth of cities 81
Cleanliness the first consideration for city streets 82
Residence streets 83
The Avenue, or traffic-street 84
The Boulevard 84
Street architecture 86
Traffic interruptions 88
The elliptical avenue 90
The planning of new subdivisions 91
The necessity for diagonal streets 93
Proposed new circuits 95
Improvement of the Chicago River 97

CHAPTER VII
THE HEART OF CHICAGO

Opportunity for creating a unified and convenient city 99
The problem of overcoming congestion in the business-center . . . 100
Solution of the problem simple and natural 100
Michigan Avenue: its importance in the city plan 100
The proposed improvement of Michigan Avenue 100
An elevated roadway 102
Bridges over the river 103
Improvement of Halsted Street 105
Slums of Chicago 106
The slum represents the failure of the city to protect its people . . . 106

CONTENTS

The Financial Quarter 107
Grant Park as a spacious and attractive public garden 108
Location of the Field Museum, the Crerar Library and the Art Institute 108
A Center of Letters 108
A yacht harbor 109
Art as a source of wealth 110
Public gifts by citizens 110
The opportunity offered for effective treatment of Chicago River banks 110
The need of a main axis for Chicago 113
Such an axis would give organic unity to the city 113
Congress Street as the grand axis 113
A Civic Center 115
Buildings to be comprised in the civic center 115
Architectural treatment of the proposed buildings 116
The landscape setting 116
Effectiveness depends on harmony and good order 117
The civic center gives coherence to the city plan 117
Great advantages which will result from the treatment proposed 118

CHAPTER VIII
PLAN OF CHICAGO

The Plan a result of systematic study 119
The cost involved in carrying out the work 119
Wealth created by the growth of population 119
The people are financially able to realize the Plan 120
Three great public works undertaken by Chicago 120
The public spirit of Chicago as shown in music, art and education 120
Gifts for the public good 121
Reasons for believing that the public will favor the Plan of Chicago 121
The Plan both practical and beautiful 121
The advantages to be derived from systematic development of Chicago 121
Elements of the Plan reviewed 121
Improvement of the Lake front an economic necessity 122
Ease of realizing the inter-urban highway system 122
The transportation problem to be worked out by the railroads 122
Additional parks necessary to the physical and mental well-being of the people 123
The attractive city a source of both wealth and satisfaction 124

APPENDIX
LEGAL ASPECTS OF THE PLAN OF CHICAGO

Introductory 127
Outer parks, boulevards, and circuits 130
City parks, squares, boulevards, and avenues 133
Lake shore development 137
Transportation problems 139
Control of lands adjacent to public improvements 139
Congested areas 151
Present borrowing and taxing powers 151
Conclusions 154

INDEX 157

LIST OF ILLUSTRATIONS

PAGE

Bird's-eye view, showing the location of Chicago on the shores of Lake Michigan, together with the surrounding towns connected with the city by radiating arteries . . . . *Frontispiece*

Wood-cut of Chicago in 1834 1

The World's Columbian Exposition, Chicago, 1893 2

    The Court of Honor, showing effect of a uniform cornice line . 3

    Plan showing orderly arrangement of buildings . . . 5

The Lake Front Park, original plan, 1896 6

    Modified plan, 1904 7

The World's Columbian Exposition; view of the Court of Honor, looking west 8

The Pyramids at Gizeh 9

The Acropolis at Athens 10

The Greek Theatre at Syracuse, Sicily 10

Plan showing Nero's Circus at Rome (First Century), Basilica of St. Peter (Fourth Century), and the present Cathedral of St. Peter (Sixteenth Century) 11

An ancient Roman circus, near the Appian Way 12

The Ponte Molle, Rome 12

Transformation of the banks of the Seine in Paris 14

Chronological views of the Place de la Bastile, Paris 15

The transformation of Paris under Haussmann: plan showing the portion executed from 1854 to 1889 . 16

Paris. Plan proposed by M. Eugene Hénard for additional radial arteries and an inner circuit boulevard on which would front the principal existing administrative buildings and many public monuments . . 17

Vienna. City center, in 1857, showing the fortifications 19

    City center, after transformations made by order of Francis Joseph in 1857 . . . 19

London. Plan of Aldwych and Kingsway connecting Holborn and the Strand . . . 20

London Traffic Commission's plan for new thoroughfares to overcome congestion, 1907 . . . 20

Original plan of Washington designed by Peter Charles L'Enfant, 1791 22

The L'Enfant plan of Washington as developed by the Senate Park Commission of 1901 . . . 23

The Washington Monument, garden, and Mall, looking towards the Capitol; Senate Park Commission plan 24

The Plaza and Union Station, Washington, begun in 1902 24

Cleveland. Group-Plan 25

    View from the civic center to the Lake 25

Plan for the development of the entire city of San Francisco 26

Bird's-eye view of the plan of development for San Francisco 26

Plans for the development of Manila, submitted to the Philippine Commission by D. H. Burnham, 1905 . 27

Plan for a summer capital of the Philippine Islands, at Baguio 28

Florence, Italy. Silhouette of towers 30

Chicago. Diagram of location with regard to the seven central States 31

Chicago, and diagram of Lake Michigan 33

Nancy, France. View of the Place Stanislas 35

Forest of Fontainebleau, France 36

Chicago. The Sheridan Road north of Glencoe 37

    The Des Plaines River; view near Madison Street bridge . . . 40

    General diagram of exterior highways encircling, or radiating from, the city . . . 40

    The shore of Lake Michigan; view at the north line of Cook County . . . 41

View of Lake Zurich, Illinois 42

xi

Chicago.   Winter view of Grant Park and the proposed harbor, looking east   43
           General map showing topography, waterways, and complete system of streets, boulevards, park-
             ways, and parks   44
Berlin.   Block plan showing the park system and proposed forest reserves   45
Vienna.   Block plan showing the park system and existing forest reserves   46
District of Columbia.   Block plan showing the park system and additions   47
London.   A view of Rotten Row in Hyde Park   48
Chicago.   View of the city from Jackson Park to Grant Park, looking towards the west .   .   .   48
           Park development proposed for the Lake shore from Jackson Park to Wilmette   .   .   48
           View of the proposed park on the south shore, looking northwest towards the city   .   .   48
           View looking south over the lagoons of the proposed park for the south shore .   .   .   48
           Section through the park proposed for the south shore   48
           The Midway Plaisance, showing the proposed waterway connecting the lagoons of Washington
             Park with those of Jackson Park   51
           Typical view across the proposed south shore park   52
England.   Henley-on-Thames: the regatta course   53
           Henley-on-Thames: a regatta   53
Versailles, France.   Plan of the palace, park, and gardens, and the great arteries leading to the gates .   .   54
                      View from the terrace, looking down the main axis   55
Paris.   View of the Sunken Garden in the Luxembourg Gardens   55
St. Germain, France.   View of an avenue in the forest and round-point   55
Chicago.   Plan of a park proposed on the main east-and-west axis of the city at Congress Street and Fifty-
             second Avenue   56
           Plan of a park proposed at Western Boulevard and Garfield Boulevard, being an extension of
             Gage Park   57
           Plan of a park proposed at the north branch of the Chicago River and Graceland Avenue   .   57
           Plan of Sherman playground and park   58
           Mark White Square   59
           Hamilton Park   59
           Sherman Park; view of field house   60
           Sherman Park; view of swimming pool   60
           Diagram of a system of freight handling for land and water transportation   .   .   .   61
           Assembling-interchange; diagrams accompanying the report of the committee   .   .   .   63
           Sketch diagram of docks suggested at the mouth of the Chicago River   64
           Sketch diagram of docks suggested at the mouth of the Calumet River   65
           Diagram of the city and surrounding country, showing railroad circuits   67
           Diagram of the city center, showing the general location of existing freight yards and railroad
             lines, the present tunnel system and proposed circuit, and connections for all these services,
             running to the central clearing yards   69
           Diagram of the city, showing complete system of inner circuits   70
Dresden.   Viaduct and railway station (Hauptbahn-hof) passing above the normal street level .   .   71
Vienna.   A railway viaduct passing over an important street   71
Chicago.   Suggested arrangement of passenger stations west of the river. Subway scheme   .   .   72
           Suggested arrangement of passenger stations west of the river. Overhead scheme   .   .   73
           Diagram of city center, showing the proposed arrangement of railroad passenger stations, the
             complete traction system, including rapid transit, subway, and elevated roads, and the circuit
             subway line   75
           Railroad rights-of-way and properties in the center of city and the existing radial arteries .   .   76
           Diagram of general scheme of street circulation and parks in relation to the areas covered by indus-
             tries and manufactures   77
Viaduct at Auteuil over the River Seine, Paris, France   78

Chicago. The center of the city looking west, showing Grant Park, the harbor, and the civic center . 79

Plan of a complete system of street circulation and system of parks and playgrounds . . 80

Plan of the street and boulevard system present and proposed 80

View looking west over the city, showing the proposed civic center, the grand axis, Grant Park, and the harbor 80

Map showing the successive city limits 81

Diagram of general scheme of street circulation and parks in relation to the population . . 82

Theoretical diagram of street circulation 83

Existing and proposed diagonal arteries 85

Paris. The Avenue du Bois de Boulogne, looking towards the Arc de Triomphe . . . 86

The Tuileries Gardens and Champs Élyseés 86

The Champs Élyseés, from the Place de la Concorde 87

View from the Arc de Triomphe along the Avenue du Bois de Boulogne . . . 87

System of traffic circulation proposed by M. Hénard for public places . . . 89

Theoretical diagram of the streets of Paris 90

Theoretical diagram of the streets of Moscow 90

Theoretical diagram of the streets of Berlin. 91

Theoretical diagram of the streets of London 91

Chicago. View of Grand Boulevard 92

View of the Lake Shore Drive 92

Plan of the city, showing the general system of boulevards and parks existing and proposed . 93

View of Drexel Boulevard 94

View of Michigan Avenue, looking north 94

Intersection of the three branches of the Chicago River 95

View looking north on the south branch of the Chicago River . . . 96

View of the south shore looking southeast over Grant Park 98

The proposed plaza on Michigan Avenue 99

Plan of the complete system of street circulation; railway stations; parks; boulevard circuits and radial arteries; public recreation piers; yacht harbor, and pleasure boat piers; treatment of Grant Park; the main axis and the civic center 100

Plan of the center of the city, showing the present and proposed street and boulevard system . 100

Proposed boulevard to connect the north and south sides of the river . . . 100

Plan of Michigan Avenue from Twelfth Street to the river, and its extension on Pine Street to Chicago Avenue 102

Proposed boulevard and parkway on Michigan Avenue and Pine Street . . . 102·

Proposed boulevard on Michigan Avenue; view looking north from a point east of the Public Library 104

View of Pine Street 105

Paris. View of the Rue de la Paix and the Column Vendôme 105

Chicago. Michigan Avenue, looking towards the south 106

Sketch plan of the intersection of Michigan Avenue and Twelfth Street . . 107

Preliminary sketch of the plaza at Michigan Avenue and Twelfth Street . . 108

Proposed Twelfth Street boulevard at intersections with Michigan Avenue and Ashland Avenue 108

Railway station scheme west of the river between Canal and Clinton streets . . 108

Alternate railway station scheme west of the river between Canal and Clinton streets . 109

Plan of Grant Park and the harbor 110

Elevation of Grant Park and harbor and the eastern façade of the city on Michigan Avenue . 110

Section looking north, taken through the proposed grand axis of the city . . 110

Bird's-eye view at night of Grant Park 112

Proposed plaza on Michigan Avenue west of the Field Museum of Natural History . . 112

The business center of the city, within the first circuit boulevard . . . 112

Chicago. Plan of the proposed group of municipal buildings or civic center 112
      Elevation showing the group of buildings constituting the proposed civic center . . . 112
      View, looking west, of the proposed civic center plaza and buildings 112
Paris. The Place de la Concorde, looking over the Seine towards the Madeleine 113
Dresden. The Zwingerhof 113
Vienna. The Ringstrasse 114
Rome. St. Peter's Cathedral 114
Chicago. View of the proposed development in the center of the city, from Twenty-second Street to Chicago
      Avenue, looking towards the east 114
Berlin. Spree Island 115
Chicago. The proposed civic center square. 116
Study for the dome of the proposed civic center 118
View eastward to Lake Michigan 119
"The Great Lakes" 124

The drawings for the Plan of Chicago were executed by Ben E. Holden, Clarence E. Howard, Chester M. Davison, Chris U. Bagge, and Leo Strelka. Mr. Holden was identified with the study of the general plan and the park system, both in general and in detail; Mr. Howard with the Center of the City and the Railroads; and Mr. Davison with the treatment of the Lake Front. The plans for the Civic Center and for Grant Park were studied by Fernand Janin of Paris, who came to Chicago in 1908 for that especial purpose. The renderings by Jules Guerin were made during extended visits to Chicago in 1907, and again in 1908. The work of both Mr. Guerin and Mr. Janin appears over their names. The Sanitary District Map of the City of Chicago has been used in compiling the plan drawings. Plate XVII is compiled from plans published in "Les Transformations de Paris."

THE COMMERCIAL CLUB OF CHICAGO

ORGANIZED 1877; UNITED WITH THE MERCHANTS CLUB, 1907.

THE MERCHANTS CLUB COMMITTEE ON THE PLAN OF CHICAGO, 1906–7. Charles D. Norton, *Chairman;* Charles H. Wacker, *Vice-Chairman;* David R. Forgan, *Treasurer;* Walter H. Wilson, *Chairman Finance Committee;* Edward B. Butler, Frederic A. Delano; Daniel H. Burnham, *Architect.*

THE COMMERCIAL CLUB COMMITTEES ON THE PLAN OF CHICAGO, 1907–08.

GENERAL COMMITTEE. Charles D. Norton, *Chairman;* Charles H. Wacker, *Vice-Chairman;* Frederic A. Delano, *Secretary;* Walter H. Wilson, *Treasurer;* Adolphus C. Bartlett, Edward B. Butler, Clyde M. Carr, John V. Farwell, Jr., Joy Morton, Charles H. Thorne; Daniel H. Burnham, *Architect.*

ON LAKE FRONT. Edward B. Butler, *Chairman;* Leslie Carter, Charles G. Dawes, John V. Farwell, Jr., Victor F. Lawson, Harold F. McCormick.

ON BOULEVARD TO CONNECT THE NORTH AND SOUTH SIDES. Clyde M. Carr, *Chairman;* Charles H. Conover, James L. Houghteling, Albert A. Sprague II., Charles H. Thorne, Frederic W. Upham, Charles H. Wacker.

ON RAILWAY TERMINALS. Joy Morton, *Chairman;* Adolphus C. Bartlett, William J. Chalmers, Charles H. Hulburd, Chauncey Keep, Franklin MacVeagh, Cyrus H. McCormick, Martin A. Ryerson, John G. Shedd, Albert A. Sprague.

THE COMMERCIAL CLUB COMMITTEES ON THE PLAN OF CHICAGO, 1908–9.

GENERAL COMMITTEE. Charles D. Norton, *Chairman;* Charles H. Wacker, *Vice-Chairman;* Frederic A. Delano, *Secretary;* Walter H. Wilson, *Treasurer;* Adolphus C. Bartlett, Edward B. Butler, Clyde M. Carr, John V. Farwell, Charles L. Hutchinson, Rollin A. Keyes, Joy Morton, Charles H. Thorne; Daniel H. Burnham, *Architect.*

ON LAKE PARKS. Edward B. Butler, *Chairman;* Edgar A. Bancroft, William L. Brown, Charles G. Dawes, John V. Farwell, Harold F. McCormick, John J. Mitchell.

ON STREETS AND BOULEVARDS. Clyde M. Carr, *Chairman;* Charles H. Conover, Thomas E. Donnelley, James L. Houghteling, Albert A. Sprague II., Frederic W. Upham, Charles H. Wacker.

ON RAILWAY TERMINALS. Joy Morton, *Chairman;* Adolphus C. Bartlett, Franklin MacVeagh, Cyrus H. McCormick, Martin A. Ryerson, John G. Shedd, Albert A. Sprague.

ON INTERURBAN ROADWAYS. Charles H. Thorne, *Chairman;* Benjamin Carpenter, Edward F. Carry, Homer A. Stillwell, Charles L. Strobel.

ON FINANCE. Adolphus C. Bartlett, *Chairman;* Charles G. Dawes, Charles L. Hutchinson, Albert A. Sprague, Walter H. Wilson.

LIST OF SUBSCRIBERS

PRIOR TO JUNE 1, 1909

Adams, George E.
Aldis, Arthur T.
Aldis, Owen F.
Alexander, William A.
Allen, Benjamin
Alvord, John W.
American Radiator Company
Armour, J. Ogden
Armstrong, Frank H.
Arnold, Bion J.
Ayer, Edward E.

Bailey, Edward P.
Baker, Alfred L.
Baker, Howard W.
Bancroft, Edgar A.
Banks, Alexander F.
Barber, Bryant H.
Barnes, Albert R.
Barnhart, Kenneth
Bartlett, Adolphus C.
Bartlett, Charles L.
Barton, Enos M.
Bates, Onward
Becker, Abraham G.
Beidler, Francis
Beifeld, Joseph
Bigelow Brothers & Walker Company
Billings, Frank
Birk, William A.
Blair, Chauncey J.
Blair, Henry A.
Blair, Watson F.
Bode, Frederick
Booth, W. Vernon
Bowen, Joseph T.
Boynton, Charles T.
Brand, Rudolph
Bremer, Herman H.
Brill, George M.
Brown, William L.
Buckingham, Clarence

Buda Foundry & Manufacturing Company
Buffington, Eugene J.
Burley, Clarence A.
Burnham, Daniel H.
Bush, William H.
Butler, Edward B.
Butler, Estate of Hermon B.
Butz, Otto C.

Canby, Caleb H.
Carpenter, Augustus A., Jr.
Carpenter, Benjamin
Carr, Clyde M.
Carry, Edward F.
Carton, Laurence A.
Chalmers, William J.
Chapin, S. B. & Company.
Clark, John M.
Clow, William E.
Cochran, J. Lewis
Cofran, John W. G.
Comstock, Charles G.
Condron, Theodore L.
Conover, Charles H.
Corwith, Charles R.
Cowan, William K.
Cowles, Alfred
Cox, Rensselaer W.
Crane, Charles R.
Crane, Richard T. Jr.
Crowell, Henry P.
Cudahy, Michael
Culver, Helen
Cummings, D. Mark
Cummings, Edmund A.
Cunningham, Frank S.

Dau, J. J.
Dawes, Charles G.
Day, Chapin A.
Deering, Charles
Deering, James

Delano, Frederic A.
Dewes, Francis J.
Dewey, Albert B.
De Wolf, Wallace L.
Dick, Albert B.
Dixon, Arthur
Donnelley, Thomas E.
Downey, Joseph
Durand, Elliott

Earling, Albert J.
Eckhart, Barnard A.
Eckstein, Louis
Edward Hines Lumber Company
Eisendrath, Joseph N.
Eitel, Emil
Ellsworth, James W.
Ewen, John M.

Fair, Robert M.
Falkenau, Victor
Farwell, Granger
Farwell, John V.
Fay, Charles N.
Felton, Samuel M.
Ferguson, Louis A.
Fetzer, John C.
Field, John S.
Field, Stanley
Findeisen & Kropf Manufacturing Company
Foote, Erastus
Foreman, Edwin G.
Forgan, David R.
Forgan, James B.
Frost, Albert C.
Fuller, William A.

Gardner, William A.
Gerstenberg, Erich G.
Gilbert, Harry K.
Glessner, John J.
Goodman, Herbert E.

xvi

Granger, Alfred H.
Greeley–Howard Company
Gregory, Robert B.
Grey, Charles F.
Grosscup, Peter S.
Gurley, William W.

Hamill, Ernest A.
Hammond, Robert R.
Hardy, F. A. & Company
Harris, George B.
Harris, John F.
Harris, Joseph
Harris, Norman W.
Hart, H. Stillson
Haskell, Frederick T.
Hately, John C.
Haugan, Helge A.
Hewitt, Charles M.
Heyworth, James O.
Heyworth, Lawrence
Holt, George H.
Hoover, Frank K.
Horton, George T.
Horton, Horace E.
Houghteling, James L.
Hoyt, William M.
Hughitt, Marvin
Hulbert, Edmund D.
Hulburd, Charles H.
Hull, Morton D.
Hurley, Edward N.
Hutchins, James C.
Hutchinson, Charles L.

Insull, Samuel
Isham, Mrs. R. N.

Jackson, George W.
James, Fred S.
Johnson, Frank S.
Johnston, Hugh McBirney
Jones, Arthur B.
Jones, David B.
Jones, Frank H.
Jones, William D.

Keep, Chauncey
Kelley, William V.
Kenna, Edward D.
Kent, William

Kesner, Jacob L.
Keyes, Rollin A.
Kimball, Charles F.
Kimball, W. W. Co.
Kurz, Adolph

Laflin, Louis E.
Lamont, Robert P.
Langhorst, Henry A.
Lathrop, Bryan
Lawrence, Dwight
Lawson, Victor F.
Lefens, Thies J.
Leicht, Edward A.
Lincoln, Robert T.
Lindgren, John R.
Linn, William R.
Lobdell, Edwin L.
Logan, Frank G.
Lombard, Isaac G.
Lord, John B.
Lowden, Frank O.
Lynch, John A.
Lyon, John K.
Lytton, Henry C.

MacVeagh, Franklin
Madlener, Albert F.
Magnus, August C.
Mandel, Leon
Mark, Clayton
Martin, William P.
Matz, Rudolph
Mayer, Levy
McCord, Alvin C.
McCormick, Cyrus H.
McCormick, Harold F.
McCullough, Hiram R.
McLaughlin, William F.
Meeker, Arthur
Mendius, Carl
Merryweather, George
Miller, Darius
Miller, Harry I.
Miller, John S.
Miner, William H.
Mitchell, John J.
Mitten, Thomas E.
Modjeski, Ralph
Morris, Edward
Morron, John R.

Morton, Joy
Morton, Mark
Murdock, Thomas

Norlin, Fred
Norton, Charles D.
Noyes, Frank B.
Noyes, La Verne W.

Ortmann, Rudolph
Ortseifen, Adam
Otis, Joseph E. Estate
Otis, Spencer

Paepcke, Hermann
Palmer, Honore
Palmer, Percival B.
Palmer, Potter, Jr.
Paper Mills Company, The
Patten, James A.
Peabody, Francis B.
Peabody, Francis S.
Pirie, John T., Jr.
Pitkin, Edward H.
Pool, Marvin B.
Pope, Henry
Porter, Henry H.
Porter, Henry H., Jr.
Potter, Edwin A.

Rawson, Frederick H
Rehm, William H.
Revell, Alexander H.
Reynolds, George M.
Rickcords, George E.
Ripley, Edward P.
Robinson, Theodore W.
Rogers, Brown & Company
Rosenthal, Benjamin J.
Rosenwald, Julius
Rubens, Harry
Rudolph, Franklin
Russell, Edmund A.
Russell, Brewster & Company
Ryerson, Edwin L.
Ryerson, Martin A.

Sard, William H.
Sargent, George M.
Scott, John W.
Scully, Arthur B.

Sears, Richard W.
Seipp, Philip W.
Selz, J. Harry
Shaffer, John C.
Shaffner, Joseph
Shedd, Edward A.
Shedd, John G.
Shirk, Elbert W.
Simpson, James
Skinner, Edward M.
Smith, Byron L.
Smith, Mrs. George T.
Smith, Orson
Smith, Walter B.
Soper, James P.
Spoor, John A.
Sprague, Albert A.
Sprague, Otho S. A.
Starring, Mason B.
Stevens, Charles A.
Stillwell, Homer A.
Strobel, Charles L.
Stumer, Louis M.
Sullivan, Roger C.
Sunny, Bernard E.
Swift, Charles H.

Swift, Edward F.
Swift, George B.
Swift, Louis F.

Theurer, Joseph
Thoman, Leroy D.
Thomas, Benjamin
Thompson, John R.
Thompson, William M.
Thorne, Charles H.
Thorne, George R.
Tilden, Edward
Tilt, Joseph E.
Turner, Edward A.

Uhrlaub, Adolph
Uihlein, Edgar J.
Upham, Frederic W.

Van Valkenburg, William
Viles, James, Jr.

Wacker, Charles H.
Walker, Henry H.
Wallace, John F.
Ward, A. Montgomery

Warner, Ezra J.
Warren, William S.
Watson, J. V.
Watson, William J.
Wells, Addison E.
Wells, M. D. Company
Wheeler, Arthur D.
Wheeler, Charles P.
Wheeler, Harry A.
Wilder, John E.
Wilder, T. Edward
Willard, Daniel
Willing, Mark S.
Willits, Ward W.
Wilmarth, Mrs. Mary J.
Wilson, John P.
Wilson, Walter H.
Winchell, Benjamin L.
Winston, Frederick S.
Winston, Payne, Strawn & Shaw
Wolff, L. Manufacturing Company
Wrenn, John H.

Young, Charles O.

PLAN OF CHICAGO

CHAPTER I

ORIGIN OF THE PLAN OF CHICAGO: THE WORLD'S COLUMBIAN EXPOSITION OF 1893 AND ITS RESULTS: THE SPIRIT OF CHICAGO

THE tendency of mankind to congregate in cities is a marked characteristic of modern times. This movement is confined to no one country, but is world-wide. Each year Rome, and the cities of the Orient, as well as Berlin, New York, and Chicago, are adding to their population at an unprecedented rate. Coincident with this urban development there has been a widespread increase in wealth, and also an enlarged participation on the part of the people in the work of government. As a natural result of these causes has come the desire to better the conditions of living. Men are becoming convinced that the formless growth of the city is neither economical nor satisfactory; and that overcrowding and congestion of traffic paralyze the vital functions of the city. The complicated problems which the great city develops are now seen not to be beyond the control of aroused public sentiment; and practical men of affairs are turning their attention to working out the means whereby the city may be made an efficient instrument for providing all its people with the best possible conditions of living.

Chicago, in common with other great cities, realizes that the time has come to bring order out of the chaos incident to rapid growth, and especially to the influx of people of many nationalities without common traditions or habits of life. Among the various instrumentalities designed to accomplish this result, a plan for a well-ordered and convenient city is seen to be indispensable; and to the task of producing such a plan the Commercial Club has devoted its energies for the past three years.

It is not to be expected that any plan devised while as yet few civic problems have received final solution will be perfect in all its details. It is claimed for the plan herein presented, that it is the result of extended and careful study of the needs of Chicago, made by disinterested men of wide experience, amid the very conditions which it is sought to remedy; and that during the years devoted to its preparation the plan has had the benefit of varied and competent criticism. The real test of this plan will be found in its application; for, such is the determination of the

III. THE WORLD'S COLUMBIAN EXPOSITION, CHICAGO, 1893.
The Court of Honor, looking towards the Peristyle.

people to secure more perfect conditions, it is certain that if the plan is really good it will commend itself to the progressive spirit of the times, and sooner or later it will be carried out.

It should be understood, however, that such radical changes as are proposed herein cannot possibly be realized immediately. Indeed, the aim has been to anticipate the needs of the future as well as to provide for the necessities of the present: in short, to direct the development of the city towards an end that must seem ideal, but is practical. Therefore it is quite possible that when particular portions of the plan shall be taken up for execution, wider knowledge, longer experience, or a change in local conditions may suggest a better solution; but, on the other hand,

IV. THE WORLD'S COLUMBIAN EXPOSITION, CHICAGO, 1893. THE COURT OF HONOR, LOOKING TOWARDS THE PERISTYLE.
This view shows the effect of an orderly arrangement of buildings and a uniform cornice line. From a painting by Mente.

before any departure shall be determined upon, it should be made clear that such a change is justified.

If many elements of the proposed plan shall seem familiar, it should be remembered that the purpose has not been to invent novel problems for solution, but to take up the pressing needs of to-day, and to find the best methods of meeting those requirements, carrying each particular problem to its ultimate conclusion as a component part of a great entity,—a well-ordered, convenient, and unified city.

This conception of the task is the justification of a comprehensive plan of Chicago. To many who have given little consideration to the subject, a plan seems to call for large expenditures and a consequent increase in taxation. The reverse is the case. It is certain that civic improvement will go on at an accelerated rate; and if those improvements shall be marshaled according to a well-ordered plan great saving must result. Good order and convenience are not expensive; but haphazard and ill-considered projects invariably result in extravagance and wastefulness. A plan insures that whenever any public or semi-public work shall be undertaken, it will fall into its proper and predetermined place in the general scheme, and thus contribute to the unity and dignity of the city.

The plan frankly takes into consideration the fact that the American city, and Chicago preeminently, is a center of industry and traffic. Therefore attention is given to the betterment of commercial facilities; to methods of transportation for persons and for goods; to removing the obstacles which prevent or obstruct circulation; and to the increase of convenience. It is realized, also, that good workmanship requires a large degree of comfort on the part of the workers in their homes and their surroundings, and ample opportunity for that rest and recreation without which all work becomes drudgery. Then, too, the city has a dignity to be maintained; and good order is essential to material advancement. Consequently, the plan provides for impressive groupings of public buildings, and reciprocal relations among such groups. Moreover, consideration is given to the fact that in all probability Chicago, within the lifetime of persons now living, will become a greater city than any existing at the present time; and that therefore the most comprehensive plans of to-day will need to be supplemented in a not remote future. Opportunity for such expansion is provided for.

The origin of the plan of Chicago can be traced directly to the World's Columbian Exposition. The World's Fair of 1893 was the beginning, in our day and in this country, of the orderly arrangement of extensive public grounds and buildings. The result came about quite naturally. Chicago had become a commercial community wherein men were accustomed to get together to plan for the general good. Moreover, those at the head of affairs were, many of them, the same individuals who had taken part in every movement since the city had emerged from the condition of a mere village. They were so accustomed to results even beyond their most sanguine predictions, that it was easy for them to believe that their Fair might surpass all fairs that had preceded it.

Then, too, the men of Chicago, trained in intense commercial activity, had learned the lesson that great success cannot be attained unless the special work in hand shall be entrusted to those best fitted to undertake it. It had become the habit of our business men to select some one to take the responsibility in every important enterprise; and to give to that person earnest, loyal, and steadfast support. Thus the design and arrangement of the buildings of the World's Columbian Exposition, which have never been surpassed, were due primarily to the feeling of

V. THE WORLD'S COLUMBIAN EXPOSITION GROUNDS IN JACKSON PARK.
Plan showing the harmonious arrangement of buildings.

loyalty to the city and to its undertakings; and secondly, to the habit of entrusting great works
to men trained in the practice of such undertakings.[1]

The results of the World's Fair of 1893 were many and far-reaching. To the people of
Chicago the dignity, beauty, and convenience of the transitory city in Jackson Park seemed to
call for the improvement of the water front of the city. With this idea in mind, the South Park
Commissioners, during the year following the Fair, proposed the improvement of the Lake

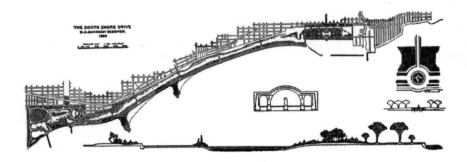

VI. THE LAKE FRONT PARK, EXTENDING FROM JACKSON PARK TO GRANT PARK, ALONG THE SOUTH SHORE
OF LAKE MICHIGAN.
Original plan, 1896.

front from Jackson Park to Grant Park. Following out this suggestion, a plan for a connection
between the two parks was drawn to a large scale, and the project was presented at a meeting of
the West and South Park Commissioners. Later this design was exhibited at a dinner given by
the Commercial Club; and many business men were emphatic in expressing their conviction that
the proposed scheme would be of enormous value to Chicago, and that it should be adopted
and carried into execution. This was the inception of the project for a park out in the Lake,
having a lagoon between it and the shore.

During the next three or four years more careful studies of the Lake front scheme were made,
and very large drawings were prepared for a meeting at the Women's Club and the Art Institute,

[1] A significant illustration of the spirit in which the World's Fair work was conceived is found in one incident. On the appointed
day the architects assembled to submit to the general committee sketches for their several buildings. There had been a luncheon,
prolonged by animated discussion. The scheme as a whole had begun to take hold of the men. The short winter afternoon was
approaching an end, when Richard M. Hunt (then the dean of the architectural profession), suffering from the severe pains of rheuma-
tism, slowly arose to speak of the Administration Building, a sketch of which he fastened to the wall. The New York architect who
followed Mr. Hunt had on his building a dome four hundred and fifty feet high. Instantly a murmur ran around the group. The
designer turned from the sketch. "I think," he said, with deliberation, "I shall not advocate that dome; and probably I shall modify
the building." There was a breath of satisfaction. The next architect had a portico extending out over the terrace. Without waiting for criticism, he said he should draw the portico back to the face of the building. As one by one each man fastened his sketch to
the wall, it was as still as death in the room; and those present could feel the great work drawing them as by a magnet; and each
was willing to sacrifice his personal ideas to secure the unity of the whole composition. Finally the last drawing was shown; the last
explanation had been made. Mr. Saint-Gaudens, who had sat in a corner all day listening, but never speaking and scarcely moving,
went over to Mr. Burnham, and taking both his hands exclaimed: "Do you realize that this is the greatest meeting of artists since the
fifteenth century?"

and for a Merchants Club dinner at the Auditorium. The newspapers and magazines, both at home and throughout the country, united in commenting on and commending the undertaking; and during the decade that has elapsed since the plans were first presented, the proposed improvement has never been forgotten, but has ever been looked upon as something sure to be accomplished. This was the beginning of a general plan for the city.

While these projects were in course of preparation, an extensive expansion of the South Parks

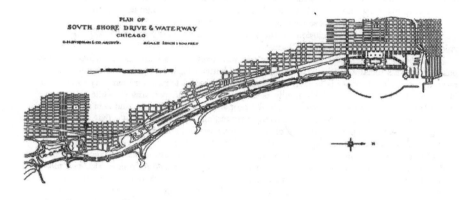

PLAN OF
SOVTH SHORE DRIVE & WATERWAY
CHICAGO
D.H.BVRNHAM & CO ARCHT'S.   SCALE 1INCH : 800 FEET

VII. THE LAKE FRONT PARK, EXTENDING FROM JACKSON PARK TO GRANT PARK, ALONG THE SOUTH SHORE
OF LAKE MICHIGAN.
Modified plan, 1904.

system was in progress, and a plan was formulated for a metropolitan park system, including an outer belt of parks and parkways. These movements were started with energy in 1903, under the general direction of the South Park Commissioners and the Special Park Commission; and the results of their work have been useful to those who have undertaken the present task.

Early in 1906 the Merchants Club arranged for the preparation of a complete project for the future development of Chicago. In order to facilitate the progress of the work, rooms were built on the roof of Railway Exchange Building, where the drawings have been prepared and the studies have been made. The Merchants Club and the Commercial Club having been merged in 1907 under the name of the latter organization, the work has continued under the auspices of that association. The committee on the plan has held several hundred meetings; during many weeks meetings have taken place daily; and throughout the entire time no week has passed without one or more such gatherings. By invitation of the Club, the Governor of Illinois, the Mayor of Chicago, and many other public officials have visited the rooms where the work was in progress, and have become familiar with the entire scheme as it was being worked out. The Department of State, through the United States consuls in various European cities, has furnished valuable information relative to civic developments now in progress. Thus the plans have had the benefit of many criticisms and suggestions, made by persons especially conversant with existing conditions.

Moreover, visitors interested in the improvement of cities and in park work of all kinds have come from both our own and foreign towns; and from them also much of value and encouragement has been gained.

In presenting this report, the Commercial Club realizes that from time to time supplementary reports will be necessary to emphasize one feature or another which may come prominently before the public for adoption. At the same time, it is confidently believed that this presentation of the entire subject accomplishes the task which has been recognized from the outset, namely:

First, to make the careful study of the physical conditions of Chicago as they now exist;

Second, to discover how those conditions may be improved;

Third, to record such conclusions in the shape of drawings and texts which shall become a guide for the future development of Chicago.

In creating the ideal arrangement, every one who lives here is better accommodated in his business and his social activities. In bringing about better freight and passenger facilities, every merchant and manufacturer is helped. In establishing a complete park and parkway system, the life of the wage-earner and of his family is made healthier and pleasanter; while the greater attractiveness thus produced keeps at home the people of means and taste, and acts as a magnet to draw those who seek to live amid pleasing surroundings. The very beauty that attracts him who has money makes pleasant the life of those among whom he lives, while anchoring him and his wealth to the city. The prosperity aimed at is for all Chicago.

This same spirit which carried out the Exposition in such a manner as to make it a lasting credit to the city is still the soul of Chicago, vital and dominant; and even now, although many new men are at the front, it still controls and is doing a greater work than it was in 1893. It finds the men; it makes the occasion; it attracts the sincere and unselfish; it vitalizes the organization, and impels it to reach heights not believed possible of attainment. This spirit still exists. It is present to-day among us. Indeed, it seems to gather force with the years and the opportunities. It is even now impelling us to larger and better achievements for the public good. It conceals no private purpose, no hidden ends. This spirit — the spirit of Chicago — is our greatest asset. It is not merely civic pride: it is rather the constant, steady determination to bring about the very best conditions of city life for all the people, with full knowledge that what we as a people decide to do in the public interest we can and surely will bring to pass.

VIII. THE WORLD'S COLUMBIAN EXPOSITION. VIEW OF THE COURT OF HONOR, LOOKING WEST.
From a painting by Moran.

IX. THE PYRAMIDS AT GIZEH.

CHAPTER II

CITY PLANNING IN ANCIENT AND MODERN TIMES: COMMERCE A LEADING MOTIVE IN CITY
BUILDING: BABYLON, EGYPT, ATHENS, AND ROME: MEDIÆVAL CITIES: THE DEVELOPMENT
OF PARIS: CITY PLANNING IN GERMANY: OVERCOMING CONGESTION IN LONDON: WASH-
INGTON A CITY BUILT ON A PLAN: OTHER AMERICAN CITIES

ROM earliest times, two motives have governed the location of
cities: either the site was selected because it offered natural
means of defense, or else commerce gathered men at a particular
point, about which they built fortifications. In either case, the
necessity of protection against enemies from without conditioned
the form and arrangement of the city. Even in this western
hemisphere the question of defense has been of moment. Louisburg and Quebec; Boston, New York, and Yorktown; Mackinac
and New Orleans; Charleston, Mobile, Vicksburg, and New
Orleans again,— are names which recall sieges and battles of three
wars; while the walled towns of Europe find their counterparts in the palisaded settlements
which sprang up in the Indian country of North America, Chicago itself being a typical example.

9

It is only within recent times that the city has been able to extend its borders free from the restraints imposed by the necessity of warding off a foe.

The first city-builder whose exploits are recorded was Semiramis, queen of Babylon; and although the history of that country, as recorded on its monuments, fails to mention even the name of this war-like ruler, we may not disregard the circumstantial accounts given by classical writers of the greatest commercial city of ancient times. Diodorus tells us that Semiramis, being of an aspiring spirit and anxious to excel all her predecessors in glorious actions, set about building a great city in the province of Babylon. First she had complete plans prepared by her architects and artists, then she assembled from all parts of her empire the men necessary for the work of construction. For the promotion of commerce, she located the city on the banks of the river Euphrates; and round about it she built a wall, very high, fortified with many turrets, and so broad at the top that thereon chariots might be driven abreast. Across the river she threw a bridge five furlongs in length, with arches having a span of twelve feet. Along either shore of the river she raised a bank as broad as the wall; and temporarily turning aside the course of the

X. THE ACROPOLIS AT ATHENS.
From a water-color by E. H. Bennett.

stream, she made in the bed of the river a passage in the form of a tunnel to serve as a connection between her two palaces, which were also lookouts whence she could command every portion of the city. Other cities on the banks of the Tigris and the Euphrates Semiramis built, and there she established traffic centers for the vending of merchandise brought from Media, Persia, India, Egypt, and other countries reached by the two great rivers, which in those ancient times vied with the Nile and the Ganges. So by her able policy she greatly enriched the merchants who trafficked in those parts, and advanced the glory and majesty of Babylon.

The ancient Egyptians, hemmed in by deserts, relied less on walls than on the defenses provided

XI. THE GREEK THEATRE AT SYRACUSE, SICILY.
From a water-color by E. H. Bennett.

by nature. Thus relieved from the necessity of building fortifications, they expended their energies in such monumental works as the Great Pyramids and temples that embody a civilization which for at least nine thousand years has been the wonder and the admiration of the world.

Means of defense having been provided, the desire of mankind for order and magnificence found expression in works of adornment, which were measured only by the love of the citizens for their city, the artistic sense developed among the people, and the means at their disposal for carrying out their conceptions. No-where else have these conditions been combined as they were in Athens during the days of Pericles. Year by year the patient excavator is bringing to the light the massive walls by which the early Athenians protected their citadel against the invader; and when security had been obtained and the tribute of the allies had accumulated in the treasury, the Greek passion for beauty found expression in public buildings which through the ages have placed the Acropolis at Athens among the world's famous places. Plutarch lays emphasis on the fact that undertakings, any one of which singly might have required for its completion several successions and ages of men, were every one of them accomplished in the height and prime of one man's political service. "Pericles' works," this same writer asserts, "were especially admired because they were made quickly to last long. For every particular piece of his work was immediately, even at that time, for its beauty and elegance, antique; and yet in its vigor and freshness looks to this day as if it were just executed. There is a sort of bloom of newness upon those works of his, preserving them from the touch of time, as if they had some perennial spirit and undying vitality mingled in the composition of them."

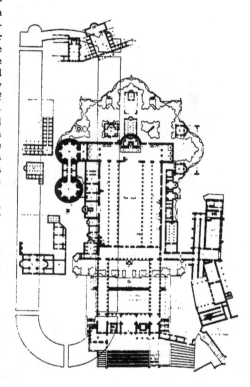

XII. PLAN SHOWING NERO'S CIRCUS AT ROME (FIRST CENTURY), BASILICA OF ST. PETER (FOURTH CENTURY), AND THE PRESENT CATHEDRAL OF ST. PETER (SIXTEENTH CENTURY). These structures were built at successive epochs, on the same site.

As Athens represents the highest expression of civic beauty which mankind has witnessed, so Rome stands for power and the magnificence thereof. Mistress of the world she styled herself; and to-day she can still lay claim to her other proud title of the "Eternal City." It is not until we come to Roman times that we begin to obtain the combination of elements which are the chief characteristics of the modern city; namely, opportunities for the healthful life of the great body

XIII. AN ANCIENT ROMAN CIRCUS, NEAR THE APPIAN WAY.
From an etching by Piranesi.

of the citizens. "Parks, gardens, commons, and public squares," says Lanciani, "have been happily compared to the lungs of a city; and if the health and general welfare of a city depend upon the normal and sound function of its respiratory organs, ancient Rome, in this respect, must be considered as the healthiest city which has ever existed on earth."[1] This writer enumerates, as existing at the end of the third century after Christ, eight commons, or green spaces, set apart mostly for foot-races and gymnastic exercises; eighteen public squares, and about thirty parks and gardens, at first laid out by private citizens for their personal comfort, but afterwards absorbed into the imperial domain by purchase, bequest, or confiscation. Besides these were the cemeteries, marble cities of the dead, shadowed by stately cypresses and weeping-willows; the sacred enclosures of the temples, with their colonnades and fountains; the

XIV. THE PONTE MOLLE, ROME.
From an etching by Piranesi.

[1] Ancient Rome, Chap. IV.

porticoes, expressly built for the sake of allowing citizens to move about pleasantly in hot or rainy weather; and lastly, the great baths, establishments provided with every possible comfort and accommodation to insure the health of the body and the education of the mind."

Out of the original market-place occupying the marshy ground between the Palatine and the Capitol, the Roman Forum was gradually evolved, with temples, treasure-houses, places for foreign ambassadors, the senate-house, the court-house, triumphal arches, and historic monuments. Here was indeed the civic center of Rome, the place of religion, business, and politics. Adjoining the Forum proper were other forums, gifts to the state, purchased at a cost, in the case of Cæsar's Forum, of $44.45 a square foot, or over four million dollars. Trajan's gift of land alone amounted to four times that sum, and the completed work was reckoned the masterpiece of Roman architecture of the golden age.

The baths of Rome, both public and private, had accommodations for 62,800 citizens at a single time, and also every Roman house was provided with bathing facilities. Beautiful porticoes enabled one to cross under shelter the whole plain of the Campus Martius, a space of between two and three miles; and similar structures connected all the great buildings of the city, serving for markets and exchanges and picture-galleries, and ministering to a thousand different wants. Lovely gardens, with thickets of box, laurel, and myrtle, with lakes and fountains, were enclosed by these porticoes, which were in themselves architectural creations of rare marbles, the floors often being inlaid with jasper and porphyry. The surrounding hills and the valleys between, once the dumping-place of the city's refuse, were converted into magnificent gardens, forming stretches of verdure in length sometimes exceeding two miles in a single composition.

To-day, after centuries of destruction and decay, Rome is taking on new life. Her population is fast increasing; since 1870 scores of millions of dollars have been spent on works of public utility and general improvement; great thoroughfares have been created, the monuments of the past have been opened to the light and air, the pestilential conditions that during the centuries of her decadence hung over the city like a pall have been removed by wise sanitation; the great estates of noble families have been given over to the public; and again the compelling power of Rome is being felt throughout the civilized world.

During the slow centuries which followed upon the destruction and decay of ancient civilization, no great works of civic utility or adornment were undertaken, and the old were no longer maintained. As the consciousness of national life again began to assert itself in Europe, and the unifying forces of Christianity and Roman law began to bind humanity together, the cities of Italy, of Germany, of France, and of England grew strong and rich by industry and traffic; and throughout western Europe the sense of permanence and power found expression in the rearing and beautification of cities. Everywhere the same spirit actuated the people, although in each land the mode of expression took on characteristic form; and since the vital principle was religion, the cathedral became the embodiment of the highest expression in civic art.

No city in the world, says Charles Eliot Norton, appeals more strongly to the poetic imagination than Venice. Rising in the dawn of modern Europe, she linked the tradition of the old civilization to the fresh conditions of the new. The destiny that ruled her beginnings seemed, as she grew, to have had no element of chance, but to have been determined by foresight and wise counsel. Her statesmen were the ablest, her merchants the most adventurous and most successful, her seamen the boldest, her craftsmen the most skillful, of their time. The affection in which she was held by her people had the depth and intensity of a passion.[1] As it was with Venice, so

[1] Church Building in the Middle Ages.

in a scarcely less degree it fared with Florence and Siena, and other independent cities of Italy, which vied with one another not only in power, but much more in beauty and in the love borne them by their citizens. And to-day their charm makes them the resort of people of taste and refinement, long after their power has waned and only their beauty remains.

1740.

1841.

1878.

XV. TRANSFORMATION OF THE BANKS OF THE SEINE IN PARIS.
Chronological views of the Petit Pont and Petit Chatelet, showing the evolution of the boulevards.

City planning, in the sense of regarding the city as an organic whole and of developing its various units with reference to their relations one to another, had its origin in Paris during the Bourbon period. Among great cities, Paris has reached the highest stage of development; and the method of this attainment affords lessons for all other cities. Paris owes its origin and its growth to the convenience of its location in view of increasing commercial conditions. Its beginnings go back to the century before the Christian era, when it was but a straggling village called Lutetia, occupying one of the islands in the Seine. On the vast level plain adjoining the town, houses could be erected indefinitely, while the numerous watercourses extending into the surrounding regions gave easy access to the trader. Fertile lands furnished an abundance of provisions; and brick-clay, lime, and sand, with timber from the neighboring forests, provided materials for building. The surroundings of Paris, so rich in all the requisites for the creation of a great city, are similar to those of London and Berlin and Chicago; and in each instance there is the same breadth in the landscape.

The architects to whom Louis XIV. entrusted his planning went far beyond the compact walled city of their day. In the open fields which the growth of Paris must sooner or later transform into streets and avenues they drew the central axis of the city. Straight, vast in width, and without limit of length, this avenue passed entirely through open country, with scarcely a dozen buildings throughout its great extent. To the noted city-builders of the seventeenth and eighteenth centuries.— Louis XIV., Colbert, Le Nôtre, Blondel, and the Academy of Architects,— Paris owes those vast reaches of avenue and boulevard which to-day are the crowning features of the most beautiful of cities. The Paris of their day was indeed a crowded, congested city; but the Paris which they conceived and laid out in the deserts and waste places was the widespreading, well-adorned, and convenient city in which to-day all the world takes delight. The Madeleine, the Place de la Concorde, the Invalides, and the great axial avenue from the garden of the Tuileries to the Place de l'Etoile,— all existed on paper decades before they were finally realized in the progress of city building. The point of interest to us is, that as Paris increased in population, the city grew according to a well-devised, symmetrical, highly developed plan; and

1780.

The dates under the views on page 14 should read 1780, 1830, 1880.

The dates under the views on page 15 should read 1740, 1841, 1878.

1830

Old Paris remained, with its dirty, crowded, ill-smelling, narrow, winding streets, the hotbeds of vice and crime. Napoleon Bonaparte was quick to see that while the Paris of the future might indeed grow in attractiveness and convenience, the Paris of the present demanded his attention. Napoleon was disturbed over the condition of his capital. He realized that the city, then numbering some seven hundred thousand people, was destined to become the home of two, three, or even four millions; and he proposed to give it a splendor never before realized by any city in the world. He began to open the Rue de Rivoli, north of the Tuileries gardens; he created the Rue Napoleon (now the Rue de la Paix) in the axis of the Place Vendôme; from the mediæval bridges he

1880.
XVI. CHRONOLOGICAL VIEWS OF THE PLACE DE LA BASTILLE, PARIS.
The evolution of the castle and moat to its present form of plaza and boulevard is shown

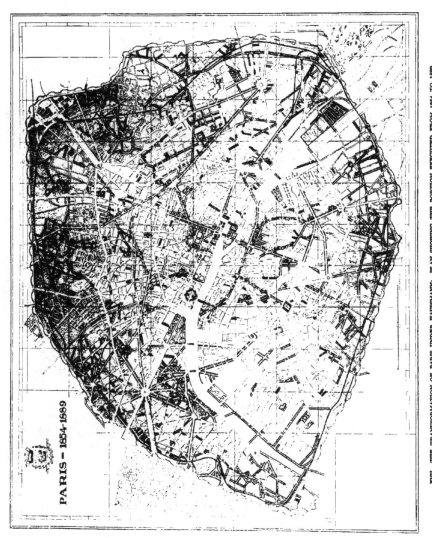

PARIS — 1854-1889

XVII. THE TRANSFORMATION OF PARIS UNDER HAUSSMANN: PLAN SHOWING THE PORTION EXECUTED FROM 1854 TO 1889.
The new boulevards and streets are shown in yellow outlined with red.

swept the superstructures, adding three superb new crossings of the Seine; he built the first sidewalks in Paris, and lighted the streets at night; and he transformed the banks of the river by the construction of three thousand meters of new quays. He also gave to Paris her great commemorative monuments, the Arc de Triomphe de l'Etoile, which was finished by Louis

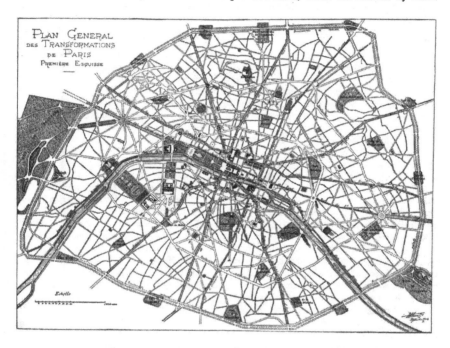

XVIII. PARIS. PLAN PROPOSED BY M. EUGENE HENARD FOR ADDITIONAL RADIAL ARTERIES AND AN INNER CIRCUIT BOULEVARD ON WHICH WOULD FRONT THE PRINCIPAL EXISTING ADMINISTRATIVE BUILDINGS AND MANY PUBLIC MONUMENTS.
The system, involving radical cuts through the blocks and widening of existing arteries, is shown by hatched lines.

Philippe, the Arc du Carrousel, and the Column Vendôme, all of which were foreshadowed in the designs of Louis XIV.

It remained for the third Napoleon, however, to accomplish the great work of breaking through the old city, of opening it to light and air, and of making it fit to sustain the army of merchants and manufacturers which makes Paris to-day the center of a commerce as wide as civilization itself. In 1853, Georges Eugène Haussmann became prefect of the Seine, the appointment being in the nature of a promotion due to the successful administration of the office of prefect in other French cities. Immediately Haussmann began a career which has established for all time his place among the city-builders of the world. As if by intuition he grasped the entire problem. Taking counsel neither of expediency nor of compromise, he ever sought the true and proper solution. To him Paris appeared as a highly organized unit, and he strove to create ideal conditions throughout the entire city. The world gives him credit for the highest success. The people of Paris have always supported those who aimed to make their city grand and beautiful. Proud, ambitious, endowed with good taste and an artistic sense, the Parisians have ever been zealous to make their city the capital not only of the state, but also of civilization.

Haussmann never overlooked the great and broad lines laid down by his predecessors; so that to a considerable extent his work was but the continuation of the plans prepared by Louis XIV. in the later years of the seventeenth century. His peculiar task, however, was to provide adequate means of circulation within the old city, by cutting new streets and widening old ones, by sweeping away unwholesome rookeries, and by opening up great spaces in order to disengage monuments of beauty and historic interest. He placed the great railway stations of Paris in a circle about the old center of the city, and opened up fine avenues of approach to them. At times he found it less expensive, and also less disturbing, to build a new street through the blocks, rather than to widen old streets; and it was his special care to create diagonal thoroughfares in order to shorten distances, and also to give picturesqueness to the street system by the creation of those corner lots which the architects of Paris have learned so well how to improve.[1]

The task which Haussmann accomplished for Paris corresponds with the work which must be done for Chicago, in order to overcome the intolerable conditions which invariably arise from a rapid growth of population. At the time he began, the population of Paris was half a million less than the population of Chicago to-day. The work was accomplished at a cost of $265,000,000. That portion of the improvements relating to the palaces was borne entirely by the nation, the remainder being divided between the nation and the city, the former paying one-third and the latter two-thirds of the expense. (It was Haussmann's theory that the money thus spent made a better city, and that a better city was a greater producer of wealth.) Experience has amply justified his contention. The convenience and beauty of Paris bring large returns in money as well as in æsthetic satisfaction.[2]

In Europe, during the last quarter of the nineteenth century, a widespread impulse towards city planning found expression in all the great towns. This movement was made possible by the fact that since the termination of the Franco-Prussian war, in 1870, there has been peace throughout Europe, and the money which theretofore had been wasted on swords and spears now found productive employment in plowshares and pruning-hooks. From out the turmoil and strife which marked the first two-thirds of the century, Germany arose united, alert, vigorous, ambitious, like a lusty youth, realizing both the opportunities before him and his own strength of body, mind, and will to take advantage of every opening. Austria, unwillingly freed from the incubus of Italy, found in union with Hungary a strength never before possessed; and Vienna and Budapest became centers of intense activity, which developed along lines of

---

[1] Baron Haussmann and the Topographical Transformation of Paris; by Edward R. Smith, Reference Librarian, Avery Architectural Library, Columbia University. The Architectural Record, 1907.

[2] A reasonable estimate, for the single year 1907, of the gold imported into France by travelers, to be spent in hotels, transportation, amusements, and purchases, is $600,000,000, a sum equal to the highest gold reserve of the Bank of France. Americans commonly exaggerate both their numbers and their expenditures in France; but one-fifth of this sum ($120,000,000) may safely be set down as their share.— *French Finance*, by *Stoddard Dewey*, *Atlantic Monthly, August, 1908*.

commercial progress, and also took on forms of convenience and orderliness which have served as examples the world over. Italy, once again shaking off the foreign yoke, became united under the rule of her own people. France, putting aside for the moment ideas of foreign domination, set herself to the task of leading all nations in the world of art and taste. England, drawing her princely revenues from every hemisphere, watched her commerce develop as her industries grew and her wealth increased.

Moreover, the past thirty-eight years of peace throughout Europe coincides with the period in which the greatest discoveries in the realm of natural forces, as applied to industry, have been made and utilized. So that the capital saved as the result of peace has yielded returns that have been increased in geometrical ratio, until we have reached the days not only of unparal-

XIX. CITY CENTER, VIENNA, IN 1857, SHOWING THE FORTIFICATIONS.

leled wealth, but also of unparalleled opportunities for increasing wealth. Moreover, peace has widened the field of traffic, so that no nation now relies merely on its own people for its commerce, but out of every nation come the finest fruits of its industry to satisfy the world's demands. And inasmuch as there are no bounds to human wants and satisfactions, the triumphs and the rewards of commerce find no limits.

All this commercial activity, suddenly developed by turning the capital of the world into productive channels, found the cities of Europe ill adapted to meet the changed conditions. The great towns, Paris excepted, were still in the swaddling-clothes of the Middle Ages; they were walled towns with narrow, tortuous streets, picturesque indeed, but absolutely unfitted for commerce or manufactures according to the modern scale. All the conditions, therefore, made imperative the transformation of the old portions of cities to meet modern demands for circu-

XX. CITY CENTER, VIENNA, AFTER TRANSFORMATIONS MADE BY ORDER OF FRANCIS JOSEPH IN 1857.
The Ringstrasse and public buildings replace the fortifications.

lation, and the extension of their borders to provide for the constant increase in population. Everywhere throughout Europe the design of the cosmopolitan city as planned by the architects of Louis XIV. became the model; everywhere the work of Haussmann in opening congested regions of old cities by means of straight thoroughfares found imitators. Vienna with

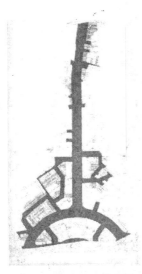

XXI. LONDON. PLAN OF ALD-
WYCH AND KINGSWAY CON-
NECTING HOLBORN AND THE
STRAND

its Ringstrasse followed the example of Paris as expressed in the boulevards of Colbert; in each case the old fortifications were cleared away to make park-like thoroughfares. The heart of old London was transformed by cutting new streets; Brussels was divided by boulevards. In Italy, Rome, Florence, and Milan, each carried out extensive schemes of improvement based on French models.

With the Germans the cutting through of new streets was undertaken for the twofold reason of facilitating traffic and of admitting light and air into a too congested and unwholesome city quarter. In Frankfort-on-the-Main, in Hamburg, in Berlin, and in Dresden it became necessary to abolish with firm hand evil conditions that had become intolerable, no matter at what sacrifice of buildings enveloped with historical associations. But the Germans have come to modify the French theory of the unconditional superiority of the rectilinear avenue; and now they seek to maintain the essential character of the city, as in the case of Darmstadt, by admitting strong curves, and, wherever desirable, by narrowing or widening the thoroughfare, making compensations by creating open spaces. They have found, also, that a too extensive clearing away of the old buildings which cluster about a great minster or cathedral results in an enhancement of effectiveness only at a sacrifice of scale and a loss of picturesqueness. As a consequence, the Germans have sought a golden mean by creating about a monumental structure free room for the beholder to see the essential parts of the building from a sufficiently remote point of view, while leaving undisturbed single structures small in scale, in order that the main building may appear to have grown out of its surroundings.[1]

In general, then, it may be said that while the French or classical theory results in monumental effects for a city and establishes unity, the German or individualistic treatment preserves for an old city a homelike feeling and a pleasing variety. It is worthy of note, however, that where city planning has been undertaken by masters, whether in France or Germany, the two theories have been used as circumstances warranted. It is only where designers are not able to handle their

[1] German City Planning; by Cornelius Gurlitt. Translated for the Metropolitan Improvements Commission of Boston, by Sylvester Baxter.

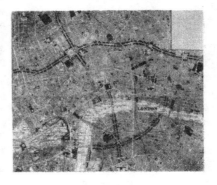

XXII. LONDON TRAFFIC COMMISSION'S PLAN FOR
NEW THOROUGHFARES TO OVERCOME CONGES-
TION. 1907.
Revised by Paul Waterhouse, F. R. I. B. A.

subject in its entirety, but have become slaves to a system, that results have been attained at great money cost and with a loss of charm and picturesqueness that by intelligent study might have beeen saved.[1]

Napoleon Bonaparte, in exile on St. Helena, one day amused himself by planning improvements for London. He would make, he said, a grand thoroughfare from St. Paul's to the Thames; and two wide streets along the Thames, one on either side of the river. He would build more bridges, and would remove from the vicinity of public buildings the mean old structures which disfigure the fine monuments. It would be easy to do this, he thought, in a city so rich as London.[2] Albert Shaw, in his work on *Municipal Government in Great Britain*, says: "If London within the lifetime of men still in their prime had taken due precautions, what errors might have been avoided! London is now creating a park system, and acquiring land that has quadrupled in value within thirty years. London is widening and straightening streets, and increasing thereby the expense of appropriating frontage that costs twice as much now as it would have cost a few years ago. The people of London suffer an inestimable loss in convenience and actual money through the haphazard nature of passenger transportation facilities."

After the great fire of September, 1666, London had the opportunity, so frequently offered in America, of rectifying those unfortunate results which occur in all cities that have grown up; and the sin of omission in the case of the British metropolis was the more unpardonable, inasmuch as plans for improvement were prepared by one of the great architects of the world, Sir Christopher Wren, only to be set aside by the perverse self-interest of the then citizens of London. Wren's plans contemplated a city with streets radiating from central points, and the locations for public buildings were arranged so as to give pleasing objects of sight at the end of long vistas,— principles of civic arrangement which the English architect fixed on paper years before the French city-builders adopted the same principles for the development of Paris.[3] The failure of Wren's scheme of 1666 has cost London millions upon millions of money to repair in part the errors which might have been avoided so easily, besides years of inconvenience and loss due to congestion of traffic. From 1855 to 1900 one project after another for bettering the conditions in London has been carried out, at a cost equal to nearly one hundred million dollars; and now the new Traffic Commission has reported a tentative plan for diminishing the congestion in street traffic by cutting two great thoroughfares: one traversing the town from north to south, the other linking Bayswater with Whitechapel, the estimated cost of the combined work being in the neighborhood of $125,000,000 for land damages alone.[4]

Recently England has taken up in comprehensive manner the whole subject of housing the working classes and of town planning. In 1890 a limited act was passed for the housing of the working classes; and in 1907 this act was supplemented by "the small holdings and allottments act." It is now proposed to extend the provisions of these acts to every urban and rural district. The powers conferred center in the Local Government Board, to which local authorities apply

[1] The magnitude of the movement for city planning in Germany is so great that literally hundreds of cities are now prosecuting schemes of systematic extension and development; and a school of city planners has grown up within the past twenty-five years, with such men as Gurlitt, Stübben, Theodor Fischer, and Baumeister among its masters. A well-edited magazine, "Der Städtebau" (City Planning) is published; and in 1903 the first German Municipal Exposition was held in Dresden.

[2] Talks with Napoleon; by Dr. Barry E. O'Meara. The Century Magazine, February, 1890.

[3] History of London Street Improvements, 1855–1897; by Percy J. Edwards. The Making of a Plan for Washington; by Glenn Brown; Park Improvement Papers; Washington, 1903. It is interesting to note, however, that the Thames Embankment improvement was a portion of Wren's scheme.

[4] Some observations on the report of the Royal Commission on London Traffic; by Paul Waterhouse. Read before the Royal Institute of British Architects. Journal of the R. I. A., May 26 and June 16, 1906.

for approval of the plans proposed; and in case these local authorities fail to make application, the Board may order schemes to be prepared and carried out. There is also a Public Works Loan Commission which authorizes loans for the purpose of carrying out the approved plans.[1]

We have found that those cities which retain their domination over the imaginations of mankind achieve that result through the harmony and beauty of their civic works; that these artistic creations were made possible largely by the gains of commerce promoted by years of peace; and

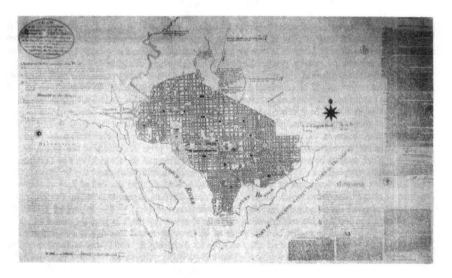

XXIII. ORIGINAL PLAN OF WASHINGTON DESIGNED BY PETER CHARLES L'ENFANT, 1791.

that intense loyalty on the part of the great body of the citizens was the chief impulse which led them to strive to enhance the prestige and dignity of their city. We have found, also, that in modern times the cities of Europe are everywhere making those changes which a rapid increase in trade and population requires, and which the awakened artistic sense of the people demands. We turn now to our own country, to note the conditions which have controlled the development of the American city, and to recount briefly some of the more noteworthy attempts that are being made in the United States to give form and comeliness to our great towns.

Washington was planned and founded as the capital of a nation. The architects of Louis

[1] Mr. John Burns now advocates the proposition that town planning schemes may be made as respects any land which appears likely to be used for building purposes; the general object being to secure proper sanitary conditions, amenity, and convenience, in connection with the laying out and use of land. To this end the Local Government Board may authorize a local authority to prepare such a town planning scheme, with reference to any land within or in the neighborhood of their area, which scheme, when approved by the Board, shall immediately take effect. The use of land for building purposes shall include provision for open spaces, parks, pleasure, or recreation grounds; and where in any town planning scheme the area extends beyond a single local authority, a joint body is provided for. Also the Board may take the initiative in preparing a plan, in case the local authorities fail or neglect to act. See Housing, Town Planning, etc., Bill, 8 Edw., 7.

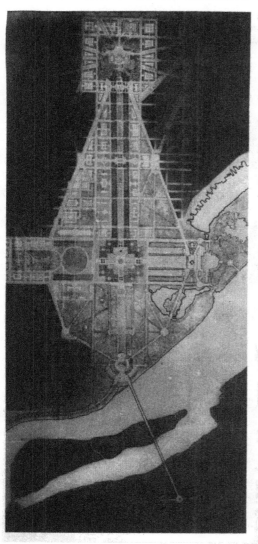

XIV. drew the lines of the new Paris beyond the walls of the existing town, and mapped avenues converging at central points where only gardens and farms then existed; and their plans were a wise provision for a not distant future. Under the direction of President Washington, and with the aid and encouragement of Secretary Jefferson, Peter Charles L'Enfant, a young French engineer, deliberately drew the map of an entirely new capital city designed to accommodate a population one-third greater than was comprised in Paris at that date. In that plan no element of civic convenience, beauty, or adornment was lacking. The entire city was regarded as a unit, and that unit was to be developed in a form not surpassed by any existing city. Upon a rectilinear system of streets L'Enfant imposed diagonal avenues of stately width, converging upon focal points designed to be the location of important public buildings, statues, or monuments commemorating historic events. The Capitol and the President's House were connected by a spacious park, and axial relations between the two structures were developed; every other building necessary for national uses was provided for; and canals, cascades, and fountains were located with reference to existing springs and watercourses. This comprehensive and magnificent plan, designed for an area which then consisted of wide swamps and wooded hills, became the laughing-stock alike of foreign traveler and American citizen. But fortunately the foundations were laid broad and deep by means of the

donation of the lands necessary for streets, avenues, and parks. Fortunately the plan was
adopted and the streets, avenues, public squares, and circles were fixed; and although the
development of the city during three-quarters of a century was slow, yet the rapid increase in

XXV. THE WASHINGTON MONUMENT, GARDEN AND HALL, LOOKING TOWARDS THE CAPITOL; SENATE PARK
COMMISSION PLAN

XXVI. THE PLAZA AND UNION STATION, WASHINGTON, BEGUN IN 1902.

The caption under illustration XXV should read "Mall" in place of "Hall."

thought for future advancement, the new plans have been carried to such a point that their general lines are well established, and already works to cost nearly $50,-000,000 are in progress, each one of which strengthens the hold of the general scheme.[1]

The plans for the improvement of Washington were prepared by the same hands that guided the artistic development of the World's Columbian Exposition in Chicago. The dream city on Lake Michigan, people said, should take on enduring form in the capital of the nation. Then as the Washington plans fired the imagination

[1] The Improvement of the Park System of the District of Columbia; LVII. Congress, First Session; Senate Report No. 166.

wealth and power that followed the ending of the Civil War found Washington ready and waiting for the improvements which have lifted it from a straggling, ill-kept town, into one of the beautiful and stately capitals of the world.

Before the opening of the twentieth century, Washington had begun to expand over the surrounding country; and there unfortunately the L'Enfant plan stopped short. Moreover, within the city there had been perversions of the plan; and there had also been additions to the park area awaiting development. Congress dealt in part with the difficulties by extending the L'Enfant plan of streets and avenues over the entire District of Columbia; and in 1901 the task of preparing a report on the development of the park system of the Federal territory and the placing of public buildings was committed to an expert commission. As Haussmann aimed in large part to carry out the work that had been planned by the architects of Louis XIV., so the Senate Park Commission sought to re-establish and reanimate the plans of L'Enfant, which had the sanction of Washington and Jefferson. In spite of much opposition on the part of those who regard only the present, and take no

XXVIII. CLEVELAND GROUP PLAN.
View looking towards the Lake from the proposed civic center.

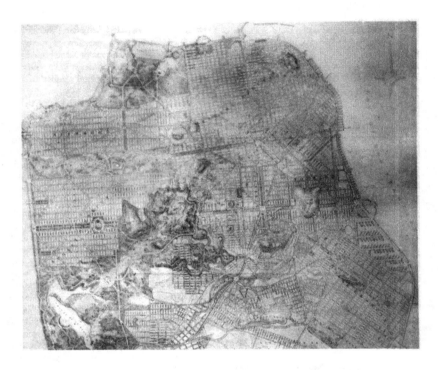

XXIX. PLAN FOR THE DEVELOPMENT OF THE ENTIRE CITY OF SAN FRANCISCO.
Report of D. H. Burnham to the Association of Improvement and Adornment of San Francisco, 1904–1906.

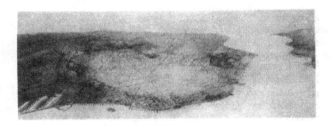

XXX. BIRD'S-EYE VIEW OF THE PLAN OF DEVELOPMENT FOR SAN FRANCISCO.
This view shows municipal center, boulevard system, and treatment of surrounding hills as parks.

of the American people, the cities throughout the country began to ask why they too should not achieve whatever of beauty and convenience their situation and their civic pride would allow. Among the first to feel the new impulse was Cleveland, a commercial city where at the time the forces of democracy were having fullest play. Taking advantage of the fact that a Federal building, a city hall, and a public library must be constructed in the near future,

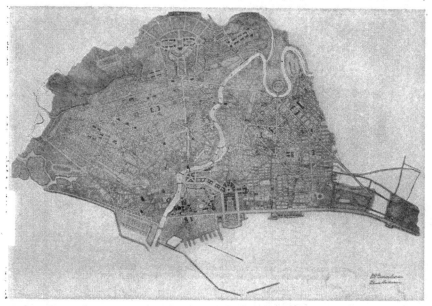

XXXI. PLANS FOR THE DEVELOPMENT OF MANILA, SUBMITTED TO THE PHILIPPINE COMMISSION BY D. H. BURNHAM, 1905.
The essential elements of this plan are the government center and system of proposed arteries radiating from it, the railway station, and the shore road.

and that a railway station on the Lake front could not long be delayed, a commission of experts was appointed to prepare a group-plan for the location of those structures, with appropriate landscape settings; and high-minded, public-spirited citizens who were behind the movement labored until they brought harmony of action among the political agencies, and so placed the plans beyond the risk of failure. The expense involved approximates $14,000,000 for public purposes, and from three to five millions additional for railway terminals, museums, and the like.

Boston has developed the most extensive park system in America, at a cost of $33,000,000, and is creating on the Charles River a tidal basin which bids fair to rival any similar work in Europe. A state commission is now studying means to relieve congestion in the city, and to extend its commercial facilities. New York is struggling with many isolated works of improvement spread over the broad domain of that city's activities; Baltimore is seeking to use the opportunity presented by a great fire to introduce order and symmetry in her street system, and also to create a connected park system; and. the citizens of St. Louis have prepared and presented a city plan for the grouping of municipal buildings, for an inner and an outer park system, for civic centers comprising small parks and playgrounds, museums, branch libraries, and like public buildings.[1] San Francisco, even before the great earthquake and fire of April, 1906, was already working on

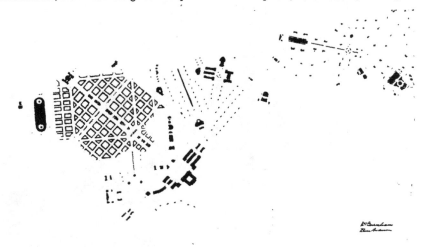

XXXII. PLAN FOR A SUMMER CAPITAL OF THE PHILIPPINE ISLANDS, AT BAGUIO.
Submitted to the Philippine Commission by D. H. Burnham, 1905.

a comprehensive plan to promote, in every practical way, the beautifying of the streets, parks, squares, and public places of the city; to bring to the attention of public officials and the citizens the best methods of instituting artistic municipal betterments; to stimulate the sentiment of civic pride in the improvement and care of private property; and, in short, to make San Francisco a more agreeable city in which to live. This latter movement resulted in a comprehensive city plan which has been adopted by the general committee of citizens and by the Board of Supervisors.[2]

Philadelphia is cutting a great parkway from Logan Square to Fairmount Park, with the expectation of extending the thoroughfare to the City Hall; is acquiring extensive additions to its large parks; and is planning for the grouping of its present buildings. Minneapolis and St. Paul have made common cause in the creation of parkways, and the last-named city is bent on securing adequate approaches for the newly completed state capitol.[3] From Providence and

[1] A City Plan for St. Louis; reports of the several committees appointed by the Executive Board of the Civic League to draft a City Plan, 1907.
[2] Report on a Plan for San Francisco; by D. H. Burnham, assisted by Edward H. Bennett; presented to the Mayor and Board of Supervisors by the Association for the Improvement and Adornment of San Francisco; edited by Edward F. O'Day, 1905.
[3] A comprehensive summary of the progress of municipal improvement in the United States is to be found in *Charities and The Commons* for February, 1908.

Hartford in the East, to Kansas City and on to Seattle in the West, the city planning is in full progress. The South also has felt the new impulse. Annapolis, the capital of Maryland, was laid out on lines strikingly similar to those embodied in Sir Christopher Wren's scheme for London; and the plan of Williamsburg, the colonial capital of Virginia, suggests the locations adopted for the Capitol and White House at Washington; so that the new plans for Roanoke, Virginia, seem like the discovery of a lost art.

No sooner had the United States come into the possession of the Philippine Islands than the War Department set about adapting the capital city of Manila to the changed conditions brought about by the influx of Americans, who are used to better conditions of living than had prevailed in those islands. While fully recognizing the value of the historic public buildings, the Department undertook to have prepared a plan for connecting thoroughfares, open spaces, driveways and promenades which should provide adequate facilities for transportation, improved sanitation, and opportunities for those particular kinds of recreation which the climate invites. As a result the expansion which is coming as the result of American occupation, will proceed on comprehensive lines. Moreover, the necessity of providing a summer capital for the rulers of our new possessions has led to the creation on the hills of Bagnio of a city laid out on a plan similar to the plan made by L'Enfant for the city of Washington, in that it provides for such public buildings as may be needed for government offices, for the service of the city itself, and for the healthfulness, convenience, and recreation of the people; and all these functions are so arranged as to make a unified and orderly city. Thus without additional expense, but merely by taking thought for the future, the two capitals of the Philippines, even in their physical characteristics, will represent the power and dignity of this nation.

It has been seen that as peace permits the expansion of cities regardless of means of defense against outside foes, and as commerce enriches the people, population increases with such rapidity as to create demands for enlarged facilities for circulation throughout the city; and that these demands are so insistent that they must be met, no matter at what cost. Also, that those cities which have made ample provision for future growth have saved largely in money while at the same time they have accomplished much in the way of convenience and orderliness. Thus it has been well said that Paris is a unified city; whereas London is a collection of towns. Moreover, it is to be noted that throughout the civilized world there is a great forward movement in the direction of transforming cities to adapt them to the improved conditions of living which the people everywhere are demanding, and which, moreover, they feel that they have the power to enforce. As a part of this movement arises the impulse to express in concrete form the feeling of loyalty to and pride in the city; and this feeling finds expression in parks and pleasure grounds, in monuments and fine public buildings, in institutions of art and learning, and in hospitals and other means of alleviating the ills of mankind. Furthermore, there has arisen the conception of the city as an organic whole, each part having well-defined relations with every other part; and the expression of this idea is now seen to be the highest aim of the city-builder.

Each city differs from every other city in its physical characteristics and in the nature of its opportunities, so that the development of every city must be along individual lines. This very fact allows full scope for the development of that peculiar charm which, wherever discovered and developed irresistibly draws to that city people of discrimination and taste, and at the same time begets a spirit of loyalty and satisfaction on the part of the citizens.

It is not to be expected that the people of Chicago will stand still while the movement for better civic conditions is sweeping over the whole civilized world; or that the stirrings of the new impulse that have begun among this people will be suffered to die out, without accomplishing the possibilities so abundantly offered to make this city pre-eminent among commercial cities.

The experience of other cities both ancient and modern, both abroad and at home, teaches Chicago that the way to true greatness and continued prosperity lies in making the city convenient and healthful for the ever-increasing numbers of its citizens; that civic beauty satisfies a craving of human nature so deep and so compelling that people will travel far to find and enjoy it; that the orderly arrangement of fine buildings and monuments brings fame and wealth to the city; and that the cities which truly exercise dominion rule by reason of their appeal to the higher emotions of the human mind. The problem for Chicago, therefore, resolves itself into making the best use of a situation, the central location and resources of which have already drawn together millions of people, and are clearly destined to assemble many times that number; and planning for that civic development which promotes present content and insures permanence.

XXXIII. FLORENCE, ITALY.
This silhouette of towers is characteristic of Italian towns in the
Middle Ages. From La Toscane.

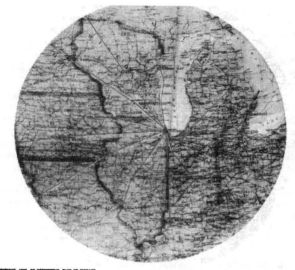

COPYRIGHT, 1909, BY COMMERCIAL CLUB OF CHICAGO

XXXIV. CHICAGO. DIAGRAM OF LOCATION WITH REGARD TO THE SEVEN CENTRAL STATES.

CHAPTER III

CHICAGO THE METROPOLIS OF THE MIDDLE WEST: REASONS FOR EXPECTING CONTINUOUS
GROWTH: THE SUBURBS: A LAKESIDE DRIVEWAY ALONG LAKE MICHIGAN: CONNECTIONS
BETWEEN OUTLYING CITIES: THE BUILDING OF GOOD ROADS

COTTONWOOD, NEAR CHICAGO.
Height, 127 ft.; diameter, 10 ft.

HICAGO is the metropolis of the Middle West, a term popu-
larly applied to the area known a century ago as the Territory
Northwest of the Ohio River. No section of the country, except
New England, has so distinct a history. Conquered by Virginia
troops at the very time when the Colonies were wresting their
independence from Great Britain, and held for the United States
by the sagacity of Franklin and the pertinacity of John Jay when
the treaty of 1783 was negotiated, the Old Northwest was the first
territorial acquisition of the new republic. Then, while the
British still held the posts and only Indians and fur-traders roamed
its forests, the Congress of the Confederation gave to the Northwest Territory in the Ordinance of 1787 a charter which con-
tained two provisions that during the years of development exercised a unifying force comparable
only to that brought about by the extension of Christianity and the civil law during the Middle

31

Ages,— the prohibition of slavery, and the encouragement of free popular education. The continuous struggle to preserve human freedom against all the forces determined to extend slavery to the fertile fields of the new West, and the establishment of schools and colleges supported from a public treasury, brought about common aims and aspirations. When the nation engaged in the struggle for its very life, this region furnished the battle-ground for the statesmen; and when war came, both the leader of the people and the commander in the field were the embodiment of the spirit of the Middle West.

The domain over which Chicago holds primacy is larger than Austria-Hungary, or Germany, or France; three thousand miles of navigable waters form a portion of its boundaries; the rivers flowing into the Great Lakes, the Mississippi, and the Ohio, give access to every part of the interior; the level prairies invite the railroad and the canal builder; the large proportion of arable land makes possible the support of an enormous population; and the abundance and range of the products of earth and forest furnish the materials for traffic. It is no wonder, therefore, that the growth of the Middle West in population and in wealth has been phenomenal; and that at the point of convenience a city of the first order has sprung up.

During the second half of the nineteenth century the population of Chicaco increased from thirty thousand to two millions of people. To-day all conditions point to continued gains. The days of chance and uncertainty are past. The days of doubtful ventures are gone, and the hazards of new fortunes. The elements which make for the greatness of the city are known to be permanent; and men realize that the time has now come to build confidently on foundations already laid.

The growth of the city has been so rapid that it has been impossible to plan for the economical disposition of the great influx of people, surging like a human tide to spread itself wherever opportunity for profitable labor offered place. Thoughtful people are appalled at the results of progress; at the waste in time, strength, and money which congestion in city streets begets; at the toll of lives taken by disease when sanitary precautions are neglected; and at the frequent outbreaks against law and order which result from narrow and pleasureless lives. So that while the keynote of the nineteenth century was expansion, we of the twentieth century find that our dominant idea is conservation. The people of Chicago have ceased to be impressed by rapid growth or the great size of the city. What they insist asking now is, How are we living? Are we in reality prosperous? Is the city a convenient place for business? It is a good labor market in the sense that labor is sufficiently comfortable to be efficient and content? Will the coming generation be able to stand the nervous strain of city life? When a competence has been accumulated, must we go elsewhere to enjoy the fruits of independence? If the city does not become better as it become bigger, shall not the defect be remedied? These are questions that will not be brushed aside. They are the most pressing questions of our day, and everywhere men are anxiously seeking the answers.

The remark is often heard, that if, after the great fire of 1871, the people had realized what the future growth of the city would be, they would have saved a vast amount of money by planning for a convenient city. The undaunted courage with which a debt-burdened community of three hundred and fifty thousand people then set about rebuilding their city must absolve them from the charge of lack of foresight. To-day there is no excuse for the second city in the United States with its destiny made manifest and its wealth secure, if it shall now fail to keep pace with the march of progress that is gathering into its ranks the progressive cities of the world.

Chicago is now facing the momentous fact that fifty years hence, when the children of to-day are at the height of their power and influence, this city will be larger than London: that is, larger than any existing city. Not even an approximate estimate can be ventured as to just how many millions the city will then contain. Mr. Bion J. Arnold, after a careful discussion of the problem of the increase that may be expected,

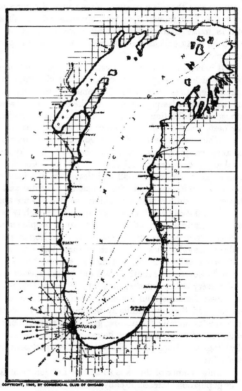

reaches the conclusion that if the national and local conditions governing the population of Chicago shall average in the future exactly as in the past the population in 1952 will be 13,250,000. Mr. Arnold hesitates to predict such an increase in population, just as the most optimistic rebuilder in 1871 would have hesitated to predict two millions in thirty years. Yet it is apparent that the tendency is towards city life. "When the Pacific Coast shall have a population of twenty millions," prophesies James J. Hill, "Chicago will be the largest city in the world." The completion of the Panama Canal, bringing about a more rapid development of the Mississippi Valley; the opening of China and Japan and the Far East to American trade and manufactures; the expansion of the wheat-producing area in the North; and the conversion of the desert lands of the West into arable acres by means of irrigation — all are factors in the growth of Chicago.

Moreover, city life has attractions that make a strong appeal to human nature. Opportunities for large success, for wealth and power and social consideration, for amusement and instruction, for the increase of knowledge and the cultivation of taste, are greater for the average person in the city than in the country. The city, therefore, is constantly drawing from the country the

XXXV. CHICAGO, AND DIAGRAM OF LAKE MICHIGAN.
Proposed roadway to connect all the towns along the shores of the Lake.

young men and women of ambition and self-reliance, who are lured thither by the great prizes which in a democracy are open to the competition of all.

When Chicago is adverted to as the metropolis of the Middle West, the meaning is that throughout this area Chicago newspapers circulate, and Chicago banks hold the banking reserves;

that in Chicago are the chief offices of the large industrial enterprises, and the market for their products. New ideas in government, in civic improvement, in the creation and maintenance of parks, and pleasure grounds are apt to appear first in the metropolis, spreading thence to the surrounding country. On high-days and holidays the great city allures the people from the neighboring parts, and sends its own people on the water or into the country for rest and refreshment, so that there is a constant interchange of comers and goers. In the art schools of Chicago more than four thousand students are gathered; the theaters draw audiences from long distances, and in music Chicago is attaining a worthy position. In Chicago great political conventions are held, party policies are determined, and from the party headquarters here national campaigns are conducted.

It is not in the spirit of boasting that these facts are stated, but rather to show the responsibility which the very pre-eminence of the city imposes, and the necessity for establishing and maintaining those standards of commercial integrity, of taste, and of knowledge which are the prerequisites of lasting success, and the only real satisfaction of the human mind. The constant struggle of civilization is to know and to attain the highest good; and the city which brings about the best conditions of life becomes the most prosperous.

While the influence of Chicago extends throughout a domain larger than any European country except Russia, there exist between this city and outlying towns within a certain radius vital and almost organic relations. The steam and the trolley railways and the automobile have opened to the city workers all varieties of life, and have made possible to a large proportion of the people a habitation amid what might be healthful and attractive surroundings. Unfortunately, however, conditions near any rapidly growing city are apt to be both squalid and ugly.

Occasionally a suburb grows up at some sightly point on the Lake shore, or gathers about some educational institution; or a group of people engaged in a common enterprise select a picturesque spot on river banks and there build homes which, by their very relations one to another, indicate neighborliness. In each of these instances a community of feeling pervades the place and finds expression in well-shaded streets, broad lawns, and homelike architecture. Too often, however, the suburb is laid out by the speculative real estate agent who exerts himself to make every dollar invested turn into as many dollars as possible. Human ingenuity contrives to crowd the maximum number of building lots into the minimum space; if native trees exist on the land they are ruthlessly sacrificed. Then the speculative builder takes matters in hand and in a few months the narrow, grassless streets are lined with rows of cheaply constructed dwellings, and with ugly apartment houses occupying the more desirable sites. In ten years or less the dwellings are dropping to pieces; and the apartment houses, having lost their newness, become rookeries.

This manner of things is as true of London or of Rome as of Chicago; it is the rule wherever population increases rapidly, because human nature is alike the world over. England, however, is remedying this evil by means of town-planning laws executed by a central board; and is endeavoring to regulate the width and direction of streets, and to provide for sufficient open spaces for the health and convenience of the people. After the English manner, a commission should be appointed to lay out all that territory adjacent to the city of Chicago which is likely to become incorporated in the city at least during the next decade. The plans should be so drawn that as subdivisions are platted the new streets shall bear definite relations to the plan of the city; that these streets shall be of suitable width, either for traffic or for residence purposes as the case may be; that building restrictions shall be made to prevent depreciation of property by the advent of undesirable classes of structures, or the erection of towering apartment houses which keep light and air from adjoining property and from the street.

Moreover, adequate provision should be made for public and semi-public buildings. In each town plan spaces should be marked out for public schools, and each school should have

XXXVI. NANCY, FRANCE. VIEW OF THE PLACE STANISLAS.
The principal avenues lead into it; a typical arrangement of public squares in small surrounding towns.

about it ample playgrounds, so that during all the year the school premises shall be the children's center, to which each child will become attached by those ties of remembrance that are restraining influences throughout life. Next to the school, the public library should have place; and here again the landscape setting should be generous and the situation commanding. The town-hall, the engine-house with its lookout tower, the police station with its court of justice, and the post-office, all naturally form a group of buildings that may be located about a common or public square, so as to form the suburban civic center.

There was a time in the older portions of the country when church and churchyard occupied the chief place in the town; and to-day enterprising real estate dealers find it to their advantage to give to one or more religious denominations building sites. But so numerous are the sects into which Christianity has divided itself, and so diverse are the nationalities to be provided for, that the suburban church building rarely offers to the eye any relief from the monotonous ugliness of the airless street which it helps to frame. Also, the old churchyards, with their serried ranks of slate headstones, their cypresses and weeping willows, and their rows of tombs, made a direct appeal to the deepest feelings of the human heart; but the disorder of the modern town cemetery would seem to carry the idea of turbulence even to the grave itself. Perhaps, in the coming times, the spirit of unity will draw people together in religion as well as in business, and such a syndication of religious effort will prevail as shall find expression in permanent buildings devoted to the moral advancement of all the people. The day of the splendid cathedral may never dawn for this country, but certainly in every community there will be buildings for the help of the unfortunate, and the amelioration of those desperate conditions which form the reverse side of great prosperity.

XXXVII. FOREST OF FONTAINEBLEAU, FRANCE.
The Croix de Franchard, an illustration of a country road inter-section.

Then, too, there are the various railway stations and the electric lighting and power buildings, semi-public structures which should be treated in such manner as to present a smiling face to the public. A well-arranged grass plot, a few shrubs, and a little regular attention will give to the plainest building a setting that, like a soft answer, will often turn away wrath from a public-service corporation.

The question of creating pleasing conditions in a suburb is not primarily a matter of money, but of thoughtful co-operation. Even the real estate agent is beginning to discover that by cutting off somewhat from the depth of his lots he can get park space that will make his land more available; and by a combination treatment he can secure for a group of houses an enjoyable area of green grass, to take the place of the narrow and ill-kept back yards which are at once unsightly and unsanitary. In every town a public-improvement commission should be formed to bring about the most orderly conditions within the town itself, and especially to act in co-operation with similar bodies in neighboring towns so as to secure harmonious, connected, and continuous improvement.

If we take arbitrarily a radius of sixty miles from the heart of Chicago and count all the territory in the semi-circumference as having definite relations with the city, the distance from center to circumference is no greater than the present suburban electric lines extend, or the automobilist may cover in a drive of two hours. The traffic over the ways leading to and from the city is already large and steady; and the near-by towns and villages along these thoroughfares may confidently look forward to the day when the tide of Chicago's growth will envelop them, and ultimately incorporate them in the city. Hence two considerations become all-important: first, the improvement of the thoroughfares, not only those leading to the great city, but also those which now form the connections between towns and which ultimately will appear as convenient diagonals within the city itself; and secondly, the arrangement of the streets of the town, together with provision for space for the public and semi-public buildings, and sufficient park and play-ground area, obtained while land is comparatively inexpensive.

The suburban movement of population will necessarily increase as the ground and buildings within the business area of the city become so valuable for commercial purposes as to preclude their use for dwellings. In the city of London a thousand policemen are detailed to guard the five thousand and more buildings left entirely empty each night. More than one-fifth of all the buildings in the "city" are thus left vacant at night and on Sunday. Moreover, London, in order to carry out improvements made to prevent congestion, finds it necessary to remove and rehouse the working-people who are displaced by tearing down buildings in the over-crowded quarters. On the site of the old Millbank prison four thousand persons removed at the time of the Holborn to Strand improvement were rehoused in convenient new dwellings built by the municipality; and more than fifty thousand people have been displaced and reinstated by reason of the various improvements. Thus the city, while drawing from the farms and small towns, also sends out swarms to be housed under more wholesome conditions.

These suburban residents are dependent on the city for a livelihood, and either directly or indirectly pay the taxes that support the municipality. They are vitally interested in adequate and convenient means of transportation, in the protection of life and property, and in well-ordered home surroundings. Thus it happens naturally that as the city grows the functions of the various governing bodies are extended over areas outside the city limits. The admin-

XXXVIII. CHICAGO. THE SHERIDAN ROAD NORTH OF GLENCOE.
From the Report of the Special Park Commission.

istrative county of London has an area of but 118 square miles; but the greater London over which the metropolitan and city police have jurisdiction comprises 693 square miles, and includes a population of two millions outside of the county. The water-board and the sanitary authorities also have authority far beyond county limits.

Boston, first among American cities, realized the advantages of co-operation between the great city and outlying districts. In 1889 the Massachusetts legislature created a metropolitan sewage commission, and later a metropolitan park commission, with jurisdiction over thirty-seven distinct municipalities; and to-day it is proposed to extend police jurisdiction and fire protection over substantially the same area. The Boston park system, developed through the co-operation of these various towns and cities, is famed for its beauty and variety. Beginning with the great ocean beach at Revere, where on a summer day one hundred and fifty thousand persons enjoy the bathing privileges, broad parkways sweep around the city, enveloping on their way great stretches of fen and lofty hills, until again salt water is reached at Nantasket, where another bathing beach as large as the first furnishes refreshment and recreation. Again, it is not without effect on the people of the outlying towns that Massachusetts Avenue keeps its name as it traverses Boston, Cambridge, Arlington, Lexington, and Concord; and that Beacon Street maintains its integrity from Boston through Brookline to Newton. Throughout the entire region one and the same spirit prevails — a spirit of love for and loyalty to the city set on three hills, which dominates the entire region. It would be no more difficult to secure the co-operation of Illinois, Wisconsin, and Indiana in planning for the continuous development of the Lake shore than it has been for New York and New Jersey to combine for the preservation of the Palisades of the Hudson and the development of their park possibilities.[1]

A highway should be built from Wilmette along the western shore of Lake Michigan to Milwaukee; and even where this road runs through intermediate towns it should be located as close as possible to the edge of the water. Such a highway should be kept somewhat back of the sand beaches and a little above them, a retaining wall being built to separate the road from the beach. The planting should be of trees and evergreens hardy enough to stand the exposure. A few miles north of Waukegan is a sand waste on which grows a dwarf juniper, the effect of which on the sand banks is that of moss of dark rich color. This could be used effectively along the shore. A similar treatment might be adopted for the edge of the water much of the way around Lake Michigan.

It needs no argument to show that direct highways leading from the outlying towns to Chicago as the center are a necessity for both; and it is also apparent that suburban towns should be connected with one another in the best manner. Isolated communities lack those social and commercial advantages which arise from easy communication one with another. A diagram has therefore been drawn for the use of the public bodies in their study of the relations of a particular town with other towns, and to suggest the locations and routes that may be followed. This diagram is not put forward as a complete study of the roads, but as a general scheme, the large details of which can be relied on and safely followed. The solid black lines are routes already open and in use as public highways; the dotted lines indicate proposed connection links not yet in existence. It is believed that the building of these roads will not be difficult or unduly expensive for any given township, as very little land will have to be acquired. The existing highways will suffice for the present, and the burden of the improvement will fall lightly on each township.[2]

---

[1] The Palisades Interstate Park Commission was organized in 1900. Mr. J. P. Morgan, the honorary president of the American Scenic and Historic Preservation Society, gave $122,500; the state of New Jersey, $55,000; and New York appropriated $410,000. With these resources the Palisades Commission has acquired most of the palisades fronting on the Hudson, from Fort Lee, N. J., to Piermont, N. Y.

[2] The commercial value of good roads was recognized by Massachusetts a quarter of a century ago, and to-day every portion of the commonwealth is provided with a network of excellent highways built under the direction of a highway commission at the joint expense

Pending the creation of a metropolitan commission for the treatment of the entire area, the public authorities or the improvement associations of each town should confer with their neighbors and agree on the routes of connecting highways; also upon the width and arrangement of roadways, sidewalks, planting-spaces and drainage, and the varieties of trees and shrubs to be used for shade and ornament.

In laying out routes, no bad kinks or sharp turns should be tolerated. The English roads, though better as to surface-finish and drainage, do not compare with the roads of France as to trend and direction; because in England there are so many abrupt and "blind" twistings, which are generally avoided in France. Liberality in road building now will be repaid many fold in the future. The aim should be to adopt the best routes, the best curves and turns, and the most perfect construction known at the present day.[1] It is the opinion of all experts on road building that taking a period of ten years, a good bed and surface carefully maintained all the time will cost less in the aggregate than the very best bed and surface if neglected. We need perfect maintenance, and organization constantly kept sharp and effective, rather than expensive first construction. Nevertheless, the best original construction will be found economical in the end. Automobiles have introduced on the roads a new sort of wear and tear, as their broad pneumatic tires, carrying great weights and moving at high speeds, press into the softer spots and suck up loose material. The result is pockmarks or rough places, which destroy the best of roads constructed according to the old-methods road building.[2]

While good highways are of great value to the terminal cities, they are of even greater value to the outlying towns, and of greatest value to the farming communities through which they pass. Good roads add an element of better living to an agricultural community; they afford ready communication with the city and reduce materially the cost of handling farm products of all kinds; and also they promote communication between farms. These state highways should invariably include a work-road for heavy loads, and also a pleasure drive. The two should be separated by a grassway and there should be grass plots at the sides, and not less than three rows of trees should be planted. The country schools should be on these highways.

At the earliest possible date measures should be taken for beginning what may be termed the outer encircling highway. Beginning at Kenosha on the north, this thoroughfare would run

of state and town; and now the work of tree planting along the roads is in progress. In Los Angeles County, California, $3,500,000 has been raised by a bond issue for laying out and improving highways — so thoroughly do the people appreciate the attractions which good roads have for the tourists who, as in Massachusetts, are a source of income to the community.

In Illinois the State Highway Commission has built two so-called experimental roads in the vicinity of Chicago, one at Wheaton and the other at Naperville. On the road at the latter town, the commission has tried both limestone and slag macadam, and also gravel treated with tar and with oil. A movement is on foot to connect the Wheaton road with Chicago by a direct highway built in a substantial manner. In a letter dated October 20, 1908, Mr. A. N. Johnson, the State Highway Engineer, says: "It is possible that some attempt will be made at the coming session of the legislature to secure means to start the construction of highways. Public sentiment in general, however, is somewhat backward, and I imagine will require longer time than is available by the next legislature to get to such a point that any considerable sum of money will be forthcoming, such as will be necessary to take this work up properly."

[1] For general information on road building there is no better reference document than the paper read by Mr. John Alvord some years ago before the Commercial Club. In general, the conclusion of Mr. Alvord and of others seems to be that there are many specifications, any of which will produce good surfaces, but that durability and lasting value in any case, must finally depend on maintenance. No road yet invented will stand up without constant care and attention being bestowed upon it, care which should begin almost as soon as the surface is first finished.

[2] No roads constructed with smooth surfaces have stood up under heavy automobile travel, except those made of asphaltum and those made like the Sheridan Road in Buena Park. The last-mentioned road has gone through two seasons of very hard usage, and although little repairing has been done, it seems unchanged as to its surface. In one section of England considerable stretches of the same sort of construction have been in service for some time, and with the same result as at Buena Park. In France two years ago, the main road from Versailles to Chartres was in first-class condition; going over the same road in June, 1907, it was found to be almost impassable, the wear upon it having come from automobiles; and yet this highway was constructed with care, on the best old-fashioned macadam formula. Asphaltum roads can be made that will not chip up or pockmark, but the surfacing must be done so that it will incorporate with the mass beneath, and not rolled on as an outer layer. A very moderate speed limit for automobiles will keep roads in good repair, for it is the high speed of the machines that is so destructive to roadbeds.

through Pleasant Prairie, Trevor, and Wilmot to McHenry, thus passing through the northern lake region. Here are the headwaters of the Fox River, lying in natural scenery of much beauty; here too are a large number of lakes and waterways surrounded by hills, the whole forming an extensive parklike territory that will become an important adjunct of Chicago life when properly improved, and when suitable connections are secured.

XXXIX. CHICAGO. THE DES PLAINES RIVER; VIEW NEAR MADISON
STREET BRIDGE.
From the Report of the Special Park Commission.

Beyond McHenry, this outer encircling highway continues on through Woodstock, Marengo, Genoa, Sycamore, De Kalb, Cortland, Sandwich, Millington, and Morris; thence it runs beside or near the Kankakee River through Wilmington, Kankakee, Momence, Shelby, and Maysville, the scenery along the route being very interesting, and much of it romantically beautiful. From Maysville the highway bends north through Valparaiso to Lake Michigan at Michigan City; or by another route from Maysville through La Crosse, Wellsboro, and La Porte to Michigan City, the total length from Kenosha around to Michigan City being approximately two hundred and fifty miles. It is obvious that such a highway, properly built and adorned, would become a strong influence in the development of the social and material prosperity of each of the cities involved, and of all the farming communities along the entire route.

The encircling highway next inside the outer one above described begins at Waukegan and passes through Libertyville to Lake Zurich; thence by two routes, one through Barrington to Elgin, the other bending around to skirt the Fox River near Algonquin and Dundee to Elgin, and on through St. Charles, Geneva, and Batavia to Aurora. From Aurora the highway continues to Plainfield, where it crosses the Du Page River, thence through Joliet, and by one route through Manhattan, Monee, Eagle Lake, Cedar Lake, Crown Point, and Hobart, to Lake Michigan; and by another route from Joliet, through Chicago Heights, Griffith, and Tolleston to Gary, on the Lake. The highway will be approximately one hundred and forty miles long, and nearly the whole of the northern part of it is very picturesque. The next highway proposed goes through a fine, rolling country west of the Des Plaines River. Beginning at Winnetka, it runs through Des Plaines, Elmhurst, and Hinsdale to Blue Island, whence the route divides into two routes, one running through Harvey and Hammond to Gary, and the other running from Blue Island to Robey, on the Lake.

The fourth of the encircling highways begins at Evanston, and passes through Niles or Des Plaines, and along the Des Plaines River to Riverside; all this part of the way, being wooded on the borders of the water, is very beautiful in its present condition. From Riverside, this high-

CHICAGO

GENERAL DIAGRAM OF EXTERIOR
HIGHWAYS
ENCIRCLING AND RADIATING FROM
THE CITY

SCALE

COPYRIGHT, 1909, BY COMMERCIAL CLUB OF CHICAGO

XL. CHICAGO. GENERAL DIAGRAM OF EXTERIOR HIGHWAYS ENCIRCLING, OR RADIATING FROM, THE CITY.
All the arteries composing the system without the city limits exist, except where shown in dotted lines. City limits shown in red tint; rivers and other waterways in blue.

way runs through Chicago Ridge to Robey or Blue Island, and from thence to the Lake, over routes already mentioned.

It will be noted that the diagram provides not only for encircling highways, but also for roads running directly to the heart of Chicago from every important town or village. And it will also be noted that nearly every stretch of roadway shown on the diagram already exists as a more or less satisfactory country road, the dotted lines indicating proposed changes or links. The system as outlined is complete, and it meets every present demand of road building for such extensive environs as those of Chicago. It is confidently believed that in the course of the next few years every mile of these highways will be improved in the best manner, and that thus Chicago ultimately will come to possess a network of surface thoroughfares equal to the requirements of future generations.

A satisfactory method of running highways is to parallel the railroads. The work-road should be next to the right-of-way; then should come the carriage driveway. Where electric railways exist, or are projected on thoroughfares, the most agreeable treatment is found in setting apart for the tracks a space which may be grassed over and well shaded. Besides adding to the comfort of the passengers, the uninterrupted use of the tracks permits high speed and thereby saves time. The improvement of the three roadways as a unit, with the appropriate planting, would give a charm to suburban travel where now there is none, while at the same time expenses of maintenance would be lessened. As a rule, the creation of highways along railroads involves only the bare cost of inexpensive land and the building of the road. The railroads are in themselves great diagonals; and by following them the shortest lines between important points are secured. Then, too, the right-of-way traversed by the tracks should be improved. The drainage should be perfect, so that pools of stagnant water shall not be an offense to the eye and a menace to health. The unsightly billboard should be replaced by shrubbery or by a wall; and the entire space should be free from the litter of papers or the accumulations of dirt and ashes.

The suburban resident is vitally interested in the means of communication between his home and his place of business. If his morning and his evening

XLI. CHICAGO. THE SHORE OF LAKE MICHIGAN; VIEW AT THE NORTH LINE OF COOK COUNTY.
From the Report of the Special Park Commission.

ride are made on the steam railway, he is interested not only in passing through pleasant scenes on his way to and from Chicago, but he is concerned also in having the railway station in his suburban town conveniently located, constructed simply but artistically, and placed amid surroundings which in themselves are harmonious and appropriate. A well-kept lawn, with shrubbery shutting out the necessarily unpleasant feature of a steam railway station; a sheltered platform well lighted at night, and a commodious station, architecturally in good taste — these accessories go a long way towards mitigating the nerve strain which every business man feels and from which too many suffer.

The electric railroads, with their frequent cars passing one's very door, have done a vast deal to bind the outlying towns firmly to the central city. More than this, they have promoted neighborliness among people of adjoining towns, and have broken up the isolation of farm life. These roads now strive to obtain private rights-of-way, excepting where for the convenience of passengers they pass through city streets; and the same observations as to good order along the routes and at the terminals that appertain to steam roads apply equally to trolley lines.

The rapidly increasing use of the automobile promises to carry on the good work begun by the bicycle in the days of its popularity in promoting good roads and reviving the roadside inn as a place of rest and refreshment. With the perfection of this machine, and the extension of its use, out-of-door life is promoted, and the pleasures of suburban life are brought within the reach of multitudes of people who formerly were condemned to pass their entire time in the city.

While the people generally have yet to be brought to appreciate the value of well-constructed highways, the universal experience is that where a stretch of good road has been built the saving in time and money is so great and so apparent that the movement gathers force rapidly, and culminates only when all main lines have been completed. Land adjacent to such roads increases in value and finds a readier sale; the farmer is no longer cut off from his market, and often he finds it possible to lessen the number of horses he keeps. The actual economies which the good road allows far exceed the increase in taxes necessary to meet the bond issue, and life on the farm becomes more profitable as well as more agreeable.

XLII. VIEW OF LAKE ZURICH, ILLINOIS.

COPYRIGHT, 1909, BY COMMERCIAL CLUB OF CHICAGO

XLIII. CHICAGO. WINTER VIEW OF GRANT PARK AND THE PROPOSED
HARBOR, LOOKING EAST.
From the original sketch by E. H. Bennett.

CHAPTER IV

THE CHICAGO PARK SYSTEM: THE MOVEMENT FOR PARK EXTENSION: PLAYGROUNDS:
OUTLYING PARK SYSTEMS IN LONDON, PARIS, BERLIN, VIENNA, AND BOSTON: PROPOSED
TREATMENT OF THE LAKE MICHIGAN SHORE: AN OUTER PARK BELT

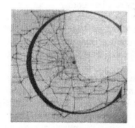

HICAGO, on becoming a city, chose for its motto *Urbs in horto*
— a city set in a garden. Such indeed it then was, with the
opalescent waters of the Lake at its front, and on its three sides
the boundless prairie carpeted with waving grass bedecked with
brilliant wild flowers. The quick advance of commerce and
manufactures, the rapid building of railroads and factories, and
the hastily constructed homes of operatives crowded out nature's
parterres of flowers. Still the motto lingered in the minds of
men, and in 1839 the struggle began to secure for the fast-growing population park spaces which should at least recall the
gardens that of necessity had been sacrificed.

In the year mentioned, a half-square on Michigan Avenue, where the Public Library now
stands, comprised the entire park system of the city of Chicago. Three years later Washington
Square was added; then followed at intervals Jefferson, Union, Ellis, and Vernon parks, each
representing the public spirit of individuals rather than the foresight of the city. In 1864 the
Common Council, having been awakened to the necessity of providing recreation places for the
growing multitudes of citizens, secured a portion of the lands which later came to be named
Lincoln Park, and the sum of ten thousand dollars was appropriated for park improvement.

At first no effort was made to provide connections among the various parks; but in 1869 a
movement was started, by those whom the practical people of that day called dreamers, to realize

the then half-forgotten and wholly disregarded motto, by framing the city of Chicago with a garden of parks and boulevards, beginning at Lincoln Park on the north and connecting Humboldt, Garfield, Douglas, Washington, and Jackson parks. The attempt succeeded; the Chicago park system came to take second place among the park areas of the United States, and was the pride and glory of the city. Substantially, park acquisition in Chicago halted there — thirty-nine years ago. Second only to Philadelphia in 1880, Chicago has now dropped to the seventh place in so far as park area is concerned; and when the relative density of population is taken into consideration this city occupies the thirty-second place! At least half the population of Chicago to-day live more than one mile from any large park, and in the congested sections of the city there are nearly five thousand people to each acre of park space. The average for the entire city is 590 persons to each acre of park. For health and good order there should be one acre of park area for each hundred people.[1]

The seriousness of present conditions being generally realized, a movement to bring about radical changes has already taken direction, and is fast gathering the force necessary to accomplish its ends. The state of Illinois has authorized the respective boards of park commissioners to connect Grant Park with Lincoln Park on the north and with Jackson Park on the south, and has granted the submerged lands along the Lake shore for that purpose, providing, however, that in all cases the commissioners must reach an amicable understanding with the riparian owners, the right of condemnation being withheld. Moreover, the state has also authorized cities, towns, and villages to grant to park authorities the right to take and improve streets not more than a mile in length without the consent of the abutting property owners, and to construct surface and elevated ways and turn the same over to public park corporate authorities.[2]

In 1899 the Chicago City Council created the Special Park Commission, at the same time adopting resolutions recognizing the value of parks in preventing crime, promoting cleanliness, and diminishing disease; also declaring the need of greater area for parks, both large and small, and providing for a systematic study of the present and future needs of the city in the matter of parks and recreation grounds. In 1903, Cook County having created a commission to secure an outer belt of parks and boulevards, co-operation between the Special Park Commission and the Outer Belt Commission was established.

At the instance of the Special Park Commission legislation has been enacted to enable the several park authorities to locate parks and pleasure grounds, of not more than ten acres in extent, in any portion of their respective districts, and to raise money by bond issues. On the South Side seventeen new parks, with a total area of 671 acres have been acquired. A feature of these small parks is the neighborhood-center building, provided with baths, gymnasia, refectory service, club rooms, and reading rooms for the district served. These "clubhouses for the people," as they are called, are in service both summer and winter. The outdoor swimming-pools and athletic fields are in charge of expert directors furnished by the authorities. The aim of the commissioners is to improve the health and morals of the people, and to stimulate local pride and patriotism; and the work has attracted international attention. The South Side expansion movement, now nearing completion, will cost about seven million dollars.

In suggesting additions to the smaller parks, the principle has been followed of placing them, as far as possible, on the proposed circuit boulevards. The intersections of these boulevards with

[1] Report of the Special Park Commission; Compiled by Dwight Heald Perkins, 1904.
[2] See Acts of May 14, 1903; May 2, 1907; April 19, 1879; June 21, 1895; May 25, 1907.

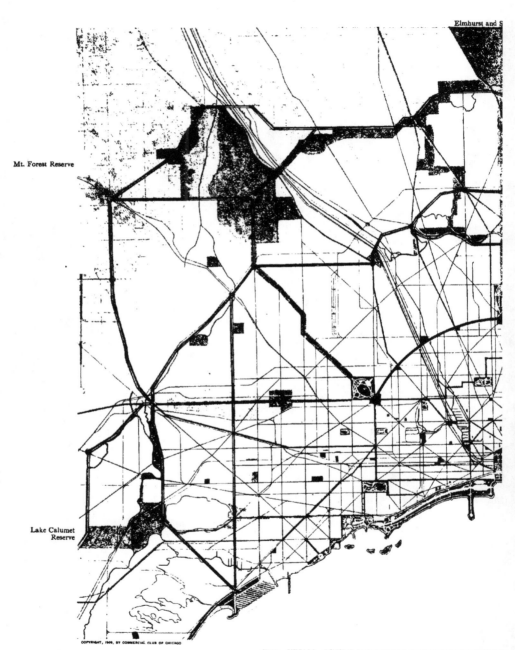

Elmhurst and S

Mt. Forest Reserve

Lake Calumet
Reserve

COPYRIGHT, 1909, BY COMMERCIAL CLUB OF CHICAGO

XLIV. CHICAGO. GENERAL MAP SHOWING TOPOGRAPHY, WATERWAYS
The parks and parkways encircle the city; they are placed in relation to the radiating arteries, and increase in area in prop
Calumet rivers, and the location of outlying townships. The elevation of t

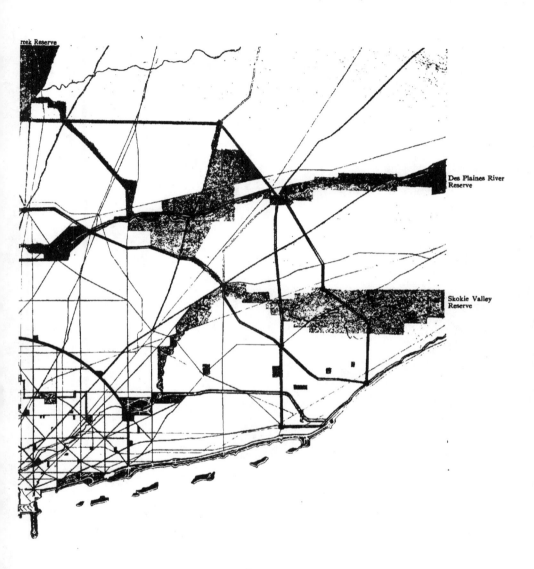

reek Reserve

Des Plaines River
Reserve

Skokie Valley
Reserve

'OMPLETE SYSTEM OF STREETS, BOULEVARDS, PARKWAYS, AND PARKS.
their distance from the center (green). Also showing railroads (red), the proposed harbors at the mouths of the Chicago and
ł is shown by increasing depth of color (orange), from the center of the city.

streets will necessarily form round-points, which should be treated as part of the park system. The same principle of placing is followed for the larger play parks, in order that they may be reached from one another by passing through a continuous line of planting. The question of density of population has been considered with reference to the relative sizes of those parks which

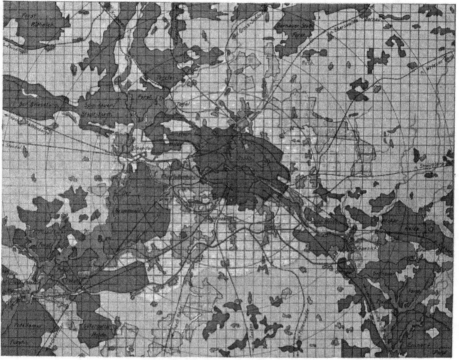

XLV.   BERLIN.   BLOCK PLAN SHOWING THE PARK SYSTEM (GREEN), AND PROPOSED FOREST RESERVES (DARK GREEN).
Reproduced from "Gross Berlin."

lie within the congested center, particularly with regard to the first circuit; and although all such parks cannot be placed adjacent to boulevards, they are shown connected with one another by important thoroughfares, so that the natural lines of travel will pass them. The smaller play parks disregard to some extent the above principles, because these are in the strictest sense neighborhood centers. The play parks and squares are thus balanced equally around the civic center, which may be said to be the center of the varying densities of population. In this way, they serve to accentuate the scheme of circuits laid down in the system of circulation on the general plan.

The report of the Special Park Commission, issued in 1904, contains a detailed study for a metropolitan park system embracing all of Cook County, together with recommendations for an outer system of parks and boulevards, in the main following the watercourses throughout the area of the county. Thus foundations have been laid for a systematic and aggressive campaign

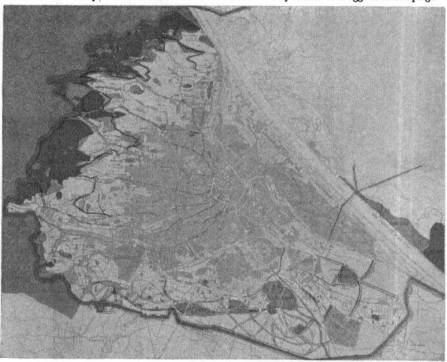

XLVI. VIENNA. BLOCK PLAN SHOWING THE PARK SYSTEM (GREEN), AND EXISTING FOREST RESERVES (DARK GREEN).
Reproduced from "Gross Berlin."

to obtain for the people of Chicago those means of recreation and refreshment absolutely necessary to a growing city. Extensive as the recommendations of the various park authorities appear, a consideration of the whole problem will show that they scarcely do more than meet the situation as it exists to-day, and that the near future will demand more ample spaces. The development of the suburban service on steam roads, the extension of the electric lines which give quick and frequent service between Chicago and cities sixty, seventy, and even a hundred miles distant, and the increasing use of the automobile have brought within the sphere of Chicago's dominating influence the towns and country for a radius of at least sixty miles from the geographical center of the city. From Kenosha on the north, around to De Kalb on the west, and thence to Michigan City on the south, all roads lead to Chicago; and this entire region might well be included in a metropolitan area within which large parks shall be located, improved, and maintained at joint expense.

XLVII. DISTRICT OF COLUMBIA. BLOCK PLAN SHOWING THE PARK SYSTEM (GREEN), AND ADDITIONS (DARK GREEN). Proposed by the Senate Park Commission.

The time to secure the lands necessary for such a system is now, while as yet the prices are moderate and the natural scenery is comparatively unspoiled. Every year of failure or neglect to act largely increases the expense and diminishes the opportunities, for all of the lands about Chicago are almost equally available for building purposes. Already the prairie state of Illinois is nearly one-half urban, and the tendency towards city life is fast increasing. At the same time the need for breathing spaces and recreation grounds is being forced upon the attention of practical men, who are learning to appreciate the fact that a city, in order to be a good labor-market, must provide for the health and pleasure of the great body of workers. Density of population beyond a certain point results in disorder, vice, and disease, and thereby becomes the greatest menace to the well-being of the city itself. As a measure of precaution, therefore, the establishment of adequate park area is necessary.

If Chicago is to equal or surpass London in size, the provision for open spaces here certainly should be no less than that which the British metropolis has found necessary. And yet London is constantly adding to its recreation grounds. As respects large parks, that city counts Epping Forest, sixteen miles to the north, which with the neighboring Hainault Forest includes 5,600 acres, an area opened by the Corporation of London in 1882, as a free and inalienable public park and place of recreation; and Bushy Park, fifteen miles to the west, comprising a thousand acres; and Richmond Park, with its 2,255 acres, not counting the famous Kew Gardens; while Windsor Great Park, 1,800 acres in extent, is but twenty-one miles from the city. Thus within a radius of twoscore miles from his city, the Londoner has at his command large parks comprising in the aggregate more than ten thousand acres; and every traveler who has found himself in London on a pleasant Sunday in summer knows well how the city empties itself of people on that day, and how every vehicle available is brought into service to accommodate the crowds seeking rest and recreation in the woods and on the Thames. On such an afternoon the Thames at Richmond is so covered with canoes and wherries that one might walk dry-shod across the river, stepping from boat to boat. The great crowd of all sorts and conditions of men and women is gay and good natured, and the scene, as looked down upon from the terraces of Hampton Court, has a charm beyond the power of words to express.

The name of Henley brings to the mind of the Englishman all that is beautiful and picturesque in the amateur aquatic life of that country. Henley is situated on the Thames in one of its most beautiful stretches; the valley is verdant; the trees are old and stately, while velvet lawns and gardens gay line the banks at frequent intervals. Back from the water the Chiltern Hills rise in a mass of green woods and waving grain. During regatta week, bunting, flags, flowers, and decorations of all kinds attract the eye, and the picturesque old place is made a scene of brightness and gayety. In the evening the many house-boats are aglow with colored lanterns; lights from boats of every sort flash hither and thither on the water, and fireworks light the heavens in beautiful colors.

Paris, which is one of the great manufacturing centers of the world, has the Bois de Boulogne of 2,250 acres

XLVIII. LONDON. A VIEW OF ROTTEN ROW IN HYDE PARK.

at its very gates; and only five miles distant, skirting the eastern boundary of the city, is the Bois de Vincennes of somewhat greater area. Thirty-seven miles distant is the forest of Fountainebleau, which covers no less than 42,500 acres, the most beautiful of all French forests; while the gardens of Versailles, with their wonderful fountains, are but fourteen miles away. Berlin has its great pine woods on the east, west, and north of the city, the park development having been made to keep pace with other radical changes which since 1878 have transformed the German capital from a badly arranged, ill-built, and ill-kept town into one of the magnificent capital cities of the world. At Vienna the forest park known as the Prater, 4,270 acres in extent, extends along the east side of the city; and so diversified are the uses to which this recreation place is put, that perhaps no other single park in the world accommodates so many people. Large as these spaces seem, no one of the cites mentioned is satisfied with its present park area; but each one is striving to enlarge its opportunities for recreation.

In 1893 Boston began the creation of its system of metropolitan parks, by the adoption of a report made that year by a special commission. Thirteen cities and twenty-six towns are now included in the metropolitan district; and upwards of ten thousand acres are controlled by a board of five commissioners. The funds for the acquirement and development of the system had been raised by loans represented by forty-year bonds issued by the State of Massachusetts, to be repaid from sinking funds made up of annual payments by the various cities and towns included within the district, except that the entire commonwealth has assumed about two and a half millions of one of the three loans, which aggregate about ten and a half millions. The annual payments for sinking funds, interest, and maintenance are made according to a table of percentages fixed by the supreme court of the state upon the report of a special commission appointed each five years. The original plan, although somewhat modified from time to time to accommodate new circumstances, has been adhered to with great fidelity as constituting the project for a complete outlying park system, to the gradual accomplishment of which the state and the district has committed itself. The appropriations, averaging between six and seven hundred thousand dollars a year for sixteen years, have been general in form; the commission has never made direct appeals or efforts to secure grants of money; but citizens concerned in the accomplishment of some particular portion of the system have interested themselves to secure the necessary funds. The woods reservations were acquired first; then Revere Beach and the banks of the lower Charles River; and lastly the twenty-seven miles of connecting parkways. After the first ten years, the legislature reviewed the entire situation, and, finding the work good, provided three hundred thousand dollars a year for four years for its continuation. Each year increases the number of friends of the system, and the necessary funds for enlargement or for special treatments, such as building ocean-front driveways, the acquisition of some specially desirable natural feature, or the construction of a connecting parkway, are provided.

The plan of Washington provides for a complete system of parks encircling the entire city, uniting Potomac Park, which stretches along the river front, with the present Zoölogical and Rock Creek parks on the north; thence by parkways to the Soldiers' Home grounds, some seven hundred acres in extent, and on to the valley of the Anacostia, where a tidal basin will be formed. The palisades of the upper Potomac, the Arlington estate, and the chain of abandoned forts on the hills overlooking the city, all become parts of the simple yet comprehensive scheme, which is but the logical development of the original L'Enfant plan. Already Washington is realizing in large measure the commercial advantages of civic beauty. People from all parts of the country are building fine residences along the broad avenues; and new business structures vie with the government office buildings in design and solidity. Thus the plans which seemed but a dream when they were first exhibited eight years ago are now so far accomplished that complete realization seems plainly in sight.

The opportunities for large parks in the immediate vicinity of Chicago are ample. First in importance is the shore of Lake Michigan, which should be treated as park space to the greatest possible extent. The Lake front by right belongs to the people. It affords their one great unobstructed view, stretching away to the horizon, where water and clouds seem to meet. No mountains or high hills enable us to look over broad expanses of the earth's surface; and perforce we must come even to the margin of the Lake for such a survey of nature. These views of a broad expanse are helpful alike to mind and body. They beget calm thoughts and feelings, and afford escape from the petty things of life. Mere breadth of view, however, is not all. The Lake is living water, ever in motion, and ever changing in color and in the form of its waves. Across its surface comes the broad pathway of light made by the rising sun; it mirrors the ever-changing forms of the clouds, and it is illumined by the glow of the evening sky. Its colors vary with the shadows that play upon it. In its every aspect it is a living thing, delighting man's eye and refreshing his spirit. Not a foot of its shores should be appropriated by individuals to the exclusion of the people. On the contrary, everything possible should be done to enhance its attractiveness and to develop its natural beauties, thus fitting it for the part it has to play in the life of the whole city. It should be made so alluring that it will become the fixed habit of the people to seek its restful presence at every opportunity.

Wherever possible, the outer shore should be a beach on which the waves may break; and the slopes leading down to the water should be quiet stretches of green, unvexed by the small irregular piers and the various kinds of projections which to-day give it an untidy appearance. Except where formal treatments are demanded, the inner shore should be a planted space. There should be lagoons, narrow and winding, along the north shore, and wider, with more regular lines, along the south shore. Both margins of these lagoons should be planted with trees and shrubs, so arranged as to leave openings of various sizes, thus making vistas of the water and the life upon it, to be enjoyed by the people passing along the driveways or living in the homes that line park stretches. These plantations should be carefully devised so as to display every form and color of foliage and blossom known to this climate; the foliage should be arranged so as to be seen here in masses and there at the end of vistas, by boatmen close at hand or far away over the waters. The aspect of these plantings from the open lake also should be studied, and especially the subject of evergreens and other forms of winter planting demands adequate attention.

Moreover, the sweet breath of plant life so abundant in nature and so agreeable to man should give greeting to those who seek the refreshment of the parks. Color of blossoms, too, should be used, not in little beds or as mere incidents, but in masses stretching broadly along the shores of the lagoons, and even upon the surface of the water itself, where aquatic plants of many varieties may be made to contribute their part in this possible paradise. The cultivation and maintenance of such stretches of natural beauty must have the co-operation of the people, to the end that the loveliness intended for all may be protected.

The building of parks along the shore is dictated by considerations of health and enjoyment. The ease with which the work can be accomplished becomes apparent when one considers that the refuse of the city seeks a dump which cannot be found anywhere else than on the Lake front. Probably 1,000,000 cubic yards of waste are annually conveyed to the Lake front from Evanston

COPYRIGHT, 1908, BY COMMERCIAL CLUB OF CHICAGO

XLIX. CHICAGO. VIEW OF THE CITY FROM JACKS
The proposed shore treatment as a park enclosing a waterway (or a series of lagoons) i
Painted for the Com

This park may be built almost without cost to the people
wastage from the city. This material aggregates at the p
acres per annum. In this manner Grant Park has alre
only a

) GRANT PARK, LOOKING TOWARDS THE WEST.
ther with the enlarged yacht harbor, recreation piers, and a scheme for Grant Park.
by Jules Guerin.

py making use of the excavated material and general
it an amount sufficient to fill as many as twenty-two
ited, and its extension down the south shore will be
ne.

A

Grand Boulevard

Cottage Grove
Avenue

Midway Plaisa

Thirty-ninth
Street

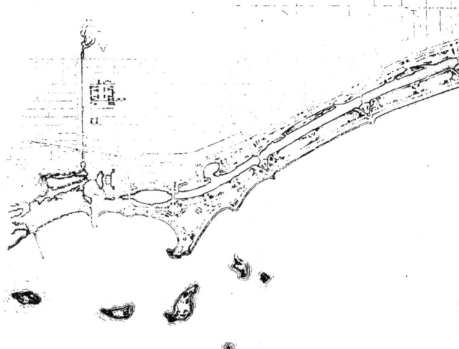

Diagram A. Lake shore from Chicago Avenue on the north

COPYRIGHT, 1908, BY COMMERCIAL CLUB OF CHICAGO

L. CHICAGO. PARK DEVELOPMENT PROPOSED FOR THE LAKE SHORE FROM JACKSON PARK TO WILMET
This park, enclosing lagoons for boating, would be a continuous playground for the people, and may be built by uti
the wastage from the city and excavated material at practically no cost.

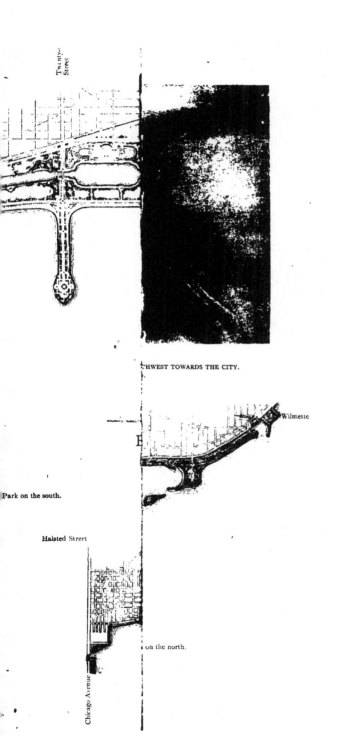

Twentye Street

THWEST TOWARDS THE CITY.

Wilmette

E

Park on the south.

Halsted Street

on the north.

Chicago Avenue

COPYRIGHT, 1909, BY COMMERCIAL CLUB OF CHICAGO

LI. CHICAGO. VIEW LOOKING SOUTH OVER THE LAGOONS OF THE PROPOSED PARK FOR THE SOUTH SHORE.
Painted for the Commercial Club by Jules Guerin.

COPYRIGHT, 1909, BY COMMERCIAL CLUB OF CHICAGO

LII. CHICAGO. SECTION THROUGH THE PARK PROPOSED FOR THE SOUTH SHORE.
A boulevard is suggested above that portion of the railroad right-of-way used for freight; additional right-of-way open to the air
to be provided for passenger trains; approaches to the outer park to run from the boulevard over the tracks.

to South Chicago, enough to fill twenty acres of ground, raising it seven feet above the surface in twenty feet of water. The necessary breakwaters having been built, this constantly growing amount of waste material can be put in place cheaply. Therefore, it is wise to provide now for the disposition of it, and to design beautiful and extensive park strips along the entire shore, which will almost build themselves in the course of another generation. Indeed both health and danger to navigation prohibit the emptying of this spoil in the Lake, as has been done in the past.

These lagoons, protected from the waves of the open Lake and sheltered from the wind by the city on one side and the park strips on the other, will be a powerful attraction toward open-

COURTESY OF THE SOUTH PARK COMMISSIONERS

LIII. CHICAGO. THE MIDWAY PLAISANCE, SHOWING THE PROPOSED WATERWAY CONNECTING THE LAGOONS OF WASHINGTON PARK WITH THOSE OF JACKSON PARK, AND EVENTUALLY WITH THE WATERWAY OF THE PROPOSED SHORE PARK EXTENDING FROM JACKSON PARK TO GRANT PARK.

air athletics, both winter and summer; they will afford a course for races for Northwestern University at the north and the Chicago University at the south. House-boats, launches, canoes, rowboats, and small sailboats will ply upon them, as well as craft for the public use, such as are usual on the Thames, the Seine, and the canals of Venice. The waterway should be lined with restaurants and pleasure pavilions and with public bath houses; swimming beaches should be constructed on their shores, which by careful designing can be made as picturesque as any inland river. Both shores should be a part of the general design, and together with the lagoon itself these shores should be owned by the park authorities, in order that the whole may be effectually policed.

Imagine this supremely beautiful parkway, with its frequent stretches of fields, playgrounds, avenues, and groves, extending along the shore in closest touch with the life of the city throughout the whole water front. What will it do for us in health and happiness? After it is finished will the people of means be so ready to run away and spend their money in other cities? Where else can they find such delightful conditions as at home? We should no longer lose so much of the cream of our earnings, now spent in other lands. When this parkway shall be created, our people will stay here, and others will come to dwell among us — the people who now spend time and large amounts of money in Paris, in Vienna, and on the Riviera. It will turn back the stream of profits which have to such a large degree gone away from us, and every one living here will feel the result of this change, for between prosperity and bad times there is often but a small percentage, and the community which can keep its earnings at home prospers.

In order to appreciate the recreation which the Lake front when properly developed will afford, one has but to recall the pleasure which similar waters afford to the people of other countries. For example, the clusters or fringes of islands in the vicinity of Stockholm form a favorite resort for the yachtsmen of Sweden, their chief rendezvous being Sandham, a pilot station on the margin of the Baltic. Tourists enjoy the exhibitions of swimming given in the public baths of Stockholm, and the canoeing on the numerous lakes and waterways. The winter sports and competitions — skating, skee-running, skate-sailing, ice-yachting, sledge-kicking, and toboganning — are famous the world over; and the Sport Park (Idrottsparken) at Stockhom is one of the features of the city.

COPYRIGHT, 1909, BY COMMERCIAL CLUB OF CHICAGO

XLIV.   CHICAGO.   TYPICAL   VIEW   ACROSS   THE   PROPOSED   SOUTH   SHORE
PARK, FOR EXAMPLE, AT WOODLAND PARK.

From South Chicago to Grant Park the treatment proposed is made up of a parkway along the actual shore line, following the right-of-way of the Illinois Central Railroad; and also a wide park strip entirely in the Lake, enclosing a series of lagoons. On the north a similar treatment is suggested, except that here the parkway is somewhat narrower than on the South Side, and an additional element is introduced in the form of a chain of outlying islands. The arrangement on the north comprises two roadways, the first following the shore as it exists to-day, while the second roadway runs within the park strip lying beyond the lagoons. In the latter parkway the line is simplified and irregularities disappear to a large extent, the outer line from North Avenue to Evanston finally becoming a double curve. This is further enveloped with a line formed by the chain of islands which it is proposed to build on the shallows. This line curves gently from the north in a southerly direction until it joins the outer park strip north of the River. This point is the beginning of the line which flows towards the south shore. A yacht harbor should be constructed at the northern end. The sport of yachting is very greatly in need of encouragement of this form, as the navigation of Lake Michigan is rather dangerous, and there is now no point north of the River to which a yacht can run for shelter. In addition to the northern yacht harbor, there should be other harbors, in the lee of the proposed islands, out in the Lake. These would be of the utmost value to yachtsmen, as they would afford from mile to mile a point of refuge in case of surprise by squalls.

For the most part, an informal landscape treatment is proposed for the two park strips;

but where the bridges cross the lagoons, a more formal treatment is introduced and pavilions are provided for the various recreation purposes. It is also proposed to create a yacht harbor just north of Jackson Park, where the shallowness of the water permits the formation of extensive meadows by filling; and also to fill in above the shoals dotting the shore, with a group of islands. Broadly stated, the treatment of the shore from South Chicago to Wilmette may be said to be one which will result in the restoration or perfection of the line already existing; while the formal treatment proposed at the bridges, which are spaced at intervals of from one to two miles, will create a rhythm which even in this broad, general scheme must have its value.

LV. ENGLAND. HENLEY-ON-THAMES THE REGATTA COURSE.

Next in the importance to the development of the Lake shore possibilities is the acquisition and improvement of forest spaces. Both the water front and the near-by woodlands should be brought within easy reach of all the people, and especially of the wage-earners. Natural scenery furnishes the contrasting element to the artificiality of the city. All of us should often run away from the works of men's hands and back into the wilds, where mind and body are restored to a normal condition, and we are enabled to take up the burden of life in our crowded streets and endless stretches of buildings with renewed vigor and hopefulness. Those who have the means and are so placed in their daily employments that they can do so constantly seek the refreshment of the country. Should not the public see to it that every one may enjoy this change of scene, this restorer of bodily and mental vigor, and will not citizenship be better thereby? He who habitually comes in close contact with nature develops saner methods of thought than can be the case when one is habitually shut up within the walls of a city. If a census of the purposes and acts of all of the people of Chicago as they affect the

LVI.   ENGLAND.   HENLEY-ON-THAMES: A REGATTA.
Illustrating the life which would develop in the lagoons of the proposed Lake Shore Parks.

general good could be made for this year of grace 1909, and again in 1933, after the creation of extensive forests in the suburbs, the percentage of improvement affecting the whole community would probably be quite surprising. The existing public parks go far in this direction, but not far enough. The spaces to be acquired should be wild forests, filled with such trees, vines, flowers, and shrubs as will grow in this climate, and all should be developed in a natural condition. Country roads and a few paths should run through these forests, but they should not be cut into small divisions. There should be open glades here and there, and other natural features, and the people should be allowed to use them freely.

In the disposition of interior parks the main consideration should be, first, to distribute the areas about the city as evenly as possible, so as to make large parks readily accessible to all citi-

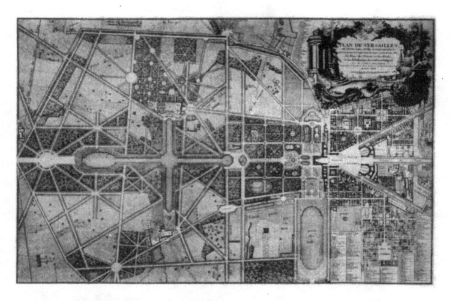

LVII. VERSAILLES, FRANCE.   PLAN OF THE PALACE, PARK, AND GARDENS, AND THE GREAT ARTERIES
LEADING TO THE GATES.

zens; and secondly, to select for improvement those localities which have the greatest charm and value as park lands. Happily nature has furnished the opportunity to combine both considerations. The wooded bluffs and ravines at the northern boundary of Cook County in Glencoe mark a natural park entrance from Lake Michigan. The virgin forest known as the Peterson woods, south of Peterson Avenue, the Gibbs woods, north of Gibbs Street, a beautiful spot on the Chicago River south of Central Avenue, are especially attractive features of this stretch. In spring the bloom of the thorn, the crab-apple, and the wild plum are features of the landscape; the ground is everywhere carpeted with flowers; there are forests of elm, oak, ash, willow, and cottonwood; and the Skokee marsh in beauty vies with the Lake itself. At a distance of a mile inland the valley of the North Branch of the Chicago River is reached. In this valley the views

LVIII. VERSAILLES, FRANCE. VIEW FROM THE
TERRACE, LOOKING DOWN THE MAIN AXIS.

are particularly beautiful, especially where the stretches are unbroken by constructions of any kind. To the north the valley stretches far beyond the county line; to the south it is framed on both sides with forest lands. In the region of Central Avenue these forest lines spread, taking in the grounds of the Glenview Golf Club, closing again between Kenilworth and Bryn Mawr avenues, where the foliage closely follows the banks of the River. The area which should be taken for this particular northern park includes upwards of eight thousand acres, and at the present time the land can be had at comparatively small expense.

The opportunity for a park area entirely surrounding the city is to be found in the extension of the Lake entrance at Glencoe westward until it reaches the valley of the Des Plaines; thence the park stretch would extend south along that valley to Riverside, and, taking in the valleys of Salt and Flag creeks, still southerly to the Drainage Canal. Turning to the east, the line would extend along the Calumet Feeder, Stony Creek, and Little Calumet River to and including Lake Calumet, and thence to the Lake front.

The Des Plaines River from the county line to Riverside flows mainly through thickly wooded country which the parkway plans include; the

LIX. PARIS. VIEW OF THE SUNKEN GARDEN
IN THE LUXEMBOURG GARDENS.

forests for the most part lie on the east side of the River, occasionally crossing to the west side. There are places of great beauty on the River banks, including Thatcher's Park at River Forest, which has been fenced in, and where an admission fee is charged. South of River Forest the parkway divides, and, passing around the cemeteries at Harlem, joins the River at Riverside. From Harlem to the southern extremity of Riverside the foliage and the scenery generally are exceptionally fine. The boulevard from Summit, running in a southwesterly direction to Spring Forest, commands fine views, particularly over the rising wooded land of Du Page

LX. ST. GERMAIN, FRANCE. VIEW OF AN
AVENUE IN THE FOREST AND ROUND-POINT.
This avenue crosses above a railroad.

County. Mount Forest is covered with trees, and presents many delightful outlooks from its height; these are particularly fine in the southwestern extremity, where the valley of the Des Plaines to the southwest and northwest, and the Sag valley to the east, all are visible. Evergreen

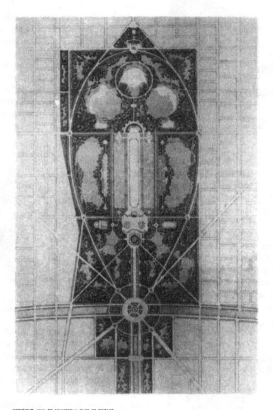

COPYRIGHT, 1908, BY COMMERCIAL CLUB OF CHICAGO

LXI. CHICAGO. PLAN OF A PARK PROPOSED ON THE MAIN EAST-AND-WEST AXIS OF THE CITY AT CONGRESS STREET AND FIFTY-SECOND AVENUE.

Park is noted for its evergreens, and Sherman farm is thickly wooded. As in the Chicago River region, the thorn, the crab-apple, and wild plum abound; and the great forests consist of elm, cottonwood, and willow, the elm seeming to predominate. The forests in the Palos region stretch south as far as the eye can reach.

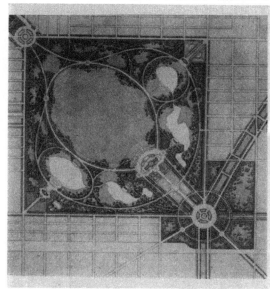

COPYRIGHT, 1909, BY COMMERCIAL CLUB OF CHICAGO

LXII. CHICAGO. PLAN OF A PARK PROPOSED AT WESTERN BOULEVARD AND GARFIELD BOULEVARD, BEING AN EXTENSION OF GAGE PARK.

The Calumet is an ample stream, and on every hand the silhouettes of steel industries give strong evidence of the coming importance of this channel as a harbor. Every effort, therefore, should be made to concentrate the vehicle traffic crossing this river at well-chosen points where great bridges might be constructed, in order to create as little friction as possible between the vessel and the land traffic. On the banks of the Calumet, in the neighborhood of One Hundred and Third Street, are large swamps capable of being developed into fine parks; the country is gently undulating, with plenty of woodland, and the view across Calumet Lake is fine. It is proposed to create a driveway around Lake Calumet, and to reclaim the low lands south of the lake without essentially changing their present topography; also to plant a belt of woods surrounding this lake park set in one of the greatest manufacturing districts in the world; and to construct roadways to form connections with the different park reservations and at the same time to become highways to the city.

The encircling system of forest parks and park connections as thus outlined, when taken in conjunction either with the existing interior boulevards and the Sheridan Road, or the proposed driveway along

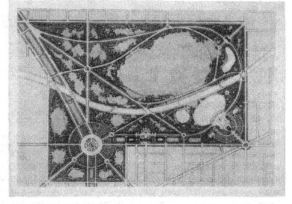

COPYRIGHT, 1909, BY COMMERCIAL CLUB OF CHICAGO

LXIII. CHICAGO. PLAN OF A PARK PROPOSED AT THE NORTH BRANCH OF THE CHICAGO RIVER AND GRACELAND AVENUE.

the Lake lagoons makes a circuit of about one hundred miles, every portion of which would serve directly an adjoining portion of the city. Such a comprehensive system of outlying parks is for the Chicago of to-day quite as practical and quite as much needed as were the boulevards of a generation ago, which have now become interior thoroughfares of priceless value. The forest preserves, with their bordering driveways, would in time come to be lined with residences and large estates, and rise in the value of the adjoining lands would permit the city to recoup in taxation many times the cost of lands now of small value.

The grouping of manufacturing towns at the southern end of Lake Michigan, and the serious attempts that have been made (especially in Pullman and Gary) to provide excellent living conditions for people employed in large operations, create a demand for extensive parks in that region; because no city conditions, however ideal in themselves, supply the craving for real out-of-door life, for forests and wild flowers and streams. Human nature demands such simple and wholesome pleasures as come from roaming the woods, for rowing and canoeing, and for sports and games that require large areas. The increasing number of holidays, the growing use of Sunday as a day of rest and refreshment for body and mind tired by the exacting tasks of the week, together with the

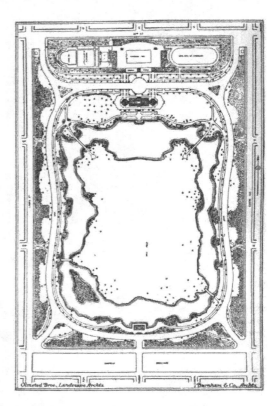

LXIV. CHICAGO. PLAN OF SHERMAN PLAYGROUND AND PARK.
The assembly hall, gymnasia, and open-air swimming pool, forming a group as the center of the composition.

constant improvement in the scale of living, all make imperative such means of enjoyment as the large park provides. Therefore, adequate provision for the growing populations that of necessity must live in restricted town areas requires that in the region south and southwest of Chicago all those marsh lands and wooded ridges which nature has thus far preserved from being taken for manufacturing purposes now should be secured for the parks that in the next

LXV.   CHICAGO.   MARK WHITE SQUARE.
View of the children's wading pool and the field house.

LXVI.   CHICAGO.   HAMILTON PARK.
View of the boys' gymnasium.

LXVII. CHICAGO. SHERMAN PARK.
Field-house seen from the west side.

generation will be required, but which will be beyond reach unless taken in the immediate future.

The development of a system of outlying large parks along the lines above indicated will give to Chicago breathing-spaces adequate at least for the immediate future; the physical character of the lands to be taken will insure a diversity in natural features most pleasing and refreshing to dwellers in cities; and the aquisition of the areas entirely around the present city will afford convenient access for all the citizens, so that each section will be accommodated. Moreover, the development of especially beautiful sections, such as the region about Lake Zurich, will give marked individuality to Chicago's outlying park system. It is by seizing on such salient features of a landscape and emphasizing their peculiar features that the charm and the dignity of the city are enhanced.

LXVIII. CHICAGO. SHERMAN PARK.
View of the open-air swimming pool.

COPYRIGHT, 1909, BY COMMERCIAL CLUB OF CHICAGO

LXIX. CHICAGO. DIAGRAM OF A SYSTEM OF FREIGHT HANDLING FOR LAND AND WATER TRANSPORTATION, TO BE WORKED IN CONJUNCTION WITH ONE ANOTHER.
(1) A central clearing and warehousing yard. (2) A north harbor at the mouth of the Chicago River. (3) A south harbor at the mouth of the Calumet River. (4) Underground freight lines interconnecting the city stations, the central yard, and the two harbors ; these lines are shown in red ; they do not represent exact locations of the routes.

CHAPTER V

TRANSPORTATION: A FREIGHT CENTER: GROUPING OF PASSENGER STATIONS: A LOOP SYSTEM

HICAGO has been made largely by the railroads, and its future prosperity is dependent upon them. In the past, however, it has been the increase in the number of roads reaching this city which has built up its commerce; but now, with twenty-two trunk lines entering Chicago from every possible direction, and with connections extending to all portions of the country, the question of numbers has ceased to be the important one.

The present problem is to handle the traffic of the railroads with dispatch and at the lowest cost. The city is too large for each railroad to attempt to maintain a separate system unrelated to that of any other except the physical connection of the tracks. The time has come to develop one common system for the handling of freight, — a traffic clearing-house. The whole perplexing and intensely intricate subject requires not only the careful study of men expert in such matters, but also a spirit of mutual forbearance and conciliation among railroad managers for the sake of promoting the general good.

Not that any one road of the entire twenty-two should be expected to make what will ultimately prove a sacrifice, but that no road should hold back from doing its full part to bring about the conditions essential to the continued prosperity of the city by the development in Chicago of a unified system of traffic handling that shall place this city ahead of any other in so far as efficiency and cheapness are concerned. The fine arts of traffic management should be studied no less than the fine arts of parks and boulevards; for unless Chicago keeps ahead of her rivals in commercial matters, the parks will become pastures, and the boulevards will be deserted.

In an address made in Chicago during the winter of 1906–7 Mr. James J. Hill laid the utmost stress on the necessity for improved railway terminals. At that time a cry was going up for more cars. Traffic was delayed, the railways being entirely unable to handle promptly the freight offered them. Mr. Hill pointed out that the main difficulty was not lack of cars, but lack of proper terminal facilities. It was a fact that hundreds and even thousands of loaded cars were at that very moment standing on the tracks in the yards of every one of the great trunk lines, which with their utmost efforts could not place these cars at the sides of the receiving platforms in the various cities. It is not an extreme statement to say that business was almost paralyzed on account of the inability of the roads to handle at the terminals the freight traffic of the country. On all the two-track lines continuous trains could have been handled from one terminus to another, if the cars could have been rescued from the disordering conditions in which they were involved and lost to use. The railroad companies were unable to make proper use of their own rolling stock and main lines, all because of the congested condition of their terminals, in which there were tracks enough, but tracks so badly placed and arranged as to deprive the roads of the full benefit of their aggregate mileage.

The bad arrangement of terminal tracks was not alone responsible for the congested condition which then prevailed at Chicago, New York, Pittsburg, and many other points. In an equal or perhaps greater degree the habit of hauling all the freight into the heart of a city and then hauling most of it out again was the cause of the trouble. If freight stations and yards located close to the center of the business district of a city were inadequate under the conditions that obtained in the winter of 1906–7, what will be the result at the next test, which will surely be a more severe one?

The conclusion is inevitable. Either nearly every one of the great railroads must increase and improve both its main line and such of its freight houses and yards as are now located in the heart of the city, or they must cease to bring all freight into the congested business center. Separate roads operating separate and independent rights-of-way to the separate and independent freight houses cannot do the work.

Year by year the railroads have gone on straightening their lines, reducing grades, and building additional tracks; and the result has been large savings in operating expenses. The time has now come to devise some plan whereby the enormous terminal costs will be lessened materially; and that city will benefit most wherein this problem shall be worked out first and best.

This report does not attempt to dictate; or to discuss the practical questions of railroading. Its aim in respect to transportation is the same as in regard to all other matters of Chicago's welfare, namely, to incorporate such generalizations as are obviously true, logical, and helpful;

because it is recognized fully that unless the railroads have power to improve their terminals, this city will be hopelessly left behind in the struggle for commercial advancement. The same spirit that is evoked to bring about other improvements is necessary also in the case of the railroads.

In order to obtain for the community as a whole the greatest economy per ton handled,

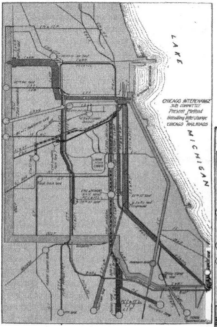

DIAGRAM A

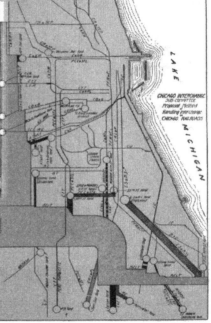

DIAGRAM B.

no goods should be carried into and out of the congested business center except those needed for construction, for retailing, or for consumption in that territory. Goods that are now brought into Chicago as a center, and from thence sold and distributed to the country outside of Chicago, should be stored at some point most convenient for the purpose,—most convenient for deposit and for reloading and carrying away to other points. It is obvious that the spot chosen be one most convenient for the shipping public as a whole; and therefore if common ground for such a great general depot can be found for all the roads, it will best answer the purposes of

LXX. CHICAGO. ASSEMBLING-INTERCHANGE; DIAGRAMS ACCOMPANYING THE REPORT OF THE COMMITTEE. C. W. HOTCHKISS, CONSULTING ENGINEER.
(A) Present method of handling interchange of freight on railroads in center of city. (B) Proposed method of handling interchange of freight on railroads by means of a belt line and clearing yards, disengaging the center of the city from existing freight congestion.

quick handling and of lowest cost per ton. A central depot, and common track facilities which should form a part of it, would bring about time and money saving both to the railroads themselves and to the trading public. For the sake, therefore, of the best interests of all the citizens of Chicago, it is proposed that great machines owned and operated in common by all the railroads be created to handle freight business.

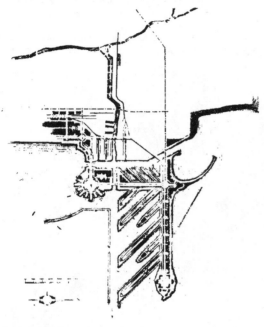

COPYRIGHT, 1909, BY COMMERCIAL CLUB OF CHICAGO

. LXXI. CHICAGO. SKETCH DIAGRAM OF DOCKS SUGGESTED AT THE MOUTH OF THE CHICAGO RIVER FOR PACKAGE FREIGHT STEAMERS.

A careful analysis of the entire freight traffic of Chicago shows that ninety-five per cent, in and out, is done by the railroads, and only five per cent is done by water. It is the opinion of leading merchants and manufacturers of this city, as well as of traffic managers of both rail and water transportation, that this average percentage of tonnage will not change in the future. This being the case, the location of a great common freight depositing and reloading station for all the roads should be located at a point most economical for them as a whole, at the common center of gravity so to speak. This center of gravity is at or near the location shown on the diagram. Here should be trackage capable of handling in the best manner all freight trains coming into or departing from Chicago, which are intended to do business other than local and suburban. It should be so arranged that individual incoming cars can be promptly placed beside the intended unloading platform or warehouse, where the goods can be handled with dispatch, and as largely as possible by machinery. The car so unloaded should be at once placed at the platform from which it is to take its new load, and then be entrained and started away to its next destination.

At this freight center may be the great warehouses of the city, arranged in reference to the tracks and service. These mutual relations must of necessity produce economy of handling goods, and economy of the closest sort. If the car and track service be perfected from the freight train standpoint, Chicago will have an advantage not possessed by any other trade center of the world, and her equipment will be fully equal to her destiny. The principal results would be the quick handling of freight trains by all the roads, their rapid unloading and reloading, and their exemption from passing into or through the crowded city. This would result in an enormous saving every year. Such a scheme can be carried out here, because the entire surrounding country is flat.

The relief from the congestion in the city now caused by bringing in and carrying out goods not to be consumed there will result in less crowding in the city, and also in the saving of its pavements, in much less dirt, and finally, in a mitigation of the smoke nuisance, because of the removal of freight engines and manufacturing to the new freight handling locality.

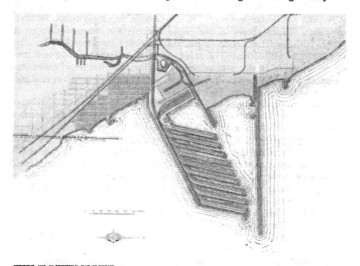

COPYRIGHT, 1908, BY COMMERCIAL CLUB OF CHICAGO

LXXII. CHICAGO. SKETCH DIAGRAM OF DOCKS SUGGESTED AT THE MOUTH OF THE CALUMET RIVER FOR BULK FREIGHT STEAMERS; ACCESS TO BE HAD WITHOUT OPENING OF BRIDGES.

Together with this freight handling center should be a harbor in connection with each of the two rivers, the Chicago and the Calumet. These two harbors should be connected underground or overhead by freight ways operated electrically, and they should also be connected with the freight handling center. The four elements, namely, freight center, two harbors, and the connecting systems, will then form one complete machine for doing almost all the transportation of goods for Chicago for all time. No doubt the present tunnel railway system should be tied up with and form part of this machine: all probably to be owned jointly by some general utility corporation. In such case any merchant or manufacturer, located wherever he may be, could, in the shortest space of time and at lowest cost per ton, receive goods from the great depository (the freight center) or send them to it for entraining.

The present underground system of tunnels already extends under all of the streets in the old business district of Chicago, and is extending on the North, South, and West Sides. It is connected with all of the railway freight stations, its floor is about 40 feet from the street surface, and is connected at that level with chambers under many of the leading commercial and manufacturing establishments and office buildings of the city, from each of which freight elevators deliver goods to and from the shipping-rooms above. Any existing tunnel system can be utilized as far as it will go in carrying out a complete system of underground distribution.

The freight handling center should become a perfect machine in itself. Trains of freight cars coming to or going from the city should be handled there, so that the individual cars may be placed at the particular warehouse from which goods are to come, and from these cars the new trains should be made up in station order. No considerable car supply should be kept on hand in this freight yard. In the course of time, when the freight business of Chicago shall have greatly increased, the present freight-car yards will be needed for storage of cars, and holding those needing repairs or rebuilding. The yards will then perform an important function, for when more cars are needed at the great central freight machine, they can be sent thither from each of the separate yards. Should a surplus of cars exist at the center of any road, this surplus can be withdrawn to that road's own yard.

One of the large retail merchants of Chicago, when in need of a fresh case of goods, now telephones to his own storehouse situated far from his shop, and through the underground tunnel quickly receives goods in a sealed car. This method of supplying the merchant's needs illustrates what will happen to all merchants when the central freight depot shall come fully into existence. A method that will work with precision, quickness, and close economy will relieve the down-town streets of freight traffic now hauled over them, and therefore make the streets cleaner and more lasting. Will not these great general facilities profoundly affect for the better the material prosperity of Chicago as a whole? When this system shall be put in operation, the better street plan, and the enlargement and improvements suggested for parks, parkways, and the Lake front, will cause the city to become permanently and highly prosperous.

In connection with the freight diagrams, the one numbered LXXIII should be considered. It shows a radical change in warehousing, and perhaps manufacturing, which will take time and cannot be put into effect abruptly, but is undoubtedly the logical outcome and ultimately must prevail. It also shows the present tendency of growth of both manufacturing and warehousing which seems to follow and cling to belt lines of railroad, especially when such lines run beside the River or Canal, where every sort of freighting economy now in vogue can be made use of. It is evident that while present methods continue in use, and until the great freight scheme can be put into operation, some common facility railroad highways must be introduced in order to improve the handling of freight in the direction of quickness and cost. The diagram (No. LXXIII) shows what these freight common facilities should be, namely:

1. An inner loop (A),
2. Loop (B), connected as shown with the inner loop,
3. Loop (C), also connected with the inner loop, and finally, loop (D).

If these three loops be wide, many-tracked, and operated for the benefit of all railroads, then the movement of freight can be increased in efficiency; and such manufacturers and warehousemen as build against the loops can be accommodated with everything needed to carry on their individual activities. Freight stations can be located on these loops wherever required, and each can be certain of quick and cheap service, the common facilities being operated by the railroads. A detail diagram for freight in the center of the city is shown in No. LXXIV.

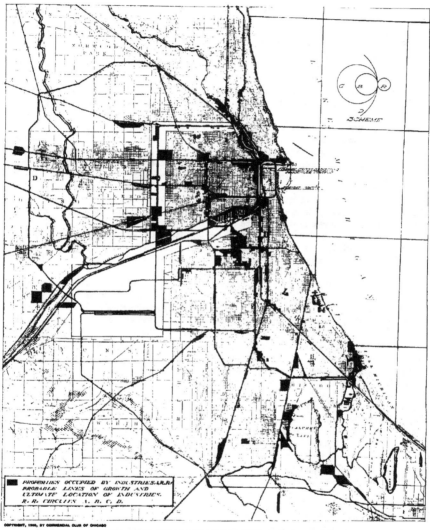

COPYRIGHT, 1908, BY COMMERCIAL CLUB OF CHICAGO

LXXIII. CHICAGO. DIAGRAM OF THE CITY AND SURROUNDING COUNTRY, SHOWING RAILROAD CIRCUITS, B, C, D, AND E, WHICH ARE, OR MAY BECOME, TANGENT TO THE INNER CIRCUIT (A).
The diagram also shows the existing industries, and the probable trend of growth away from the center of the city.

It is proposed to extend the freight lines to the Lake front piers and harbors. The excursion-boat piers, as well as the recreation piers and those at the harbors, are to be thus connected. It is probable that many of the present freight houses of the railroads will remain and carry on their functions as at present, except as to goods now hauled into and out of Chicago, although intended solely for outside trade. As they are already connected by tunnel, they can be and will be used for the city-consumption trade, and to supply the great number of smaller retailers and others who cannot afford to operate separate individual freight elevators from their shops to the tunnel railroad.

At the present time much of the near-by farm stuff for housekeepers, hotels, and restaurants is brought into the city on wagons which load late in the afternoon and travel at night, reaching the general market at South Water Street or West Market at dawn. Much if not all of this freightage can be done cheaper to the truck farmers, and more satisfactorily to the consumer, by cars run at night on the trolley and elevated lines. Between one and seven o'clock in the morning these roads should render this important service. The saving of wear and tear on road-beds due to the elimination of heavy teaming is, all by itself, enough to recommend the adoption of the above suggestion. Besides, the convenience of both producer and consumer is to be considered, and also the saving of time and the cheapening of provisions.

The proposed street plan of Chicago is based on a system of circuits and radials. This is also true of the railroad and traction systems. As shown on the accompanying diagrams, the heart of Chicago is surrounded by a circuit of railways, which may be said to follow Michigan Avenue, Canal Street, Sixteenth Street, and Kinzie Street. Following the same lines, a subway circuit may be constructed for handling freight, and another for passengers, the latter running, however, on Twelfth and Washington. To this circuit would be tangent three others enclosing areas increasing in size around the center of the city as above described. By means of these circuits a complete system of distribution of passengers and freight may be secured. To the inner circuit will relate the various services of distribution of the elements of life, produce, and commodities for manufacture; and on it should be placed the freight substations, the markets for general produce, the main post-office, and postal substations. The various services for water, sewers, power, telephone, and telegraph, also may be schemed on the inner circuit as a basis. To it will also correspond the inner circuit of boulevard circulation.

Although these various circuits do not correspond in exact detail to one another, they may be said to be virtually superposed, and to serve not only the intensely active center of the city, but also the enclosing zone as far as the second boulevard circuit — Michigan Avenue, Twenty-second Street, Ashland Avenue, and Chicago Avenue — an ideal condition if the main circulation of the streets be left free and uninterrupted in its working.

The center line on which balance the circuit A, and all the others to a greater or less degree, is the axial line of Congress Street. The two great arteries, Halsted and Congress streets, may be said to form the grand crossing, at the intersection of which it is proposed to place the civic center. The base of this civic center touches the west side of the inner circuit, tangent to which are all the other circuits. The importance of this inner circuit will thus be seen. The tangent or line of coincidence extends from Lake Street to Sixteenth Street. It may be used as the clearing-house for all the interests above described, coming to and going from the heart of the city.

The passenger lines entering the densely inhabited parts of the city should not cross each other or carriage roads at grade. Much has been done already, and much more is proposed to

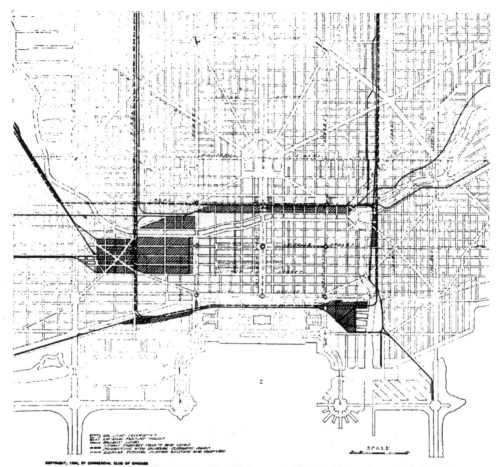

COPYRIGHT, 1908, BY COMMERCIAL CLUB OF CHICAGO

LXXIV. CHICAGO. DIAGRAM OF THE CITY CENTER, SHOWING THE GENERAL LOCATION OF EXISTING FREIGHT
YARDS AND RAILROAD LINES, THE PRESENT TUNNEL SYSTEM AND PROPOSED CIRCUIT, AND CONNECTIONS FOR
ALL THESE SERVICES, RUNNING TO THE CENTRAL CLEARING YARDS.

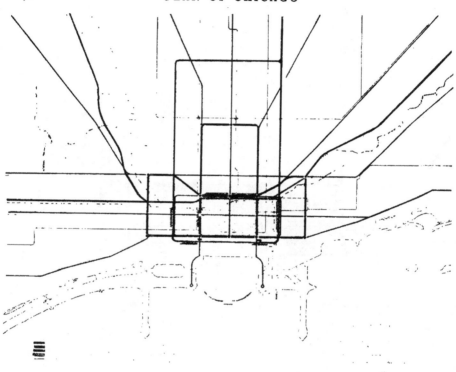

COPYRIGHT, 1908, BY COMMERCIAL CLUB OF CHICAGO

LXXV. CHICAGO. DIAGRAM OF THE CITY, SHOWING COMPLETE SYSTEM OF INNER CIRCUITS.
(1) General traction subway circuit. (2) General railroad freight circuit.

eliminate grade crossings. In European cities, and in some American cities as well, the railroads have taken great pains to beautify their rights-of-way, a step very important to the roads
themselves, to individual passengers, and to the community at large. Cleanliness and pleasing
treatment of the roadways, the embankments, the drainage channels, the fences, the yards, and
the stations, large and small, insure better service on the part of the railroad employees, while the
appearance of the city is immensely improved thereby.

The terminal stations in the city should be either above or below the street levels. They
should be centrally located, but always arranged so as to avoid the closing of streets. The two
best available locations for permanent passenger stations for all the roads are, first, between
Canal and Clinton streets from Lake Street to Twelfth Street, and on Twelfth Street widened

as proposed.   In the case of the terminal stations between Canal and Clinton streets, the tracks either under or over street grades may be allowed to extend out to the street curb lines and possibly farther. Whether under or over the grade, the railroads should be allowed to occupy this entire space. In case the overhead system be adopted, there should be two open plazas, one preferably at Washington Street and the other at Congress Street; and the plazas should have no tracks above them, except passovers on each side of the plazas.

LXXVI. DRESDEN. VIADUCT AND RAILWAY STATION (HAUPT BAHN-HOF) PASSING ABOVE THE NORMAL STREET LEVEL, ILLUS- TRATING THE TYPE PROPOSED IN THE OVERHEAD SCHEME FOR RAILWAY STATIONS WEST OF THE RIVER.

In case of overhead installation, the roads may, for the present, burn coal in their locomotives. In case of depressed rights-of-way coal cannot be burned unless the spaces from street to street over the railways be kept open. In the long run, it will be very costly to do this, because all this space from street to street, so long as not needed by the railroads, could be used for markets, commercial booths, and warehouses, the rentals reducing the cost of operation to the road.

In case of elevation, the viaducts over the streets should have sidewalk lights between the rails, and these viaducts should be freed of posts, deep girders being used; the walls and pavements should be as nearly white as possible. The Eighth Street subway under the Union Station yard at Washington, D.C.,

LXXVII. VIENNA. A RAILWAY VIADUCT PASSING OVER AN IMPORTANT STREET.

is a good example of what such a structure should be. There is no reason why these viaducts should not be very attractive when brilliantly lighted. Each should have a handsome police house in the center, with windows arranged to give a clear view of the entire space included

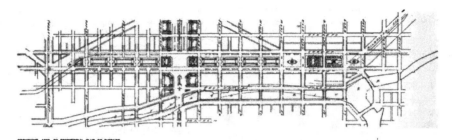

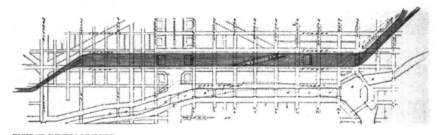

COPYRIGHT, 1909, BY COMMERCIAL CLUB OF CHICAGO

LXXVIII. SUGGESTED LOCATION AND ARRANGEMENT OF THE RAILWAY PASSENGER STATIONS WEST OF THE
RIVER. SUBWAY SCHEME: 1. PLAN OF STREET LEVEL. 2. PLAN BELOW STREET LEVEL.

under the tracks. There is no reason why this construction, even if elevated, should not present a very pleasing appearance as seen from Canal Street or Clinton Street. Whether there are buildings or only unoccupied spaces beneath, they can be enclosed by masonry walls extending high enough above track level effectually to screen the trains from view. Such a structure would be similar in general effect to the great Roman aqueducts. It might be made not only of practical value, but at the same time a highly interesting and even a grand architectural detail lending orderly distinction to that part of the city.

The Twelfth Street location would extend from State Street west to the South Branch of the Chicago River, straightened as shown on the diagram, according to the design for the passenger stations of Chicago which was made and published years ago. Here the purpose is to care for passenger service of every sort, except that of roads coming in on the West Side system. These stations should open on the great Twelfth Street Boulevard, which in front of the stations should be two hundred and fifty feet wide, and east and west of the stations should be one hundred and eighty feet in width. This boulevard would begin to rise at Michigan Avenue, and at the final elevation, which is at the level of the main floor of the stations, should pass over the River on a double-deck bascule bridge. This thoroughfare should come to the present street level at Canal Street, where there is to be a round-point from which a new street should extend to the civic center. As a one hundred and fifty foot wide boulevard, Twelfth Street should continue

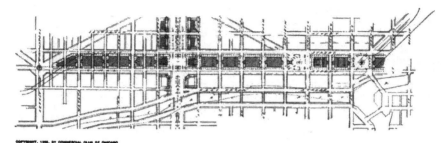

COPYRIGHT, 1908, BY COMMERCIAL CLUB OF CHICAGO

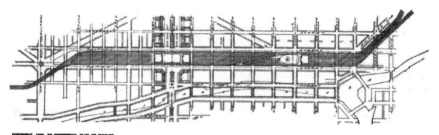

COPYRIGHT, 1908, BY COMMERCIAL CLUB OF CHICAGO

LXXIX. SUGGESTED LOCATION AND ARRANGEMENT OF THE RAILWAY PASSENGER STATIONS WEST OF THE
RIVER. OVERHEAD SCHEME: 1. PLAN AT STREET LEVEL. 2. PLAN ABOVE STREET LEVEL.

westward until it joins the West Park Boulevard now existing on the same line, west of Ashland
Avenue. The present rights-of-way of the railroads passing under Twelfth Street can go into
business use without loss to the corporations owning them. The freight systems and trackage for all of these roads should be underneath the proposed passenger stations and their yards.

No more modern or perfect machine could possibly be devised for both passenger and
freight in a great city's heart than that included in the two schemes above shown and
explained. Of necessity they should have an ideal street-car connection with all parts of the
city. To accomplish this result it is proposed:

First, to carry the elevated loop along the side and east of the West Side passenger system;
along the side and south of the Twelfth Street passenger system; thence over to the Alley L as
at present, around by Lake Street and across to the West Side passenger station, forming a
complete overhead circuit.

Second, there should be a surface street-car circuit following the same route, with minor
circuits within it.

Third, there should be an underground street-car system following substantially the same
route as first mentioned above, but extending under the main branch of the River and running
east and west at or near Michigan Street. Two extensions of this service are shown north of the
River, two south of Twelfth Street, and one west, at or near Ashland Avenue.

This entire system of stations and street-car routes is shown on diagram marked No. LXXX. If carried out, many times the present number of people can be handled in the center of Chicago; and all · streets can be kept open on their present level north and south, east and west, giving every possible opportunity for circulation on foot and in wagons and carriages, since surfaces would be available for carrying people below and above the present grades.

The better circulation of people on the streets and on street-car systems is not all or even the principal gain anticipated. Of first importance is the restoration to general business of the territory from State Street to the South Branch of the River, and from Van Buren Street south to Twelfth Street. This area is almost as large as our present central business district of Chicago, in which there can now be no extension of such of our great industries as can succeed only when operated in the very center of the business district. Present conditions are crowding out enterprising men and vast capital. This new area must be added to the old, and by no other means than those proposed can this be done. The regions north of the main River and west of the South Branch are filling up solidly and very rapidly with business, such as is not and never will be done on the old location from Van Buren Street to Water Street; meanwhile there is the most urgent necessity of extending the space for the kind of business that is and always will be done on such a location as the one proposed. If this is the case now, what will be the case ten years hence? We cannot act too promptly in regard to creating and maintaining perfect street circulation, car circulation, and extension of area for the heart of Chicago. We cannot get ready too soon for the enormous extension of all those facilities the necessity for which is already pressing.

By the arrangement of passenger stations at Canal and Twelfth streets, the business center is convenient for pedestrians, and with the addition of the underground and overhead loops, the entire business district is within easy and comfortable reach. This applies to both through and suburban passenger traffic.

This report does not go into details of the roadways and stations, either trunk or intra-mural. Routes are suggested which seem to be the natural and logical ones. The expert engineers will find the best solutions of the constructive and mechanical problems as they arise. But all citizens are interested to see that the best and most comprehensive general schemes shall be adopted, and that in carrying out of any one of them, every detail shall be designed and executed with regard to its effect on the senses as well as on the basis of mere mechanical or constructive excellence. A million Chicago people who habitually use railway facilities will possess a higher average of good citizenship when the irritation of nerves is reduced to the minimum, and within a few years most of the waking hours of a million Americans will be spent in the business center of Chicago, where unpleasant sights and sounds should be abolished. The community will get far more out of its million workers when their nerves cease to be wracked by irritating conditions.

Again, the noises of surface and elevated road cars is often excruciating. It is not denied that this evil can be largely mitigated. These conditions actually cause misery to a large majority of people who are subjected to the constant strain, and in addition they undoubtedly cause a heavy aggregate loss of money to the business community. For the sake of the state, the citizen should be at his best, and it is the business of the state to maintain conditions conducive to his bodily welfare. Noises, ugly sights, ill smells, as well as dirty streets and workshops or offices, tend to lower average efficiency. It does not pay the state to allow them to continue. Moreover,

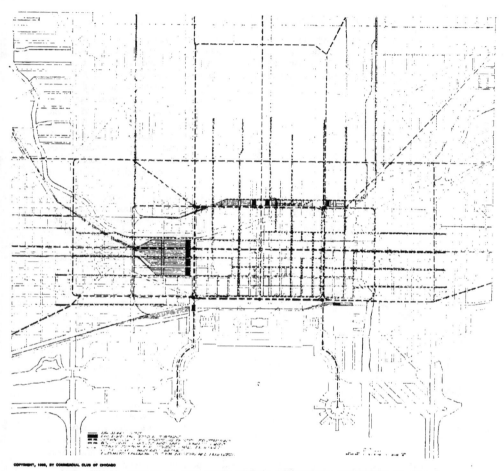

COPYRIGHT, 1909, BY COMMERCIAL CLUB OF CHICAGO

LXXX. CHICAGO. DIAGRAM OF CITY CENTER, SHOWING THE PROPOSED ARRANGEMENT OF RAILROAD PASSENGER STATIONS, THE COMPLETE TRACTION SYSTEM, INCLUDING RAPID TRANSIT, SUBWAY, AND ELEVATED ROADS, AND THE CIRCUIT SUBWAY LINE.

The last is designed,— (A) To connect all railroad stations with one another. (B) To connect passengers from all points of the city within and without the center with the railroad stations by transfer from the subway line proposed in the Arnold Report. (C) To supplement by transfer the interchange of passengers from traction lines going through the center from the North, South, or West to any point in the city.

citizens have pride in and loyalty to a city that is quiet, clean, and generally beautiful. It is not believed that "business" demands that our present annoying conditions be continued. In a state of good order all business must be done better and more profitably. With things as they should be, every business man in Chicago would make more money than he does now.

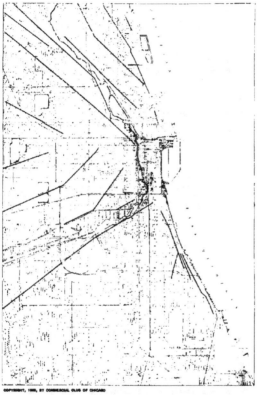

COPYRIGHT, 1908, BY COMMERCIAL CLUB OF CHICAGO
LXXXI. CHICAGO. RAILROAD RIGHTS-OF-WAY AND PROPERTIES IN THE CENTER OF CITY AND THE EXISTING RADIAL ARTERIES.

In regard to the mail service of Chicago this report can have little to say. Only expert public officials trained in handling the mails are capable of discussing it; and apart from the pneumatic tube or other circulatory system it does not affect our special problem. From motives of economy the Federal Government has incorporated post-offices in the same buildings with United States courts and other public offices. The time has come for a change in this respect, and it is to be hoped that such a building or buildings as this service will need in order to do its great and fast-growing business will be located where needed for post-office purposes, and be designed as to subserve these special functions. The Federal Government should work out a complete scheme for handling the mail matter of Chicago. The location of the central post-office and substations should be determined with a view to economical reception and distribution, all having reference to one another, to the railway mail stations in the city and suburbs, and, as before stated, to the general system of railway circuits. If it be possible to determine the future route of overhead, surface, and elevated street-car systems, they should be brought into the consideration of the Chicago mail service scheme. Strict economy and quick collections and delivery are all involved in this study.

The general trend of improvement is in the direction of central plants for heating, lighting, and power, because such plants are found to do the work more economically than separate stations. The individual buildings would, in such a case, cost less initially by leaving out much of the mechanical work now installed; and also they would make saving by greater cleanliness, due to improved atmospheric conditions. For it stands to reason that the abolition of a large majority of the smokestacks of the down-town district would improve the air we breathe, and relieve us of much of the cost of cleaning buildings, inside and out, and of protecting goods.

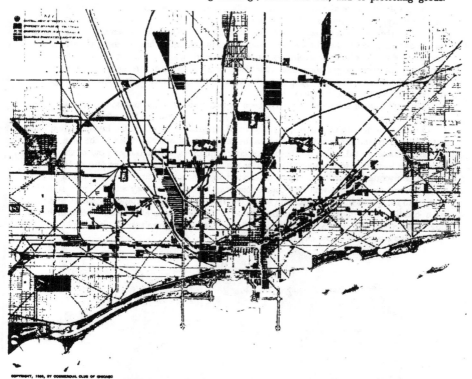

LXXXII. CHICAGO. DIAGRAM OF GENERAL SCHEME OF STREET CIRCULATION AND PARKS IN RELATION TO THE AREAS COVERED BY INDUSTRIES AND MANUFACTURES (RED). THE CENTER OF INDUSTRIES IS INDICATED BY A STAR. RAILROAD PROPERTIES AND LINES IN BLUE.

The embellishment of stations and station grounds of railroads first began in this country on the Boston and Albany and the Pennsylvania roads. It is now a feature all over the country; it adds immensely to the pleasure and comfort of travel, and especially of suburban travel. So strong is this attraction that many an owner of a large subdivision in the suburbs not only recognizes it, but he puts into practice at and near the station all the arts of landscaping at his command. In a very few places especial pains have been taken to plant for winter effect, as well as for effects depending on full foliage and blossoming shrubs. New winter effects should be studied in the parks, boulevards, playgrounds, and for all stations. It generally calls for expenditure of thought; but very little, if any, extra expenditure of money is involved in procuring charming results.

As a rule, the general aspect of our suburban stations is not pleasant. They should be bright, cheery, and inviting in a high degree. More study, not more money, is needed for this work. Let the architectural schools and societies take up this topic; it demands artistic imagination as well as skill. Let the man who undertakes this problem think of the hundreds or even thousands of people who must habitually use the given station, and let him do his utmost to bring into being for these people something that shall be a joy to them. A delightful station conduces to cheerfulness as a man goes to work and as he comes home, while a shabby or neglected station produces the opposite effect.

The problems of transportation have been viewed entirely from the standpoint of the paramount interests of Chicago as a commercial city. It has been assumed that what is for the greatest advantage to the city as a whole, will also be of the greatest benefit to the transportation lines both collectively and individually. Just as the realization of other portions of the plan call for harmonious and united action on the part of civic authorities, so the carrying out of the recommendations in respect to transportation will necessitate unity of action on the part of the managers of transportation facilities. Each must yield in some particulars in order to bring about the great end sought; but whatever concessions may be called for, they will be found insignificant when compared with the great gain which will result to the transportation systems themselves from creating here in the central metropolis of the United States a complete system of handling both freight and passenger traffic so as to promote the convenience of the people, and to enhance the commerce of the city of Chicago.

LXXXIII. THE VIADUCT AT AUTEUIL OVER THE RIVER SEINE, PARIS, FRANCE.

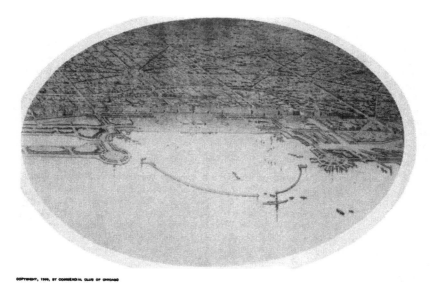

COPYRIGHT, 1909, BY COMMERCIAL CLUB OF CHICAGO

LXXXIV. CHICAGO. THE CENTER OF THE CITY LOOKING WEST, SHOWING GRANT PARK, THE HARBOR, AND THE CIVIC CENTER.

CHAPTER VI

NATURAL FEATURES OF CHICAGO: NECESSITY FOR COMPREHENSIVE TREATMENT OF THE STREET SYSTEM: STREETS WITHIN THE CITY: THE RESIDENCE STREET, THE AVENUE, AND THE BOULEVARD: STREET ARCHITECTURE: THE STREETS OF CHICAGO: PROPOSED NEW CIRCUITS

 HICAGO has two dominant natural features: the expanse of Lake Michigan, which stretches, unbroken by islands or peninsulas, to the horizon; and a corresponding area of land extending north, west, and south without hills or any marked elevation. These two features, each immeasurable by the senses, give the scale. Whatever man undertakes here should be either actually or seemingly without limit. Great thoroughfares may lead from the water back into the country interminably; broad boulevards may skirt the Lake front, or sweep through the city; but their beginnings on the north, on the south, or on the west must of necessity be points that move along determined lines with the growth of population. Other harbors have channels winding among islands or around jutting promontories until the landlocked basin is reached; but Chicago must throw out into the

open water her long arms of piled-up rock in order to gather in safety the storm-tossed vessels. Other cities may climb hills and build around them, crowning the elevations with some dominating structure; but the people of Chicago must ever recognize the fact that their city is without bounds or limits. Elsewhere, indeed, man and his works may be taken as the measure; but here the city appears as that portion of illimitable space now occupied by a population capable of indefinite expansion.

Whatever may be the forms which the treatment of the city shall take, therefore, the effects must of necessity be obtained by repetition of the unit. If the characteristics set forth suggest monotony, nevertheless such are the limitations which nature has imposed; and unless the problem is faced squarely no treatment proposed will seem adequate or will prove lastingly satisfactory. On the other hand, the opportunity now exists to create out of these very conditions a city which shall grow into both convenience and order, and shall possess all the means of making its citizens prosperous and contented.

It is in the grouping of buildings united by a common purpose — whether administrative, educational, or commercial — that one must find an adequate method of treatment; or again, in far-stretching lines of lagoons, inviting the multitudes to seek recreation along the endless miles of water front; or in broad avenues where the vista seemingly terminates with a tower by day, or in the converging lines of lights by night, in each case the mind recognizing that there is still space beyond. Always there must be the feeling of those broad surfaces of water reflecting the clouds of heaven; always the sense of breadth and freedom which are the very spirit of the prairies.

At no period in its history has the city looked far enough ahead. The mistakes of the past should be warnings for the future. There can be no reasonable fear lest any plans that may be adopted shall prove too broad and comprehensive. That idea may be dismissed as unworthy a moment's consideration. Rather let it be understood that the broadest plans which the city can be brought to adopt to-day must prove inadequate and limited before the end of the next quarter of a century. The mind of man, at least as expressed in works he actually undertakes, finds itself unable to rise to the full comprehension of the needs of a city growing at the rate now assured for Chicago. Therefore, no one should hesitate to commit himself to the largest and most comprehensive undertaking; because before any particular plan can be carried out, a still larger conception will begin to dawn, and even greater necessities will develop.

The two prime considerations for every large city are, first, adequate means of circulation; and second, a sufficient park area to insure good health and good order. In those portions of the city where congestion has brought about hindrances to traffic and consequent waste, new streets must be created at whatever present cost. Chicago has now reached that point in its growth when the congestion within the city demands new and enlarged channels of circulation, in order to accommodate the increasing throngs that choke the narrow and inadequate thoroughfares. There is need, also, for an orderly arrangement of public and semi-public buildings, and for proper approaches to such structures, to express the power and dignity of the city. One thinks of Paris, not as a place of so many millions of people, but as the beautiful capital, in which the artistic sense of the French people has found fullest expression. London impresses one, not so much on account of its size, but because of those monuments which the genius of the Anglo-Saxon race has reared to mark great events and to commemorate great names in the progress of civilization. In Berlin, in Vienna, and in every great city of Europe it is the plan of

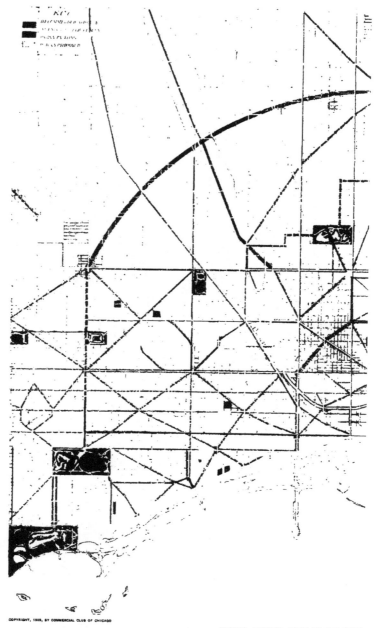

COPYRIGHT, 1909, BY COMMERCIAL CLUB OF CHICAGO

LXXXVI. CHICAGO. PLAN OF THE STREE
Proposed additional arteries and street widenings (orange); the present park system (green); the prop
of those already existing, and around the center of the city they serve

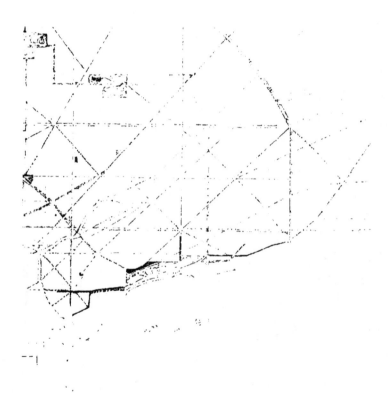

.EVARD SYSTEM PRESENT AND PROPOSED.

.s and playgrounds (hatched green). The proposed diagonal arteries are in every instance extensions
·onjunction with rectangular streets, the proposed circuit boulevards.

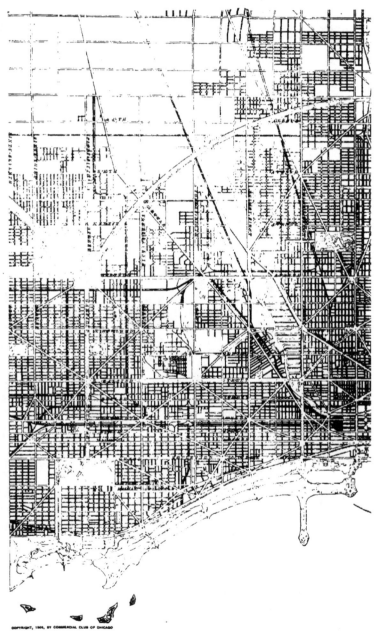

COPYRIGHT, 1909, BY COMMERCIAL CLUB OF CHICAGO

LXXXV. CHICAGO. PLAN OF A COMPLETE SYSTEM OF STREET CIRCULATION AND SYSTEM OF F
RELATED

PLAYGROUNDS, PRESENTING THE CITY AS AN ORGANISM IN WHICH ALL THE FUNCTIONS ARE
NOTHER.

COPYRIGHT, 1909, BY COMMERCIAL CLUB OF CHICAGO

LXXXVII. CHICAGO. VIEW LOOKING WEST OVER THE CITY, SHOWING THE P
Painted for the Commerci

POSED CIVIC CENTER, THE GRAND AXIS, GRANT PARK, AND THE HARBOR
Club by Jules Guerin.

the city, the character of its monuments, the impressive location of its public buildings, the picturesqueness of its thoroughfares, the development of its parks and gardens, or the treatment of its water front that give the character and charm which create individuality and interest.

COPYRIGHT, 1908, BY COMMERCIAL CLUB OF CHICAGO

LXXXVIII. CHICAGO. MAP SHOWING THE SUCCESSIVE CITY LIMITS, AND A LINE TRACED FROM THE SITE OF FORT DEARBORN THROUGH THE PRESENT CENTER OF POPULATION, REPRESENTING THE GENERAL TENDENCY OF GROWTH.

In all growing cities it has been necessary, as it is now necessary in Chicago, to break through the conditions imposed by the lack of an adequate and comprehensive plan at the beginning, and to create, at large expense, those thoroughfares and boulevards and public squares which the increasing demands of population and the larger requirements of civic life require. The longer the beginning has been postponed the harder has been the task and the greater the expense; but whatever the labor and however large the cost, the result has always been found more than compensation for the outlay. And so it will be with Chicago. Every year of postponement will deprive its citizens of advantages they might have enjoyed had they carried out improvements the necessities of which have been universally acknowledged.

People flock to those cities where conditions of work are good, where means of recreation abound, and where there are attractions for the senses and the intellect. Persons of wealth and refinement seek such cities as their abiding-places; and those who have accumulated wealth in a city bent on improvement remain there. Moreover, there is no stronger appeal made to the American citizen of to-day than comes from the call of one's native or adopted city to enter upon the service of creating better surroundings not only for one's self, but for all those who must of necessity earn their bread in the sweat of their brows. Nor is the call of posterity to be denied.

To love and render service to one's city, to have a part in its advancement, to seek to better its conditions and to promote its highest interests, — these are both the duty and the privilege of the patriot of peace.

The thoroughfares of a city may be divided into three classes: the street, by which is meant

COPYRIGHT, 1909, BY COMMERCIAL CLUB OF CHICAGO

LXXXIX. CHICAGO. DIAGRAM OF GENERAL SCHEME OF STREET CIRCULATION AND PARKS IN RELATION TO THE POPULATION.

The various densities of population, ranging from o to 25 persons per acre to 250 to 300 per acre are indicated by differ-ent densities of red color.   The center of population is indicated by a star.   Railroads are shown in blue.

the general type of artery; the avenue, on which tides of traffic and travel surge back and forth; and the boulevard, designed primarily as a combination of park and driveway. The first con-sideration for all thoroughfares is cleanliness, which is the result of a good roadbed kept in thor-ough repair, and unremitting care on the part of the city cleaning department. In the con-gested retail district the desirable street width is from 80 to 100 feet, about equally divided between sidewalks and roadway. Here the pavement should be smooth and noiseless; there should be frequent islands of safety for the pedestrian crossing from side to side, and occasional subway crossings; and the lighting, the signs, and every accessory of the street should be arranged with regard to the dictates of good taste. For streets carrying heavy tonnage a width of from

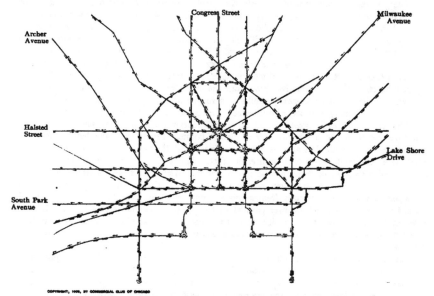

COPYRIGHT, 1909, BY COMMERCIAL CLUB OF CHICAGO

XC. CHICAGO. THEORETICAL DIAGRAM OF STREET CIRCULATION, SHOWING EXISTING LINES OF TRAVEL (BLACK), AND PROPOSED SUPPLEMENTARY LINES (ORANGE).
Circulation from north to south and east to west is already established by the rectilinear system of streets. There is need of additional facilities to be provided by street widenings and new arteries. Circulation towards the center is partially established, but the arteries need extending and developing, and circulation across the city from the northwest to the south and east and from the southwest to the north is lacking. It is proposed to remedy this lack by extending existing diagonal streets.

70 to 90 feet is desirable, with a roadway width of a little more than one-half the entire space, and here the pavements should be of the most enduring character, regardless of noise.[1]

On residence streets the area devoted to pavement may well be lessened to from 20 to 36 feet, according to the amount of traffic, in order that greater area may be obtained for trees and grass plots. This is highly desirable where, as in some sections is inevitable, houses are crowded

---

[1] The report to the Street Paving Committee of the Commercial Club on the street paving problem of Chicago, by John W. Alvord, C. E., and an opinion by John S. Miller, Esq., on maintenance and repair of Chicago streets (1904) is at once so comprehensive and so compact a document that it is sufficient simply to call attention to it. After discussing tendencies in this country and Europe, Mr. Alvord reaches this conclusion: "Everywhere the main result is the same. So soon as wealth and population increase to the point where luxury and comfort can demand it, the economical and more durable pavements of stone or granite on heavily traveled streets give way to pavement of shorter life and higher maintenance cost, but of immensely greater comfort to the public in the cessation of noise, smoothness for traffic, and ease with which they may be kept in condition."

together or apartment buildings abound, so that the smaller children may have playgrounds close at hand, and restful shade may prevail.   A well-kept grass plot in front of the house induces habits of neatness and comfort within; and cool shade brings people from cellars and dark rooms out into the light, thus contributing to good order and a higher morality.

The greatest disfigurement of the residence street is found in the varied assortment of poles which crowd out the trees along the space between curb and sidewalk.   There are trolley-poles, electric lighting poles, poles for telephone wires, and poles for police and fire-alarm purposes. The natural development of the city will relegate the greater portion of such service into conduits controlled by the municipality and occupied in common by the city and the various public service corporations.   So fast as streets are cleared from these obstructions, the municipality should take over the planting and maintenance of all trees in street spaces; so that the planting may be effective and attractive throughout the entire way.   The present method of leaving such work to individuals necessarily results in a ragged appearance of the street, and also fails to provide that diversity in variety of trees which gives beauty and individuality to the thoroughfare.

The avenue or traffic street should be of sufficient width to draw to itself the streams of traffic passing from one point in a city to distant points.   Provision should here be made not only for vehicular traffic, but also for street car lines; and the two currents may well be separated, so as to avoid interference with each other.   This end may be obtained as in Paris by a road lined with trees, or there may be subdivision into various roadways, of which one is dominant.   These thoroughfares, when conforming to the rectilinear street system, should be developed at intervals sufficiently frequent to accommodate the traffic that naturally would be drained into them from the narrower parallel streets and from the intersecting streets.   In order, however, to care for the traffic which flows from northeast to southwest, and from northwest to southeast, and vice versa, diagonal avenues become a necessity, in order to save time and consequent expense.

Few cities have been laid out with sufficient foresight to provide for such diagonals.   It has usually happened that at first a small city area has been developed, in which the need of diagonal thoroughfares was not felt; and then as the city expanded subdivision after subdivision has been added, wherein the original street system has been followed, with no care or thought for the increased traffic which growth begets.   The one idea of those who make new subdivisions is to secure the utmost space to sell immediately, leaving the future to take care of itself.   Hence it happens that, as a rule, when diagonal streets become of prime necessity they must be created at large expense, and with great temporary inconvenience.   Yet whatever the expense, such thoroughfares must be opened; and the city itself is the gainer in each instance, not alone by the saving of time, but also in the increased valuations for taxation which such improvements inevitably bring about.   Fortunately for Chicago a considerable number of diagonals already exist, and the large part which they play in promoting circulation offers the best argument for their extension and completion.   Blue Island and Milwaukee avenues, the happy survivals of old country roads, now carry great streams of traffic, while Ogden and Archer avenues and other lesser diagonals are of large utility as time-savers.

The third class of thoroughfares are the boulevards properly so called; the streets from which all heavier traffic is excluded; the streets lined with commodious and even fine dwellings; the streets where grass and shrubs and trees assert themselves, and where there may well be continuous playgrounds for the children of the neighborhood, such as many Chicago boulevards now

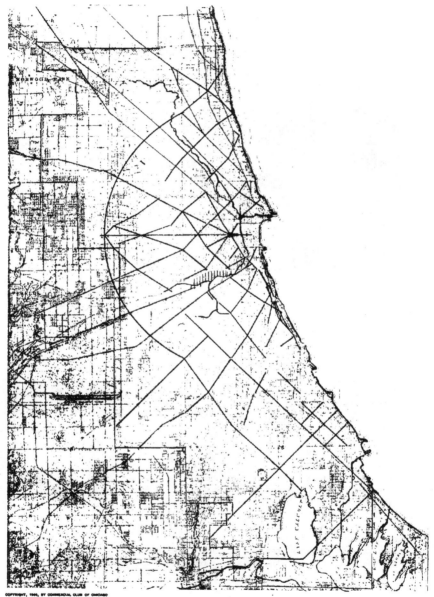

COPYRIGHT, 1908, BY COMMERCIAL CLUB OF CHICAGO

XCI. CHICAGO. EXISTING AND (IN RED) PROPOSED DIAGONAL ARTERIES.

provide. If in certain sections buildings for light manufactures abut upon these thoroughfares, the working people will then enjoy a maximum of fresh air and light; and so will work

XCII. PARIS. THE AVENUE DU BOIS DE BOULOGNE, LOOKING TOWARDS THE ARC DE TRIOMPHE.

with greatest effectiveness. The boulevard also affords appropriate sites for statues and fountains, and all other forms of adornment pleasing to the eye, making attractive the city. The smaller parks may well be adjacent to the boulevards, or may be expansions of them, thus providing for larger playgrounds, for places of assembly, and for displays of plants and flowers, and rare and beautiful trees, which appeal to the almost universal love of nature. The principle governing the grouping of boulevards and avenues is the establishment of through connection, so that one thoroughfare shall lead into another, and that circulation shall be everywhere promoted but never impeded.

Along the curved avenues and the diagonals the architectural design should avoid the building up of the thoroughfare structure by structure, each one following the whim of its owner or the struggle for novelty on the part of its architect. Without attempting to secure formality, or to insist on uniformity of design on a large scale, there should be a constant display of teamwork, so to speak, on the part of the architects. The former days when each architect strove to build his cornice

XCIII. PARIS. THE TUILERIES GARDENS, AND CHAMPS ÉLYSÉES BEYOND, FORMING THE MAIN AXIS OF THE CITY.

higher or more elaborate than the adjoining cornice are giving place, happily, to the saner idea of accepting existing conditions when a reasonable line has been established. There is as much reason why façades should live together in harmony as there is for peace among neighbors. In the case of open spaces, effectiveness of architectural design is to be obtained only by a large unity in the entire composition. The harmonious treatment of the buildings facing the circle opposite the railway station in Rome and on the Place Vendôme in Paris, and the plan adopted for the plaza in front of the Union Station at Washington, all prove that an imposing effect can be produced by a unified and grandly simple design. In Paris when attempt was made to alter some of the houses in the Place Vendôme, the owners were forbidden to do so, because the proposed alterations would have spoiled the architectural symmetry of that circle.

Chicago, being a comparatively new city, escapes one

XCIV. PARIS. THE CHAMPS ÉLYSÉES, FROM THE PLACE DE LA CONCORDE, SHOWING THE ARC DE TRIOMPHE IN VISTA.

difficulty experienced in the re-formation of cities of the Old World; here there are no buildings possessing either historical or picturesque value which must be sacrificed in order to carry out the plans necessary to provide circulation for a growing metropolis. The absence of monumental structures, however, imposes other obligations on the city planner. All the boulevards of Paris were established on the models of the boulevards of Louis XIV., with two lines of trees bordering the driveways, and lines of houses on each side of the street, so that the mass of verdure almost entirely obscures the view of the façades. In the new streets the houses are to have a different system of alignment, so as to form a broken line which will admit of alternate

XCV. PARIS. VIEW FROM THE ARC DE TRIOMPHE ALONG THE AVENUE DU BOIS DE BOULOGNE.

masses of masonry, and masses of green. In this manner the boulevards will gain in artistic effect; while at the same time the line of the façades will be lengthened, thereby making the interior of the dwellings more healthful and agreeable. Much the same effect is produced in many Boston and some Washington apartment buildings, which are constructed on three sides of a court, leaving a mass of green open to the street.

In laying out new thoroughfares or treating old ones it must be remembered that with respect to traffic streets the increase in population is constantly making larger demands for width, and that on residence streets the city should not be burdened unnecessarily with the cost of street construction and maintenance. Moreover, there is great economy in the distinct separation of residence streets from traffic streets. Whenever a street railway seizes upon a residence street of ordinary size, that street immediately begins to undergo transformation into a business street; and this change while working its slow way causes depreciation in land values which, save on favorably located corners, amounts to virtual confiscation. With good planning these ruinous transformations become unnecessary, and the purchase of a home then becomes a stable investment and not a gambling hazard. Again, in every country experience has proved that the clear and even remorseless cutting of main lines through the district to be developed, and the division of great blocks into traffic arteries and service streets is the soundest economy, as well as the most effective means of reaching the sought-for end.

The second form of traffic interruption, arising from the intersection of lines of movement, is complicated by reason of the fact that here the pedestrian movement, as well as the vehicular movement, must be taken into consideration. There are times when men gather in the streets for patriotic purposes, as on the Fourth of July and Decoration Day; or because of an eager desire to learn the news of great events, like election results. The right of the people to assemble for discussion is fundamental. All these requirements must be met by the creation of open spaces, which appropriately may be adorned by the statues of men of achievement, or may be ornamented with fountains and memorials of various kinds. These spaces for assembly and for embellishment should be arranged so as to allow traffic to flow unvexing and unvexed. Nothing could be more of a makeshift than the arbitrary regulations of the police in many of our cities, where long detours are imposed on the wayfarer and vehicle alike, in order to diminish that congestion which it is the task of the city planner to prevent. Yet in no city in the world has this intricate and perplexing problem been completely solved.

It is charged against the French system of "star-places" that they invite congestion by concentrating traffic; and doubtless they are open to this accusation when placed on great traffic thoroughfares, unless pains are taken to insist on a movement similar to that of a whirlpool, so that each entering vehicle shall be required to move around the circumference until its particular street shall be reached. The solution of a gentle junction of two lines in a common line for a certain distance, like that of a railway, has advantages which the city planner will not overlook. Whatever the form taken in a particular instance, the angles in the lots produced by the junction should be studied in order that the open space may not seem to be unfinished, and also that the architect may not be compelled to utilize sharp points unfitted for architectural treatment.

It should be borne in mind that directness is not the only consideration. Traffic wagons when loaded naturally seek the shortest course, but the great majority of vehicles and of pedestrians as well are lured out of the direct line to streets made attractive by the shops, the trees, or other embellishments. Often it happens that unattractive streets, in spite of being shorter, are quite deserted because they are spotted with vacant sites, ugly buildings, and dreary spaces. Beauty allures while ugliness repels in city architecture as in everything else. Moreover, every consideration which affects the planning of a city as a whole is truly architecture, and wherever there is evidence of foresight and the relation of one part to another, there the mind finds the highest satisfaction. Paris is the international capital because in its planning the universal mind recognizes that complete articulation which satifies the craving for good order and symmetry in every part.

If Chicago were to be relocated to-day, it would still be placed at the spot where it now is; and if the streets were again to be mapped, the same general system would be adopted, because

XCVI. SYSTEM OF TRAFFIC CIRCULATION PROPOSED BY M. HÉNARD FOR PUBLIC PLACES.
A continuous gyratory movement reduces conflict of currents to the minimum.

the present rectilinear street system best comports with the line of the Lake front which nature has unalterably fixed. The rectilinear system certainly accords with the ideas of rightness inherent in the human mind; and also it involves a minimum waste of ground space. Moreover, the River, for the most part, allows the use of the right-angled system without playing havoc with the orderly arrangement of the streets. It is only when and as the city increases in population that diagonals become necessary in order to save considerable amounts of time and to prevent congestion by dividing and segregating the traffic. Thus it happens that no rectilinear city is perfect without the diagonal streets; and conversely, having the rectilinear system, the creation of diagonals produces the greatest convenience.

Now, while it happens that the planning of a new city imposes straightness as a duty, and diagonals as a necessity, it is equally true that a virtue should be made of these hard-and-fast conditions. There is a true glory in mere length, in vistas longer than the eye can reach, in roads of arrow-like purpose that speed unswerving in their flight; and when and where the opportunity of level ground permits, this glory should be sought after. Older cities may indeed bend and curve their new streets to preserve what is picturesque or historic; but new cities, built on level country, should see to it that as subdivisions are platted, the streets and avenues shall be adequate to bear the traffic which will come to them from the city itself, and that such thoroughfares shall form an integral part of the entire system of circulation.

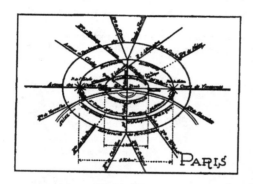

REPRODUCED FROM "LES TRANSFORMATIONS DE PARIS," BY M. E. MÉNARD
XCVII. THEORETICAL DIAGRAM OF THE STREETS OF PARIS.

At the same time the elliptical avenue may be used to introduce variety, and especially to serve as a link to connect parks. Chicago had no encircling fortifications to turn into boulevards such as those which beautify and distinguish the cities of Vienna, Brussels, Rouen, Milan, and especially Paris; but such avenues may well be created in order to relieve the monotony of the straight streets. One such great parkway is shown on the plans, and it requires but a glance to recognize the effectiveness of such a thoroughfare.

Having discussed the general principles applicable to the arrangement and development of streets within a city, we come to the specific problem. The city of Chicago now extends for about twenty-six miles along the Lake front, and has a width of not more than seven miles. It is apparent that as population increases, the entire territory between the present western boundaries and the Des Plaines River will become thickly settled, and that as this occupation proceeds the pressure of the increased numbers to

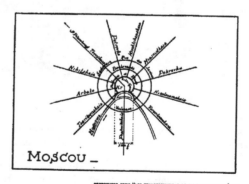

REPRODUCED FROM "LES TRANSFORMATIONS DE PARIS," BY M. E. MÉNARD
XCVIII. THEORETICAL DIAGRAM OF THE STREETS OF MOSCOW.

reach the business district and the Lake front will work serious congestion, unless additional thoroughfares shall be created in order to add to transit facilities inadequate even at the present time. Obviously it is idle to expect those who plat subdivisions for the mere purpose of selling land to make provision for a circulatory system sufficiently comprehensive to meet the requirements of a growing city. That task belongs to the city itself, and the only way in which it can be accomplished is by the preparation and adoption of a plan for platting all those lands adjacent to the city which are reasonably certain to be included within the enlarged boundaries. The entire territory extending westward to the Des Plaines should be laid out to meet future requirements, with the requisite area for residences, as well as wide thoroughfares for traffic, well-planned diagonals to gather and distribute the travel, and adequate park spaces. As the architects of Louis XIV. laid out streets and avenues of Paris far in advance of occupation, and as the United States government adopted a plan for the development of the entire District of Columbia in accord with the original L'Enfant plan, so the authorities of Chicago should see to it

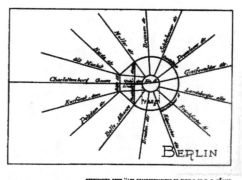

REPRODUCED FROM "LES TRANSFORMATIONS DE PARIS," BY E. E. HÉNARD
XCIX. THEORETICAL DIAGRAM OF THE STREETS OF BERLIN.

that when and as new subdivisions are platted in any portion of Cook County not now included within the city boundaries, the thoroughfares in those subdivisions shall be fitted to care for the traffic that will be imposed upon them by reason of their location in relation to the business district.

The functions of the diagonals and circuits proposed for the area impinging upon the business district are three in number: first, to allow traffic seeking the center to reach its destination expeditiously; secondly, to divert from the center traffic not having its objective point within the central area; and, thirdly, to afford direct passage through the center in those cases where such crossing is necessary.

The matter of widening avenues by means of regulating the frontage is largely one of conservation. That is to say, along streets where residences predominate the thoroughfare should be widened by acquiring all the property to the line of the buildings, so that as the street changes its character from a residence to a business thoroughfare it shall not be narrowed at the very time when greater width is desirable. In short, the city should

REPRODUCED FROM "LES TRANSFORMATIONS DE PARIS," BY E. E. HÉNARD
C. THEORETICAL DIAGRAM OF THE STREETS OF LONDON.

acquire and own the front yards, just as the Federal government owns the space between houses and sidewalks in Washington. For example, Chicago Avenue gives one the impression of a

splendid boulevard, owing to the fact that the buildings are set well back from the street; but eventually the avenue will be narrowed to 100 feet, unless the yard spaces shall be acquired, as acquired they can be at small expense, so long as the purpose is to keep the space open.

The diagonals are the most useful and necessary arteries. Those belonging to the first circuit passing around the business center are as follows:

Chicago Avenue and Lincoln Park Boulevard to Milwaukee Avenue and Canal Street, crossing the river north of the junction of its three branches;

From the intersection of

CI. CHICAGO. VIEW OF GRAND BOULEVARD.

Washington and Canal streets running to Halsted and Congress streets;

From Halsted and Congress streets to Twelfth and Canal streets, and from the latter intersection across the river at Sixteenth Street to Archer Avenue at State Street and Cottage Grove Avenue at Twenty-second Street.

For the most part, these diagonals would run through wholesale and manufacturing districts, passing near some of the railroad freight yards and intercepting the traffic to the city from the other outlying freight yards. This traffic, once having reached the circuit, would make use of it as a means of getting around the congested district.

CII. CHICAGO. VIEW OF THE LAKE SHORE DRIVE.

As the city increases in population, its retail and business district necessarily expands also, the rise in values of the real estate forcing the wholesale interests farther away from the center.

Traffic on these circuit arteries would thus change in character, and they might eventually be made boulevards to carry traffic of every description except that of heavy teaming. The argument for the circuit as described is equally strong when considered with regard to any form of

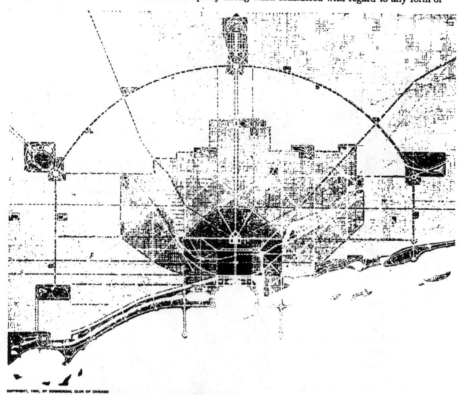

COPYRIGHT, 1909, BY COMMERCIAL CLUB OF CHICAGO

CIII. CHICAGO. PLAN OF THE CITY, SHOWING THE GENERAL SYSTEM OF BOULEVARDS AND PARKS EXISTING AND PROPOSED.

The boulevards are planned to form a continuous system of circulation; the parks are related closely to the boulevard system, and are located, wherever possible, in connection with them.

traffic. It is based on a general experience in other cities, which proves that there is a gradual evolution from mere utility to a service of a lighter and more agreeable character. For example, the Square of the Innocents in Paris, once a cloistered cemetery, is now a playground, and serves as a breathing space for the densely populated neighborhood. Some such evolution will come in the case of the present freight yards lying along the river, which ultimately will be abandoned for freight purposes, just as the fortifications of Paris and Vienna have been transformed from absolute utility to useful purposes of an entirely different nature.

CIV. CHICAGO. VIEW OF DREXEL BOULEVARD.

When the freight yards shall be abandoned as industrial sites a large tract of territory will be available for public purposes, and the growing population might easily demand the space for recreation; and the fact that the available space lies along the river will be of double advantage, since river banks furnish an agreeable variety when they extend throughout a city.

In addition to the diagonals shown on the diagram are the existing roads running beside the great railway rights-of-way. Some of these already extend far out in the country, and also penetrate inside the city. All of them should be improved, and missing links should be supplied. When, at perhaps no distant day, the railroads entering the city come to be operated by electricity, no better highways can be imagined. They should be broadened, ornamented, and made to serve as great arteries. Outside the city limits, and often inside them, these highways beside the railways penetrate populous districts, where they are of increasing importance. They should be drained, paved, and planted in the best manner, and it is of first importance that

CV. CHICAGO. VIEW OF MICHIGAN AVENUE, LOOKING NORTH.

there should be no grade crossings of carriageways and railways. This work of improvement which is already in progress inside the city should be carried on until every crossing within the territory shown on the main diagram or encircling highways shall be eliminated.

In time the streets within the business center will be taxed to the utmost on the surface, on the overhead tramways, and underneath the present grades. Knowing this, it is important to provide means to divert as much as possible the movement of people around the center when business or pleasure does not necessitate passing into or through it. The topography of Chicago is such that this may be accomplished readily. The shore of the Lake bends rapidly away toward the northwest north of North Avenue, thus placing the center of population of that section so far west that traffic can go directly to the South Side without passing through the business district, if only means to this end be provided; and at the same time the people of the West Side can easily reach the North and South Sides, south of the business districts, without passing through the center.

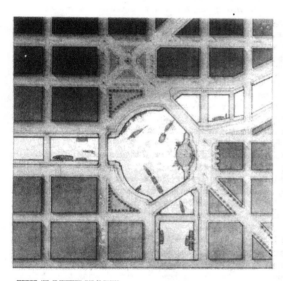

COPYRIGHT, 1808, BY COMMERCIAL CLUB OF CHICAGO

CVI. CHICAGO. INTERSECTION OF THE THREE BRANCHES OF THE CHICAGO RIVER.

Plan suggested to facilitate traffic circulation by means of two additional bridges placed as proposed for the north-and-south boulevard at Michigan Avenue, on a level above the present street, and connected eventually with streets to be built on either side of the River.

The streets should be arranged and improved so as to provide for such lines of travel. At present, nearly every one going from one section of the city lying outside of the center to another section outside of the center comes into the business district and passes through it on his way. This movement includes pedestrians, passengers on the elevated and surface cars, and wheeled vehicles; it also includes teams and trucks of every description, including those for fire and police services. It is obvious that direct and well-improved thoroughfares should enable this traffic to pass outside the congested center from one section to another.

The main portion of the proposed grand circuit would extend from a park at the intersection of Graceland and West avenues, around to Gage Park, thence on Fifty-fifth Boulevard to Michigan Avenue, and thence north to Graceland Avenue at the Lake, a distance of nearly thirty miles. This great circuit can be utilized for continuous playgrounds sweeping around the center and connecting the dense populations that will inhabit the North and South Sides; and thus it will be of inestimable value. To this circuit traffic would come from considerable distances on either side of it, then follow its line until reaching a street leading directly to that portion of the city for which it is destined. By such a route congested business and manufacturing territories may be avoided, and thus it would serve the purpose of many diagonals that otherwise must be created. As a continuous park it would furnish breathing space and playgrounds for a very large number of people, and become a most popular avenue for pleasure as well as for necessary circulation. Moreover, the great circuit seems to be the line most normal to all the great existing radials, and thus it would be the most economical method of furnishing quick and easy communication. Also it expresses in an ideal manner what is aimed at by all inner circuits, which are angular because of the prohibitive cost of making them follow a continuous curve; and also because a curve for the inner circuits would not develop the necessary articulation with existing important rectangular streets. The degree of curvature of this outer circuit parkway insures an extremely noble effect along its entire length and makes many picturesque angles with the intersecting streets. As a whole, it is intended to be a stately highway, such as does not now exist in any city.

The next circuit inside the grand one now largely exists in the form of the great park boulevards of Michigan Avenue, Grand Boulevard, or Drexel Boulevard to Washington Park, Fifty-fifth Street to Gage Park; thence by the West Park boulevards through the West Parks, back by Diversey Boulevard to the Lake, and south to Michigan Avenue. Another circuit is on the same route as the one last mentioned, except that it does not extend so far to the south as Fifty-fifth Street, but goes west to McKinley Park as shown on the diagram.

A circuit of very great ultimate importance would extend on Michigan Avenue from Chicago Avenue to Twenty-second Street; thence on Twenty-second Street to Halsted; on Halsted diagonally to the corner of Ashland and Twelfth streets; thence north on Ashland to Union Park; from Union Park diagonally to the corner of Chicago Avenue and Halsted, thence east on Chicago Avenue to the Lake. This route should be a great thoroughfare, affording every facility for the movement of people on foot, in carriages, or in streets cars, and for teams as well. It should be very wide and well planted.

The innermost circuit utilizes Michigan Avenue, Twelfth Street, and Canal Street; thence diagonally to Halsted and Congress streets; thence again diagonally to Washington and Canal streets; thence on Washington Street to the Lake. This circuit should have an underground and an overhead loop for passengers, except that the overhead line should swing over Wabash Avenue instead of over Michigan Avenue.

The following existing east-and-west streets should be widened and much improved: Graceland Avenue, Diversey Boulevard, North Avenue, Indiana Avenue, Chicago Avenue, Washington Street, Congress Street extended and very much widened. Twelfth Street should become a great viaduct, beginning at grade at Michigan Avenue and extending elevated over to Canal; and it should not be less than 180 feet in width as shown on drawings. Sixteenth Street and also Twenty-second Street should be widened. It would be wise, also, to widen each of the section-limit streets running east and west, and also the half-section streets.

South Park Avenue (which is the extension of Grand Boulevard) should be carried over the Illinois Central right-of-way from Twenty-second Street to Grant Park, over which it should pass to that railroad's north freight yards; thence over the yards and the main branch of the river, and on until it connects with the Lincoln Park Lake Shore Drive on the North Side. This would form a continuous outer boulevard connecting the Lincoln Park and South Park systems with the utmost correctness, and in a fine manner. This way would enable people to pass by

COPYRIGHT, 1909, BY COMMERCIAL CLUB OF CHICAGO

CVII. CHICAGO. VIEW LOOKING NORTH ON THE SOUTH BRANCH OF THE CHICAGO RIVER, SHOWING THE SUGGESTED ARRANGEMENT OF STREETS AND WAYS FOR TEAMING AND RECEPTION OF FREIGHT BY BOAT, AT DIFFERENT LEVELS.

Examples of the arrangement exist at Algiers, Budapest, Geneva, and Paris.

the business center when they do not desire to enter it, and would be an additional thoroughfare to and from the center.

The cost of this improvement would amount to comparatively little for condemnation of private property; the space to be taken would be only that necessary to widen Grand Boulevard to Twenty-second Street, and to carry through the route on the North Side portion. The right-of-way over the railroad from Twenty-second Street to Grant Park, and from Grant Park to the river should be obtained without cost.

The Chicago River, which gave to the city its location and fostered its commerce, has become a dumping spot and a cesspool; bridges of every possible style and condition span it at irregular intervals and at all angles; and year by year riparian owners have been permitted to encroach upon its channel until there are to be found as many as four lines of docks, each newer one having been built further into the stream. Tunnel-backs have restricted its depth for purposes of navigation. The widening proposed by the Sanitary District authorities and the fact that almost all the docks are in a dilapidated condition will combine to make changes imperative. The opportunity should be seized to plan a comprehensive and adequate development of the river banks, so that the commercial facilities shall be extended, while at the same time the æsthetic side of the problem shall be worked out.

Boulevards should extend from the mouth of the river along the North and South branches and on both sides, at least from the mouth of the river to North Avenue on the North Branch and to Halsted Street on the South Branch. These thoroughfares would be an important factor in the relief of traffic congestion down town; they should be raised above the normal traffic level in order to afford greater facility of circulation, and to allow warehouses to be constructed below the roadway. This upper level would thus connect the points on the river at which the street scheme calls for an elevation, as in the case of the north-and-south connecting boulevards, the junctions of the three branches of the river, and Twelfth Street. These boulevards apart from their practical advantages would become the most delightful route to the Lake.

We have now considered with some detail the disposition of the streets and avenues surrounding the intense business center of Chicago. While this outer city area is occupied mainly by dwellings, certain streets along which transportation lines pass, come to be lined with shops throughout their entire length, so that one passes from the center of affairs into the residence district without noting the transition. As a rule, however, the density and importance of the buildings decrease from the center to the circumference; and in corresponding manner the highways of circulation and exchange may diminish in width. It is essential, however, to provide encircling or belt thoroughfares which act as collectors of traffic, and also as distributors of it; so as to prevent the inextricable congestion which inevitably arises when masses of people gathered along converging lines attempt to penetrate the center at a single point. However difficult it may be to provide against such congestion in the case of older cities, a reasonable system of circulation in connection with the business center of a comparatively new city like Chicago should be accomplished with comparative ease. The widening of some streets and the construction of needed arteries is made less difficult by reason of the fact that the buildings which cover the greater part of Chicago's area beyond the business center are not of a permanent character, and in the natural order of things they must be replaced by others more substantial. Provision should be made now so as to ensure that, as the transformation progresses, sufficient land area shall be left unoccupied to provide good sanitary conditions, and attractive streets as well.

The three requisites for this outer region, therefore, are: first, convenient means of access to the main business center and to the subordinate centers, which are the day's working-places; secondly, equally convenient means of access to the water and the fields and forests, where the hours of recreation and refreshment are passed; and, thirdly, as much light and air as possible for the dwellings and the schools, where the home-keepers are occupied with their daily tasks, and where the children are trained, either for weakness or for strength, as physical conditions largely determine.

CVIII. CHICAGO. VIEW OF THE SOUTH SHORE LOOKING SOUTH-
EAST OVER GRANT PARK.

COPYRIGHT, 1909, BY COMMERCIAL CLUB OF CHICAGO

CIX. CHICAGO. THE PROPOSED PLAZA ON MICHIGAN AVENUE.

CHAPTER VII

THE HEART OF CHICAGO: OPPORTUNITY FOR CREATING A CONVENIENT AND UNIFIED CITY: MICHIGAN AVENUE AS THE BASE OF A GREAT COMPOSITION: THE WIDENING OF HALSTED STREET: A GROUP PLAN FOR THE FIELD MUSEUM, THE CRERAR LIBRARY, AND THE ART INSTITUTE: CONGRESS STREET AS THE MAIN AXIS OF THE CITY: THE CIVIC CENTER

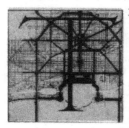

HE Heart of Chicago is that portion of the city area between Halsted Street and the Lake, and between the main river and Twelfth Street. Within the next few years these boundaries will be enlarged to include Chicago Avenue on the north, Ashland Avenue on the west, and Twenty-second Street on the south. The treatment of this area, having a length of appproximately three miles north and south, and a width of four miles from Ashland Avenue to the ends of the two great piers planned to extend into the Lake at Chicago Avenue and again at Twenty-second Street, involves the most serious problems encountered in the plan of the city.

As the population of Chicago spreads itself over the area between the Lake and the Des Plaines River the pressure on the Heart of Chicago must of necessity increase in geometrical ratio. The ground, being devoted to business purposes, will become so valuable that the buildings will rise to the height permitted by law. These buildings will be used for offices by corporations whose plants are scattered throughout the wide territory of which Chicago is the metropolis; for shops and banks; for hotels; for theatres and other places of entertainment; for railroad passenger terminals; for churches and public or semi-public structures, all of which will be resorted to by hundreds of thousands of people who must pass daily into and out of this comparatively small area.

The main problem to be solved is the disposition of the various streams of traffic, so that people may reach expeditiously the places to which their daily vocations call them. This prob-

99

lem may be postponed, or it may be solved inadequately; but sooner or later, as experience teaches, some solution must be found. Postponement multiplies ultimate cost, and meantime creates a constantly increasing burden of discomfort and loss of business. True economy, therefore, dictates that the present moment, when already congestion is a menace to the commercial progress of the city, shall be seized upon as the proper time to begin a thorough regeneration of the street system within the Heart of Chicago. Fortunately, the general lines on which the changes should be made are determined by opportunities so obvious that the development of a dignified and thoroughly convenient composition would seem to come about quite naturally. All that is necessary is to take advantage of existing possibilities by combining the various elements into a consistent whole. By so doing a unified city, wherein each portion will have organic relation to all other portions, will result.

In considering the Heart of Chicago as a single composition it is desirable to begin with the base line. Obviously this is found in Michigan Avenue, which is already a broad thoroughfare, and is now in process of being widened to a width of 130 feet throughout that portion which is bordered by Grant Park. At the present time, Michigan Avenue is the main connecting thoroughfare between the North and South Sides; but it is much more than this. Office buildings, hotels, clubs, theatres, music-halls, and shops of the first order as to size and architecture line the western side of the avenue, the Park opposite their fronts insuring light, air, and an agreeable outlook. So desirable has this thoroughfare become that extensions of it to the north or the south must enhance the value of the abutting real estate, because of the increased opportunities such extensions will create for continuing the building of structures of the highest class.

Michigan Avenue is probably destined to carry the heaviest movement of any street in the world. Any boulevard connection in Michigan Avenue which fails to recognize the basic importance of the avenue will be a waste of money and energy. Any impairment of the capacity of this street at any point along its entire front, any weakening of this foundation, is an error of the first magnitude.

At the present time the northern limit of this foundation of street circulation on the Lake front is the water-tower on Chicago Avenue, and the south limit is the intersection of Twelfth Street and Michigan Avenue. This avenue or parkway should be made as spacious as possible along its entire length. It should be wide enough to provide two broad parallel roadways: one to be used by those who wish to visit the shops, hotels, or theatres, and the other for the passage of those who do not care to stop on their way through the city. Between these roadways should be a broad sidewalk, and the walk next to the buildings also should be very broad. This roadway should be made attractive by effective planting. The trees framing the boulevard may well be of the clipped variety in order to carry out the architectural effect; and the lamps and other accessories should be designed so as to give finish and unity to the composition.

The limit of width is fixed by the physical conditions of Michigan Avenue between Randolph Street and the river. Here the distance between the west side of Michigan Avenue and the west line of the Illinois Central property is 246 feet. Michigan Avenue north of Randolph Street is now 66 feet wide. The business blocks between Michigan Avenue and Beaubien Court are 130 feet deep, and Beaubien Court is 50 feet wide; a total of 246 feet. Therefore 246 feet is the limit of possible width, and this is recommended as the width of the proposed boulevard connection, every foot of which is part of this Lake front parkway — the great base of Chicago's street circulation.

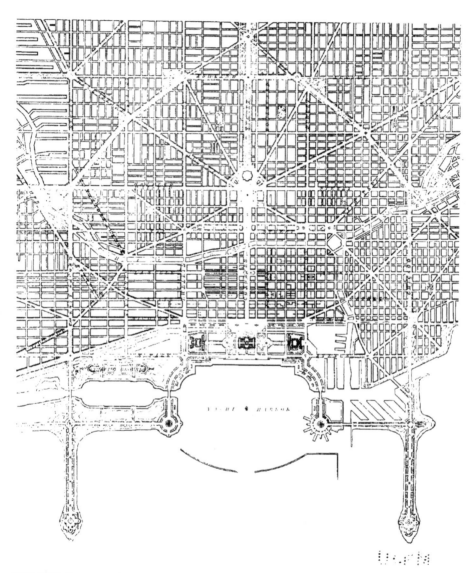

COPYRIGHT, 1909, BY COMMERCIAL CLUB OF CHICAGO

CX. CHICAGO. PLAN OF THE COMPLETE SYSTEM OF STREET CIRCULATION; RAILWAY STATIONS; PARKS, BOULEVARD CIRCUITS AND RADIAL ARTERIES; PUBLIC RECREATION PIERS, YACHT HARBOR, AND PLEASURE-BOAT PIERS; TREATMENT OF GRANT PARK; THE MAIN AXIS AND THE CIVIC CENTER, PRESENTING THE CITY AS A COMPLETE ORGANISM IN WHICH ALL ITS FUNCTIONS ARE RELATED ONE TO ANOTHER IN SUCH A MANNER THAT IT WILL BECOME A UNIT.

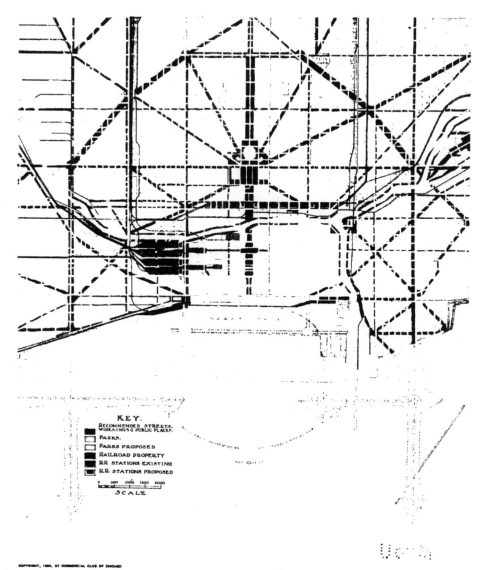

KEY.

RECOMMENDED STREETS,
WIDENINGS & PUBLIC PLACES.

PARKS.

PARKS PROPOSED

RAILROAD PROPERTY

R.R. STATIONS EXISTING

R.R. STATIONS PROPOSED

0   500   1000   1500   2000
SCALE

COPYRIGHT, 1909, BY COMMERCIAL CLUB OF CHICAGO

CXL CHICAGO. PLAN OF THE CENTER OF THE CITY, SHOWING THE PRESENT STREET AND BOULEVARD SYSTEM.
The proposed additional arteries and street widenings (orange); the present parks (green); and proposed new parks and playgrounds within present shoreline (hatched green); the present railway properties, lines, and stations, and the proposed new
stations arranged on a circuit boulevard (dark blue).

Randolph Street

COPYRIGHT, 1909, BY COMMERCIAL CLUB OF CHICAGO

CXII. CHICAGO. PROPOSED BOULEVARD TO CONNECT THE NORTH AND SOUTH SIDES OF THE RIVER; VIEW LOOKING NORTH FROM WASHINGTON STREET.

The boulevard is raised to allow free flow of east-and-west teaming traffic under it, and both Michigan Avenue and Beaubien Court are raised to the boulevard level. The raised portion throughout its entire length, from Randolph Street to Indiana Street, extends from building line to building line. It is approached from the cross streets by inclined roadways or ramps; these may be changed to the east side or omitted.

Painted for the Commercial Club by Jules Guerin.

In a study of this problem several years ago, "along lines that will not only meet the present requirements of the city, both as to convenience and beauty, but which for years to come will meet the needs of the city," committees of the City Council, the Real Estate Board, the architects, the South Park Board, and the Lincoln Park Board, after consultation with the Mayor of Chicago and other interested citizens, recommended the condemnation of all of the land lying between Michigan Avenue and Beaubien Court from Randolph Street to the river, in order that an adequate thoroughfare might be provided. These committees, which contributed very much to a proper understanding of the conditions, were convinced of the necessity of taking all of the property rather than a strip of it. This parkway should be reserved exclusively for the use of pedestrians and lighter vehicles. It is the one great thoroughfare that can be so dedicated, and commercial traffic should be excluded from it and amply provided for elsewhere.

From Twelfth Street to Chicago Avenue the only east-and-west streets crossing Michigan Avenue that carry a heavy commercial traffic are the four east-and-west streets immediately south of the river, and the four east-and-west streets immediately north of the river. These eight east-and-west streets, together with the tracks and sidings of the Chicago and Northwestern railway on the north bank of the river, are the only points where commercial traffic comes into collision with the north-and-south movement on the Lake front parkway. Naturally the commercial cross-traffic that flows east and west through these eight streets is particularly dense, being created by the railway terminals, docks, and warehouses east of Michigan Avenue, both north and south of the river. By actual count on a given day it was found that between the hours of 8 and 10 o'clock in the morning the pedestrian movement at the crowded crossing at the intersection of Michigan Avenue with Randolph Street was 12,484. In short, 104 people, sixty per cent of whom were probably women and children, passed this corner every minute. On the same morning it was ascertained that between 7 and 10 o'clock 893 trucks and light vehicles moved in the intersection of one of these streets and Michigan Avenue. Confusion and delay attendant upon the concentration of such masses are certain to increase as the Illinois Central, the Michigan Central, and the Wisconsin Central railways improve their terminals, as the warehouses of this district are increased, and as more docks or harbors are developed at the mouth of the river.

By the plan for the connecting boulevard, which would begin its rise at Randolph Street, heavy traffic would be diverted into Lake Street and other streets north, making the Randolph Street intersection safer for pedestrian movement. The other streets crossing under the parkway would be freed almost entirely of cross-traffic, and the loss of time resulting from impeded movement would be reduced to the minimum.

Evidently if this Lake front parkway is to be dedicated solely to the use of the people, with commercial traffic excluded, it cannot be carried across these east-and-west streets at the present level of Michigan Avenue, without depressing these east-and-west streets. After an investigation by engineers all thought of such street depression has been abandoned. Therefore the boulevard connection must be elevated from Randolph Street on the south to Indiana Street on the north, if collision between two classes of traffic, both of which are better served when kept apart, is to be avoided.

It is not, however, necessary to carry the connecting boulevard very high. The present grade of Michigan Avenue at Randolph Street can be raised one foot, or a little more, without difficulty, so that from the street level at this point to the level of the boulevard connection one block north, at the corner of Lake Street and Michigan Avenue, the total rise would be about

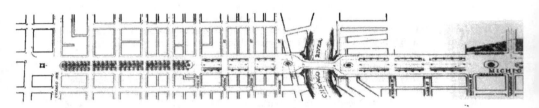

RIGHT, 1909, BY COMMERCIAL CLUB OF CHICAGO

CXIII. CHICAGO. PLAN OF MICHIGAN AVENUE FROM TWELFTH STREET

The proposed double roadway is designed to accommodate the immense volume of traffic which will be attracted to the Lake front. The west roadw
interference from stationary vehicles. The boulevard proposed is raised above the three streets north and south of the River (as shown in illustration No. CV
traffic-teaming belo

COPYRIGHT, 1909, BY COMMERCIAL CLUB OF CHICAGO

CXIV. CHICAGO. PROPOSED BOULEVARD AND
View looking west across Grant Park, sh

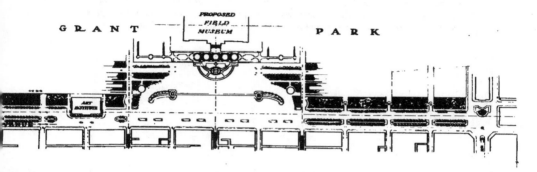

GRANT — PROPOSED FIELD MUSEUM — PARK

RIVER, AND ITS EXTENSION ON PINE STREET TO CHICAGO AVENUE.
or shopping traffic and carriages waiting for the crowds attending public functions; the eastern roadway carries traffic through the business section without
ating an artery free from heavy teaming traffic at its crossings from the North to the South Sides. A double-deck bridge accommodates the north-and-south
ht vehicles above.

ON MICHIGAN AVENUE AND PINE STREET.
elation of the park to the boulevard.

eleven feet, with a grade of two and seven-tenths per cent. From Lake Street to South Water Street the surface of the boulevard connection would rise only three feet more on a grade of three-fourths of one per cent. North of South Water Street the surface would rise very slightly to the bridge, from which point it would continue to the north practically on a level, until descending

CXV. CHICAGO. PROPOSED BOULEVARD ON MICHIGAN AVENUE; VIEW LOOKING NORTH FROM A POINT EAST OF THE PUBLIC LIBRARY. ALSO DEVELOPMENT OF THE PROPERTY EAST OF BEAUBIEN COURT, IN WHICH A RAIL-WAY STATION MIGHT BE INCORPORATED.

on a gentle grade to Lincoln Park Boulevard, near Indiana Street, or to Ohio Street. The grades suggested are less than those existing on Fifth Avenue in New York.

Not one roadway only, but the whole boulevard connection, 246 feet wide, should rise gradually from Randolph Street, and every store and building, both on the east side and on the west side of the parkway, north as well as south of the river, would naturally open on the level of the boulevard, exactly as the shops or hotels open on Michigan Avenue south of Randolph Street. Furthermore, every building facing on the boulevard connection would have direct access to the lower level under the elevation (except for a portion of one block at each end), so that goods could be brought into the buildings conveniently. This lower level, well lighted, ventilated, and protected from weather, would afford ideal conditions for handling commercial traffic. Part or all of it could be solidly filled in if the authorities and the property owners deemed this more

CXVI. CHICAGO. VIEW OF PINE STREET.
The Waterworks tower is shown as a marker in the vista of the proposed boulevard to connect the North and South Sides.

desirable; it would not be necessary to have all of the lower level open. From this lower level at street intersections there would be inclined roadways or ramps, giving comfortable facilities for pedestrians or carriages to reach the parkway. It would not be necessary to place these ramps at exactly the points where they are shown in the design; but they could be moved to the east side of the parkway if for any reason that side offered an advantage; or they could be eliminated if considered unnecessary.

The proposed bridge has two decks. The lower one, being designed for commercial traffic, would provide for the present heavy teaming moving north and south over the Rush Street bridge, without interrupting the teaming during the construction of the new parkway, as the old bridge could be retained until the completion of the new one.

The grade on the lower level approach up to the heavy teaming deck from the south would be 2½ per cent as compared with the present grade of nearly 5 per cent up to the present Rush Street bridge, and 5 per cent up to the present Dearborn Street bridge. The advantage of the double-deck bridge recommended in this plan is set forth in the statement of general requirements in the report made by the commission of engineers to the Board of Local Improvements on the proposed north-and-south boulevard connection. The engineers say: "The bridges over the river may be of either the bascule or the vertical lift type, and two single bridges may be used, one to accommodate boulevard

CXVII. PARIS. VIEW OF THE RUE DE LA PAIX AND THE COLUMN VENDÔME.

traffic, the other for team traffic; or one double-deck bridge may be used, the upper deck to accommodate boulevard traffic, the lower deck for team traffic. In the case of two bridges, the present Rush Street bridge may be continued in service during the construction of the new boulevard bridge, and after completion of the latter may be temporarily used as a team traffic bridge. Eventually, however, Rush Street bridge will have to be replaced by a new bridge, and during the construction of the latter it will be necessary to divert the team traffic to other crossings.

COPYRIGHT, 1909, BY COMMERCIAL CLUB OF CHICAGO

CXVIII. CHICAGO. MICHIGAN AVENUE, LOOKING TOWARDS THE SOUTH.
Proposed double roadway running to a plaza at its intersection with Twelfth Street, and a suggestion for buildings to surround the place, including rearrangement of the Twelfth Street railway station.

This will cause some inconvenience to this traffic, which is very heavy. The double-deck bridge avoids this difficulty, as it can be completed and put in service without disturbing Rush Street bridge; so that all the traffic of that bridge, both team and boulevard traffic, can be at once transferred to the new bridge when this is ready."

In the plan here presented, the surface of the elevated boulevard connection at Lake Street would be only 11 feet higher than the present Michigan Avenue, and the upper deck of the new bridge would be only 16 feet higher than the surface of the present Rush Street bridge, and only 9¼ feet higher than the surface of the Jackson Boulevard bridge. Looking south, a pedestrian would see before him Grant Park and the improved Michigan Avenue; the view along the river,

both east and west, would offer an interesting picture of the business activities of the city; on the north the wide avenue would end at the water-tower, beyond which can be seen the waters of Lake Michigan opposite the Lake Shore Drive. Thus the plan presents one of the most magnificent highways of the world. It seizes and develops the finest opportunity which Chicago possesses for this purpose. The people of Chicago, during the past twenty-five years, have expended more than $220,000,000 in permanent improvements. This fact proves conclusively that the city is bent on increasing its traffic facilities; yet because there has been no comprehensive plan for develop-
ment of city thoroughfares, much of this work must now be done over again. The proposed connecting boulevard is but one detail in the plan of a great city, but it is one of the most important. Unless the Lake front is dealt with as one great thoroughfare, there is no excuse for the expenditure of a large sum of money on a single span of it.

This great improvement will come because it is a part of a plan which provides a basis of street circulation, and which will weld and unify the three detached sides of Chicago; because it will improve facilities for commercial traffic, and at the same time preserve for the people the uninterrupted use of their greatest and most attractive highway.

No less important than

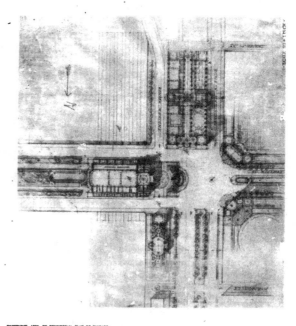

COPYRIGHT, 1909, BY COMMERCIAL CLUB OF CHICAGO

CXIX. CHICAGO. SKETCH PLAN OF THE INTERSECTION OF MICHIGAN AVENUE AND TWELFTH STREET.

the widening and extension of Michigan Avenue is the improvement of Halsted Street, often called "the king of streets" by reason of its extreme length. This street begins near the Lake, two and a half miles north of Lincoln Park, and thence runs directly south through the center of population of Chicago to the southern city limits and beyond them to Chicago Heights, a distance in the city of over twenty miles. This street will inevitably be called upon to bear a very heavy burden of traffic. One of the longest business streets in the world, it is bound to become also one of the most important. The necessity for widening Halsted Street becomes apparent when one considers that this thoroughfare, situated midway between Michigan and Ashland avenues, is already congested by reason of the traffic poured into it by those important diagonals, Milwaukee Avenue on the northwest and Blue Island Avenue on the southwest.

The conditions now prevailing near the intersection of Chicago Avenue and Halsted Street need thorough transformation. There the smoke from railroad shops and yards and from standing locomotives combines with the soot sent up by nearly four hundred trains that come and go each day. Steamships, tugs, and other river craft add their contribution; the near-by tanneries and the garbage wagons contribute their odors; the great coal docks, with their noisy buckets and intermittent engines, increase the din; and the streets are covered with the sawdust,

COPYRIGHT, 1909, BY COMMERCIAL CLUB OF CHICAGO

CXX. CHICAGO. PRELIMINARY SKETCH OF THE PLAZA AT MICH-
IGAN AVENUE AND TWELFTH STREET LOOKING SOUTHEAST.

coal, and dirt spilled from the thousands of wagons that constantly use this crossing. Close to this intersection is a cosmopolitan district inhabited by a mixture of races living amid surroundings which are a menace to the moral and physical health of the community.

The electrification of the railways within the city, which cannot be long delayed, will serve to change radically for the better the dirt conditions in this neighborhood; but the slum conditions will remain. The remedy is the same as has been resorted to the world over: first, the cutting of broad thoroughfares through the unwholesome district; and, secondly, the establishment and remorseless enforcement of sanitary regulations which shall insure adequate air-space for the dwellers in crowded areas, and absolute cleanliness in the street, on the sidewalks, and even within the buildings. The slum exists to-day only because of the failure of the city to protect itself against gross evils and known perils, all of which should be corrected by the enforcement of simple principles of sanitation that are recognized to be just, equitable, and necessary. It is no attack on private property to argue that society has the inherent right to protect itself against abuses; and when the city itself leads the way by the creation of broad streets well paved and cleaned, restrictions against overcrowding, defective drainage, and the heaping of waste in yards and side streets are but a logical sequence. In respect to street cleanliness and adequate air-

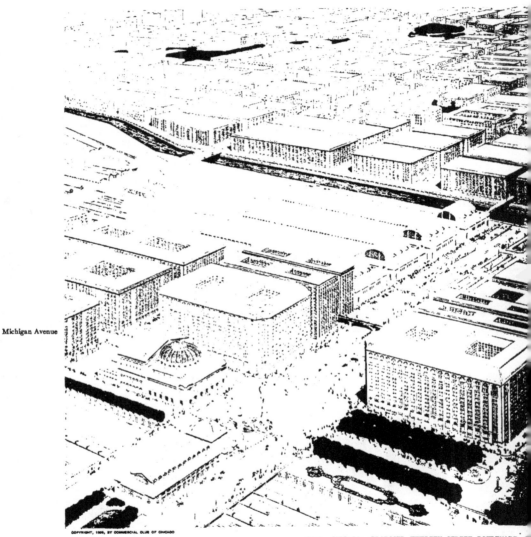

Michigan Avenue

COPYRIGHT, 1909, BY COMMERCIAL CLUB OF CHICAGO

CXXI. CHICAGO. PROPOSED TWELFTH STREET BOULEVARD A
The proposed railway terminals are shown fronting on the Boulevard at its level, which is raised to allow north-and-south traffic to flow
the intersection of Twelfth and Canal streets a diagonal thoroughfare is shown extending to the proposed c
Painted for the Com

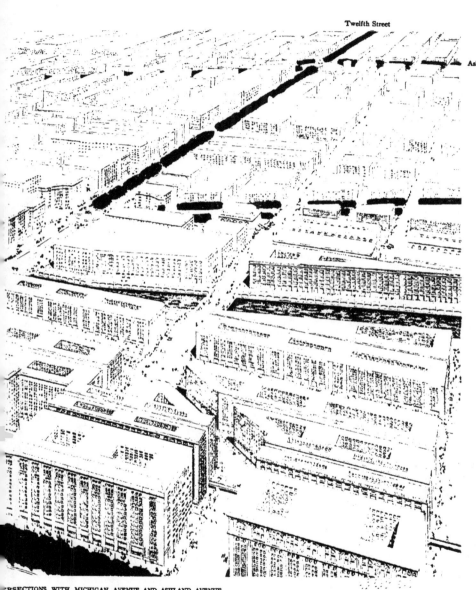

Twelfth Street

Ashland Avenue

ERSECTIONS WITH MICHIGAN AVENUE AND ASHLAND AVENUE.
Access to the Boulevard is provided at alternate streets. The rise begins at Michigan Avenue and may end at Canal Street. From
Between this diagonal and the River is shown the beginning of the proposed West Side railway stations.
by Jules Guerin.

COPYRIGHT, 1909, BY COMMERCIAL CLUB OF CHICAGO

CXXII.   CHICAGO.   RAILWAY STATION SCHEME WEST OF THE RIVER BETWEEN
This plan provides for the railways at a leve
Painted for the Comme

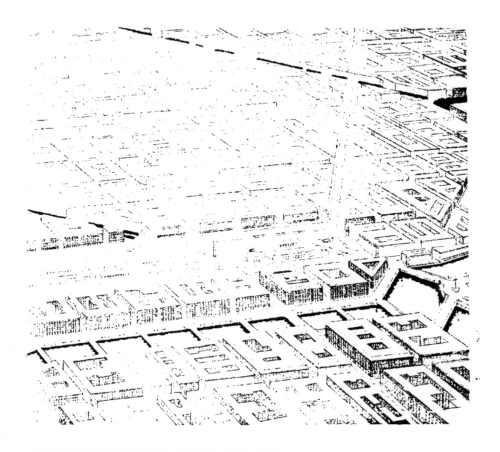

AND CLINTON STREETS, SHOWING THE RELATION WITH THE CIVIC CENTER.
.hat of the street, with the stations above.
ab by Jules Guerin.

space, Chicago may well take a lesson from Berlin, where the streets are kept clean by daily washings, and where a property owner may build on only two-thirds of his land, leaving the remainder for a court. Chicago has not yet reached the point where it will be necessary for the municipality to provide at its own expense, as does the city of London, for the rehousing of persons forced out of congested quarters; but unless the matter shall be taken in hand at once, such a course will be required in common justice to men and women so degraded by long life in the slums that they have lost all power of caring for themselves.

In other localities in Chicago besides the one adverted to like conditions prevail, and must be dealt with in similar manner.

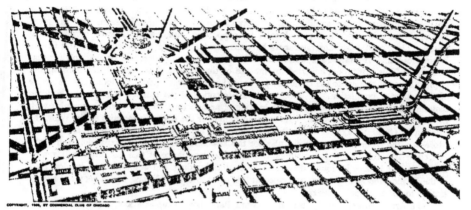

COPYRIGHT, 1909, BY COMMERCIAL CLUB OF CHICAGO

CXXIII. CHICAGO. ALTERNATE RAILWAY STATION SCHEME WEST OF THE RIVER BETWEEN CANAL AND CLINTON STREETS.
This plan provides for the railways at a level above that of the streets.

It is proposed ultimately to widen La Salle Street from Van Buren Street south and to connect it with Wentworth Avenue, also widened; likewise to widen La Salle Avenue from the river north,— changes which will come about with the new arrangement of railway stations. By this means a much needed thoroughfare can be opened between the North and the South Sides; and when this is accomplished an open space should be created at the intersection of La Salle and Congress streets, around which should be grouped great business exchanges. This area would become the financial heart of the city, being directly connected in the best manner with the existing banking and office-building neighborhood. Such an axis as La Salle Street, running from the South Side north to Lincoln Park, and having no street cars on its surface, would seem to be demanded for that future time (perhaps not so far off) when the inhabitants of the city shall number several times as many as to-day. Canal Street, also, should be widened and extended, as has already been discussed in the chapter on Transportation.

The opportunity for one of the most comprehensive, convenient, and dignified compositions known to city planning anywhere comes from the combination of elements already existing in

Chicago, together with the manifest needs of the city in the immediate future.   Chicago, unlike many American cities, has not been drawn away from the water.   The creation of Grant Park adjacent to the Lake and extending along the entire business front of the city is of inestimable value.

Grant Park readily lends itself to the function of a spacious and attractive public garden. The location of the Field Museum in the center of this space is a special instance of good fortune.   The purpose of this building is to gather under one roof the records of civilization culled from every portion of the globe, and representing man's struggle through the ages for advancement.   Hence it must become a center of human interest, making appeal alike to the citizen and the visitor; to those who are drawn by curiosity and those who come for study.   The very size of the building required to hold and display such collections as are being formed fits it to play an important part in the architectural development of the city.[1]   At the same time the great size of the area in which it is placed calls for supporting buildings, to answer corresponding needs.   The South Park Commissioners have arranged also for the location of the new Crerar Library building in Grant Park, and a fund of over one million dollars will be available for that structure.   This institution, intended for the use of the student of social, physical, natural, and applied science, renders to the community a special service which permits a location irrespective of the center of population.   It is the expressed intention of the trustees to make the building monumental in character and classical in style of architecture, so that it will harmonize with the design of the Field Museum.[2]   As meeting center for the scientific societies of the West, the location in Grant Park, near the buildings devoted to music and art, seems most appropriate. Moreover, the space set apart on the plan for this structure allows for that expansion in the way of lecture and convention halls which the growing importance of this institution will render necessary.   If it shall be found desirable, the central building and administrative headquarters of the Public Library might also be located at this point, thus establishing here a center of letters, similar to the Sorbonne in Paris.

The Art Institute, already located in Grant Park, now occupies a site, a portion of which is needed for the widening of Michigan Avenue; and at the same time the increase in the collections will soon necessitate a larger structure than the one now in use.[3]   When the new gallery and school shall be built, the location should occupy the same relative position north of the Field Museum that is proposed for the library group on the south.   The plan shows a gallery of the fine arts, together with a school of art, comprising lecture halls, exhibition rooms, ateliers, and general administration quarters.   To complete this composition would be open-air loggias and gardens, the whole group being akin to the great art museums and schools of Europe.   In Boston the new art museum now under construction in the Back Bay district has been located in the midst of the most attractive surroundings, near the fine group of buildings recently erected for

[1] The Field Museum of Natural History, established in 1894, at the close of the World's Columbian Exposition, was made possible by the gift of one million dollars by Marshall Field, who at his death in 1906 bequeathed a further eight million dollars, one-half for the erection of a building, and one-half for endowment.   Another half million has been contributed by various individuals; and to the $25,000 annual income aside from the endowment, about $100,000 for maintenance will be raised annually by taxation.   On the collections representing anthropology, botany, geology, and zoölogy, over two million dollars has been expended, and the institution (now occupying temporary quarters in Jackson Park) has a staff of directors and curators, a library of 50,000 titles, a well equipped publication bureau, and other appropriate accessories.   By a contract between the South Park Commissioners and the trustees of the Field Museum, dated January 31, 1907, the site in Grant Park was set aside for the new building.

[2] The Crerar Library had its foundation in the bequest made by the late John Crerar, a resident of Chicago from 1862 until his death in 1894.   The endowment fund is upwards of $3,400,000.   The new building will have accommodations for a million volumes, and provisions will be made for extensions when necessary.

[3] The collections of the Art Institute now give the galleries a rank among the first three or four in the country.   The present building was opened in 1893.

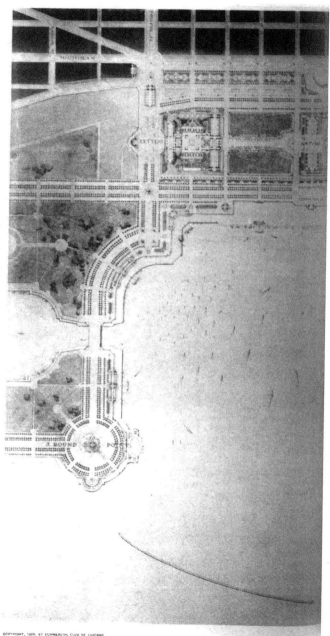

COPYRIGHT, 1909, BY COMMERCIAL CLUB OF CHICAGO

CXXIV. CHICAGO. PLAN OF GRANT PARK
Three main groups of buildings devoted to letters, science, and arts; meadows, pla...

From a ...

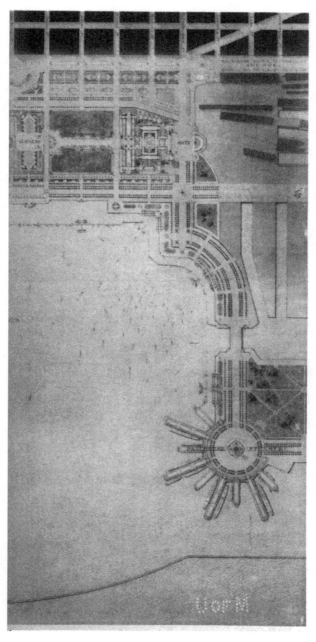

SHOWING PROPOSED ARRANGEMENT.
ues; yacht clubs, at the water's edge; passenger steamer landings and lagoons.

Twelfth Street

COPYRIGHT, 1909, BY COMMERCIAL CLUB OF CHICAGO

Halsted Street

COPYRIGHT, 1909, BY COMMERCIAL CLUB OF CHICAGO

Congress Stree

AND HARBOR; THE EASTERN FAÇADE OF THE CITY ON MICHIGAN AVENUE, A

Chicago River

the Harvard Medical School, and near other educational institutions which have been established on lands reclaimed by the city in much the same manner that Grant Park has been created. In New York the large extension of the Metropolitan Art Museum in Central Park indicates clearly the growing demand for great galleries adapted for the exhibition of works of the fine arts.

The assembling in Grant Park of three monumental groups so as to form one composition offers opportunity for treatment impressive and dignified in the highest degree. It is such opportunities which when properly utilized give to a city both charm and distinction, because of the satisfaction which the mind obtains in contemplating orderly architectural arrangements of great magnitude both in themselves and in relation to the city of which they thus become an integral part. On the other hand, the failure to realize such possibilities inevitably creates dissatisfaction over lost opportunities; and this feeling increases with the years and is shared by all the people.

Economy, as well as effectiveness, dictates the adoption of a group plan; for the buildings have kindred uses, and should express relationship both in their architecture and also in their landscape settings. Indeed they may well be found together by porticos to protect the visitor against sun and rain; and such porticos would offer abundant means of adornment by statues, paintings, and commemorative inscriptions. One has only to recall the impressiveness of the Peristyle at the World's Fair to understand the value of the colonnade as an adjunct to buildings beautiful in themselves.

The landscape setting of the Grant Park group offers opportunities of the highest order. The broad terraces need for their relief the green of trees and the judicious use of parterres; and the walks and driveways, if well located, will give the sense of unity, while at the same time adding to the convenience of the visitor.

It should be realized clearly that as Michigan Avenue is widened and extended, the great traffic which this thoroughfare is sure to bear will come to require large open spaces for gatherings of people to witness parades and pageants and for similar occasions. Much of the passing from north to south will utilize the lakeside drive; and at gala times, when the harbor is illuminated, the terraces of Grant Park will afford unsurpassed views of the spectacle. Such pleasures make a universal appeal, and give charm and brightness to the life of people who must of necessity pass long summers in the city.

The yacht harbor, planned to extend the entire length of the park, is enclosed on the north and south by broad recreation piers stretching for a mile and a half into the Lake; and provision is made for transit lines reaching to the ends of the piers, so as to make these places parks of decided value. The movement among the yachts and small craft; the life of the club-houses by day and the bright lights by night already lend interest to the Lake front; and as the city grows, the increased boating facilities will afford opportunities for indulging in one of the most universally popular sports, while at the same time imparting life to the otherwise monotonous stretch of water.

Such a treatment for Grant Park is not only feasible, but it requires no radical change in present procedure. It is the obvious and natural manner in which the work will be conducted unless some violent change or some regrettable failure to act shall work distortion in a plan that must commend itself to the judgment of those who study the whole problem of the development of the Lake front in its relation to the city of Chicago. No additional expense is involved; for public money is being spent continuously to accomplish the same ends. The plan merely provides for the most effective and satisfactory manner of expending that money.

The advantages of developing Grant Park as the intellectual center of Chicago cannot be overestimated; for art everywhere has been a source of wealth and moral influence. Already the students at the Art Institute number more than four thousand, and as art collections and opportunities for study increase Chicago will draw pupils from many states. The influence of this training in raising the standard of public taste and in creating demands for better physical conditions must be manifest. The possession of Saint-Gaudens' statue of Lincoln is a distinction to the city of Chicago, in the same sense that the Sistine Madonna enriches Dresden. Take the Louvre from Paris, the Rubens collection from Antwerp, the National Gallery and the British Museum from London, the Public Library and the Art Museum from Boston, the Metropolitan Museum from New York, and the Library of Congress from Washington, and the commercial loss to those cities would be very considerable. When Chicago realizes all the advantages of the location in Grant Park of three great groups of buildings devoted to the intellectual and æsthetic cravings of man, it must be apparent that the city will have a great asset in the gifts of those public-spirited citizens who have found satisfaction in leaving to the public useful memorials of the successful lives of the givers.

Public-spirited citizens have left precious legacies by providing for the intellectual and æsthetic needs of the people; and it should be esteemed a high privilege as well as a sacred duty to administer those gifts in such a manner as to accomplish the most effective results from the benefactions. So to manifest appreciation encourages others to emulate the good example; and simply by taking thought the city gains constantly by the addition of monuments which benefit the whole community.

South of Grant Park, and extending along the lagoon between Twelfth and Twenty-second streets, the plans show a great meadow developed as an athletic field, with central gymnasium, outdoor exercising grounds, swimming beaches, and such other features as have been found advisable in the playground parks.

Another great opportunity comes from the fact that the river flows through the center of the business district. It has been the experience of European cities that the banks of a river, although at first devoted only to commercial purposes, sooner or later are transformed into places which combine business uses with drives and promenades for traffic and for the pleasure of the people. The treatment of the Thames in London, the Seine in Paris, the Danube in Vienna and Budapest, the Scheldt at Antwerp, the Riverside Drive in New York, and the proposed Potomac Quay at Washington are, all of them, instances of a development which indicates clearly what must also result to the Chicago River when the city comes to give attention to other needs in addition to those of commerce and manufactures.

The grouping of railway passenger terminals along Canal and Twelfth streets will add another element of good order, convenience, and architectural dignity; for it is not to be conceived that as the railroads replace their present inadequate structures the new buildings will be less important or less dignified than those which have been built in other cities. It is to be supposed rather that the greatest railway center in the world will be able to command terminal stations equal in every respect to any that have been constructed elsewhere.

An adequate study of existing conditions in the Heart of Chicago must show the necessity of providing adequate means of circulation from west to east throughout the business center. Chicago Avenue is already a wide thoroughfare capable of carrying the heavy traffic which inevitably it will be called upon to bear; and the widening of Twelfth Street is required as a means

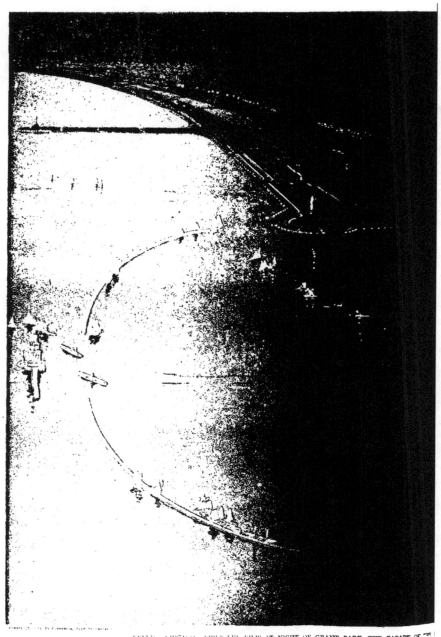

CXXVII. CHICAGO. BIRD'S-EYE VIEW AT NIGHT OF GRANT PARK, THE FAÇADE OF THE
Painted for the Com

OSED HARBOR, AND THE LAGOONS OF THE PROPOSED PARK ON THE SOUTH SHORE.
Jules Guerin.

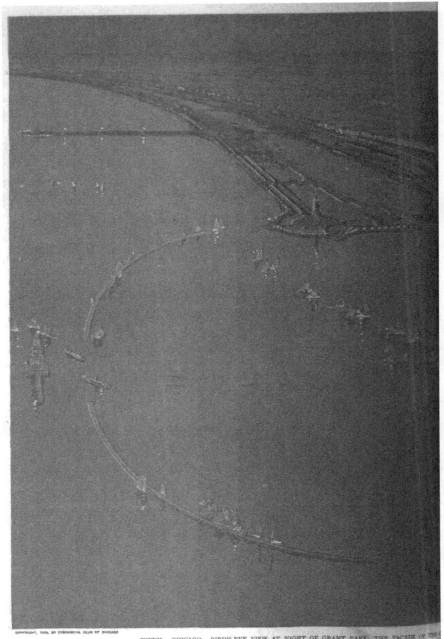

COPYRIGHT, 1909, BY COMMERCIAL CLUB OF CHICAGO

CXXVII. CHICAGO. BIRD'S-EYE VIEW AT NIGHT OF GRANT PARK, THE FAÇADE OF THE
Painted for the Com

POSED HARBOR, AND THE LAGOONS OF THE PROPOSED PARK ON THE SOUTH SHORE.
Jules Guerin.

CXXVIII. CHICAGO. PROPOSED PLAZA ON MICHIGAN AVENUE WEST OF THE FIELD MUSEU
Painted for the C

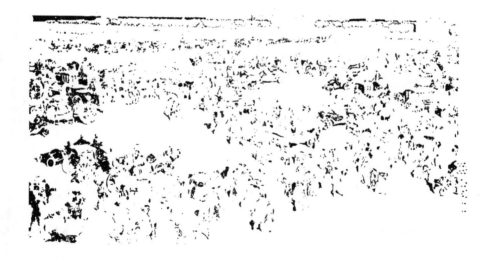

HISTORY IN GRANT PARK, LOOKING EAST FROM THE CORNER OF JACKSON BOULEVARD
by Jules Guerin.

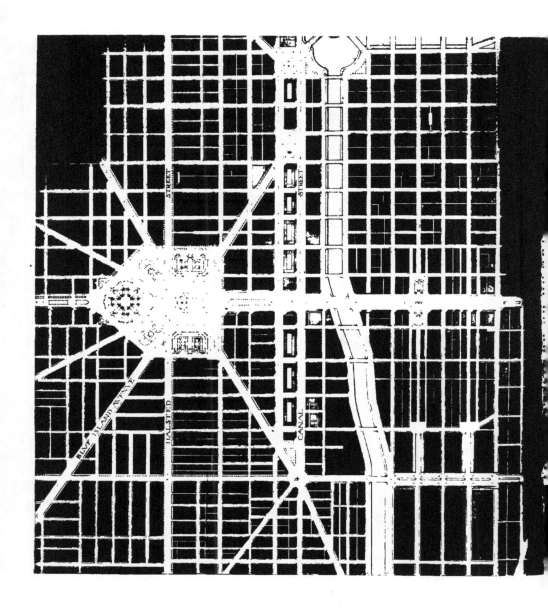

COPYRIGHT, 1909, BY COMMERCIAL CLUB OF CHICAGO

CXXIX. CHICAGO. THE BUSINESS CENTER OF THE CITY, WITHIN THE FIRST CIRCUIT BOULEVARD, SHOWING THE PROPOSED GRAND EAST-AND-WEST AXIS AND ITS RELATION TO GRANT PARK AND THE YACHT HARBOR; THE RAILWAY TERMINALS SCHEMES ON THE SOUTH AND WEST SIDES, AND THE CIVIC CENTER.

···, BY COMMERCIAL CLUB OF CHICAGO

X. CHICAGO. PLAN OF THE PROPOSED GROUP OF MUNICIPAL BUILDINGS OR CIVIC CENTER, AT THE INTERSECTION OF CONGRESS AND HALSTED STREETS.

· plan indicates a possible orderly and harmonious arrangement of public buildings grouped for the purpose of administration, near the center of population · central building is planned not only to dominate the place in front of it, but also to mark the center of the city from afar, and it is in part a monument to the spirit of civic unity.

COPYRIGHT, 1908, BY COMMERCIAL CLUB OF CHICAGO

CXXI. CHICAGO ELE

CXXXII. CHICAGO. VIEW, LOOKING WEST, OF THE PROPOSED CIVIC CENTER PLAZA AND BUILDINGS, SHOWING IT AS THE CENTER OF THE SYSTEM OF ARTERIES OF
CIRCULATION AND OF THE SURROUNDING COUNTRY.
Painted for the Commercial Club by Jules Guerin.

COPYRIGHT, 1909, BY COMMERCIAL CLUB OF CHICAGO

CXXXII. CHICAGO. VIEW, LOOKING WEST, OF THE PROPOSED CIVIC CENTER PLAZA AND BUILDINGS, SHOWING IT AS THE CENTER OF THE SYSTEM OF ARTERIES OF CIRCULATION AND OF THE SURROUNDING COUNTRY. Painted for the Commercial Club by Jules Guerin.

of giving access to the Lake front to the dense population west of the River, which is now practically shut off from the enjoyment of this most attractive feature of Chicago life. It would be desirable to widen several of the east-and-west streets that pass through the present business district,

CXXXIII. PARIS. THE PLACE DE LA CONCORDE, LOOKING OVER THE
SEINE TOWARDS THE MADELEINE.
This square is one of the great circulatory centers, placed on the grand axis
of the city (the Champs Elysees) and the circuit of the grand boulevards.

but such a course would be inexpedient, on account of the prohibitive cost of the land and buildings abutting on those thoroughfares. For this reason it is not proposed to widen east-and-west streets north of Congress. It is within reasonable financial possibility, however, to develop a great avenue, extending from Michigan Avenue throughout the city and westward indefinitely. This would result in providing for all time to come a thoroughfare which would be to the city what the backbone is to the body. Thus, and thus only, is it possible to establish organic unity, and, in connection with the improvement of the streets above mentioned, to give order and coherence to the plan of Chicago.

The selection of Congress Street for development into a broad cross avenue is urged by many considerations. First, this particular street coincides substantially with the center of the business district; and also is about equidistant from the other east-and-west streets (Twelfth and Washington, and Twenty-second and Chicago Avenue) which most readily lend themselves to development as arteries in the street system; and it is also equidistant from the two great east-and-west railroad rights-of-way at Kinzie and at Sixteenth streets. Secondly, the very fact that Congress Street now exists only in disconnected portions, and that the buildings throughout the proposed

CXXXIV. DRESDEN. THE ZWINGERHOF.
A formal arrangement of architecture and public gardens in the
center of a city.

cutting are comparatively inexpensive, offers a very strong argument for its selection on the score of economy. The widening of another street would mean the destruction of two frontages in order to obtain sufficient width without encroaching on the building space on parallel streets. Thirdly, Congress Street stands in such relations to Grant Park that its use as a central axis of the city allows park and avenue to sustain reciprocal relations in the highest degree conducive both to convenience and to good order. Fourthly, the opening of Congress Street would create, in combination with Van Buren Street on the north and Harrison Street on the south, a triple set of arteries at the center of things. There are no arguments favoring the selection of another street which present such a combination of advantages as is to be found in the choice of Congress Street. The diagram showing business occupancy indicates that Congress Street is already very near the center of the great commercial activities, and also that this center has steadily moved in a southwesterly direction.

CXXXV. VIENNA. THE RINGSTRASSE, SHOWING THE PUBLIC BUILDINGS GROUPED ABOUT SQUARES AND GARDENS ALONG ITS COURSE.

Thus far the argument for the selection of Congress Street has dealt with purely practical questions, which in themselves would seem to be conclusive. The choice of Congress Street is quite as logical from an æsthetic point of view. In a sense the Field Museum will be one of the important buildings in the city. The site selected is exactly opposite the intersection of Congress Street with Michigan Avenue. To create a great cross avenue without utilizing the element of symmetry which this noble building stands ready to furnish would be to set at defiance every law of civic order, and to perpetrate a crime against good taste that could never be atoned for. It is inconceivable that in the present state of public taste any people would permit such a barbarism.

The new Congress Street should be created with a width, from Wabash Avenue westward, of from 200 to 250 feet to Canal Street; and thence to the civic square the width should approxi-

CXXXVI. ROME. ST. PETER'S CATHEDRAL, SHOWING THE APPROACH.

mate 300 feet. The roadways should be divided for the various kinds of traffic, and it should furnish opportunities for the highest class of adornment known to civic art. Theaters, public and semi-public buildings, retail shops, and all the other structures which are to be found on

COPYRIGHT, 1908, BY COMMERCIAL CLUB OF CHICAGO

CXXXVII. CHICAGO. VIEW OF THE PROPOSED DEVELOPMENT IN THE CENTER OF THE CITY, FROM TWENTY
AND LA
Painted for the Comm

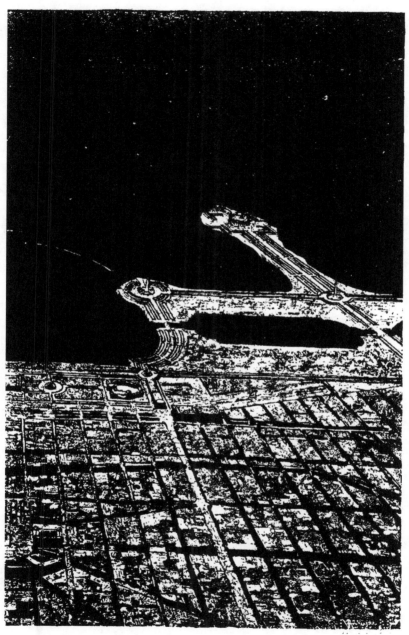

D STREET TO CHICAGO AVENUE, LOOKING TOWARDS THE EAST OVER THE CIVIC CENTER TO GRANT PARK
HIGAN.
lub by Jules Guerin.

frequented streets would come to be built along a thoroughfare which from the time of its opening would be of the first importance.[1]

As it is proposed to group in Grant Park the buildings pertaining to art, literature, and
science, so it is planned to create on the axis of Congress Street a composition representing the
dignity and importance of the city from the administrative point of view. Where Congress
Street intersects Halsted Street, a civic center should be established. At this center radiating
arteries naturally converge. The population in Chicago has stretched itself along the Lake
shore; but the center of density has moved steadily in a southwesterly direction. Beginning
with the original Fort Dearborn reservation, the line of density of population passes through the
present location of the City Hall and the Court House, thence a little to the south of the proposed
civic center. Moreover, the point selected for the civic center is the center of gravity, so to speak,
of all the radial arteries entering Chicago. Even now the proposed center is not far in advance

CXXXVIII. BERLIN. SPREE ISLAND, IN THE HEART OF THE CITY.

of the growth of the city; while at the same time land values in the area selected are not excessive.

The buildings comprised in the civic center naturally fall into three divisions, represented by
the City of Chicago, by Cook County, and by the Federal Government; and inasmuch as a single
building would be insufficient to accommodate the offices either of the city or of the general government, there should eventually be three groups. Of these three the city group would predominate, with the city hall as the central building. The city administration building should accommodate the mayor and the common council, together with the clerks and officers directly connected
with the administrative and legislative departments; also the headquarters of the fire department; the offices of the board of education, including those of the superintendent of schools;
the offices of the city attorney, the auditor, the board of assessors, the tax collectors, the license
department, the board of local improvements, the elections bureau, and others of like character.

Ultimately there should be a separate building for the department of public works; but for
the immediate future one wing of the administrative building may be set apart for the engineers
and surveyors, for the electrical department, and the departments of sewers, water, and gas, and
the superintendent of streets. The need of special quarters for this division of the public service

[1] While Congress Street is the ideal location for the grand axis, the development of one of the parallel streets and a corresponding change in the site of the Field Museum and of the civic center might be resorted to, if obstacles to the use of Congress Street arise
which shall seem insuperable.

arises not only from the extent and character of the work of the various bureaus, but also because of the great number of people who of necessity resort to them in order to obtain permits for constructing and repairing buildings, for establishing electrical, gas, and water connections, and to transact the vast amount of business arising in a department that affects every business, institution, and home.

The department of public health, requiring extensive laboratories, should include an emergency hospital, rooms for the commission on insanity, and a detention place for the insane, as well as a bureau of vital statistics; offices for the health, food, and milk inspectors; quarters for the coroner, including autopsy and inquest rooms and a public morgue.

The hall of records should be accessible to the courts and the other departments of the public service, and to the general public. The building should be so constructed as to secure its contents from possible danger from fire or the results of dampness; and it should be so arranged and administered as to make the records immediately available.

The court-house building offers architectural opportunities of the first order; and here again the dignity, majesty, and impartiality of justice should be made manifest in every appointment, so as to teach the lesson that "obedience to law is liberty." The highest of the city courts, with chambers for the judges; the grand jury quarters; trial jury rooms, with accommodations for lodging juries over night; the offices of the district attorney; the marriage license department; and the law library should be housed in this edifice.

To the building used as the police headquarters would be assigned the central police court with its official clerks, stenographers, bailiffs, bond and warrant officers; the city prison, with its complement of vaults for criminal records of all kinds; the headquarters of the chief of police and of the staff of detectives; a drill-room, assembly-room, gymnasium, and practice gallery for shooting, and arsenal. One reason for making this building one of the civic group is to promote the convenience of the citizens who are called to the court for jury duty or as witnesses.

The central administrative building, as shown in the illustrations, is surmounted by a dome of impressive height, to be seen and felt by the people, to whom it should stand as the symbol of civic order and unity. Rising from the plain upon which Chicago rests, its effect may be compared to that of the dome of St. Peter's at Rome. The buildings are shown raised on terraces one story in height. These terraces would give great dignity to the structures, and would mark the transition from them to the great open space on which they front. The motifs surmounting the terraces, with such other accessories as refuges, shelters, subway stations, balustrades, and lamps, would combine to unite the square into an harmonious whole. The group of buildings may be connected by subways, or even bridges treated in the form of colonnades or arcades of a decorative character, all contributing to the general effect of the square.

Space at the civic center should be reserved for the next county building which Cook County will build when the present one becomes too small to accommodate the county business. Experience shows that in this country a public building is no sooner finished than it is found not sufficiently extensive to provide for the public business that it was meant to serve.

The designs for this square and its buildings are suggestions of what may be done, for the report does not seek to impose any particular form on structures that when executed must carry out a program written by the growing necessities for adequate accommodations for administrative offices and the rapidly developing demand on the part of the public for order and beauty in the arrangement of these elements of city life.

COPYRIGHT, 1909, BY COMMERCIAL CLUB OF CHICAGO

CXXXIX. CHICAGO. THE PROPOSED CIVIC CENTER SQUARE, SHOWING THE GROUP OF SURROUNDING BUILDINGS, CROWNED BY THE CENTRAL DOME.

The administration building, located on the main axis, is placed in such a manner that, while dominating the square, it does not obstruct the flow of traffic which will be poured into this open space from the streets reaching it, and in particular from the great radial arteries. The latter thoroughfares are schemed to center upon an obelisk in the middle of the square, the base of which it is proposed to combine with a decorative fountain, treated with the greatest richness, since it will be located on the spot which is to be the center of interest in the city.

The Federal group should be only less extensive than that devoted to city purposes. The Chicago Federal Building, completed in 1905, is already inadequate. Indeed it has been the custom of the general government to attempt to house many and divergent departments of administration under one roof. In a great city like Chicago the dignity and the business of the United States courts demand a building exclusively for that one purpose. The post-office is now seeking a site on the West Side. Thus the opportunity is at hand to begin the civic center group with a building of importance, by locating it in connection with ground reserved on the plan as a public square which finally shall be surrounded with administrative buildings. The custom-house and the internal revenue office; the various offices of the engineers employed on lake and river improvements and surveys; the lighthouse service; the inspectors of steam vessels; the life-saving service; the recruiting officers for the army and the navy; the emigrant inspectors; and the various other officials charged with enforcing the rapidly growing body of laws for the protection of health and the promotion of good order,—all this army of employees of the United States should have suitable quarters in buildings erected for the exclusive use of the government. The Federal buildings alone, if they are to be adequate to the demands of the public business, would require a group of buildings of the first order in so far as architecture and location are concerned.

The civic center will be dependent for its effectiveness on the character of the architecture displayed in the buildings themselves, in their harmonious relations one with another, and in the amount of the space in which they are placed. Surely, the results attained at the World's Columbian Exposition in 1893 so amply proved the truth of these principles that it is not necessary to enlarge upon them. The attainment of harmony, good order, and beauty is not a question of money cost, for in the end good buildings are far cheaper than bad buildings. What is required is enlightened understanding and competent planning; the great buildings of the world are simple and inexpensive when compared with many of the over elaborate structures of the present day; but for centuries they have served their important purposes and the people will not give them up, because they have become part and parcel of their life. They typify the permanence of the city, they record its history, and express its aspirations. Such a group of buildings as Chicago should and may possess would be for all time to come a distinction to the city. It would be what the Acropolis was to Athens, or the Forum to Rome, and what St. Mark's Square is to Venice, — the very embodiment of civic life. Land should be acquired in quantity sufficient to carry out a plan commensurate with Chicago's needs, and with her dominating position in this region. This plan first should be worked out by the architects, and then should be realized by the concerted action of the community.

Important as is the civic center considered by itself, when taken in connection with this plan of Chicago it becomes the keystone of the arch. The development of Halsted Street, and Ashland and Michigan avenues, flanked by the great thoroughfares of Chicago Avenue and Twelfth Street, will give form to the business center; while the opening of Congress Street as the great central axis of the city will at once create coherence in the city plan. Nowhere else on this continent does there exist so great a possibility combined with such ease of attainment. Simply by an intelligent handling of the changes necessary to accommodate the growing business of Chicago, a city both unified and beautiful will result. The Lake front will be opened to those who are now shut away from it by lack of adequate approaches; the great masses of people which daily converge in the now congested center will be able to come and go quickly and without discomfort; the intellectual life of the city will be stimulated by institutions grouped in Grant Park; and in the center of all the varied activities of Chicago will rise the towering dome of the civic center, vivifying and unifying the entire composition.

COPYRIGHT, 1909, BY COMMERCIAL CLUB OF CHICAGO

CXL. STUDY FOR THE DOME OF THE PROPOSED CIVIC CENTER.
From a study by F. Janin.

COPYRIGHT, 1908, BY COMMERCIAL CLUB OF CHICAGO

CXLI.   VIEW EASTWARD TO LAKE MICHIGAN.

CHAPTER VIII

THE PLAN OF CHICAGO: THE RESULT OF SYSTEMATIC STUDY: THE COST INVOLVED IN CARRY-
ING OUT THE WORK: THE PEOPLE ARE FINANCIALLY ABLE TO REALIZE THE PLAN: THE
ELEMENTS INVOLVED: HOW THE COST MAY BE DIVIDED: THE FINAL RESULT.

HE plan of Chicago as presented in illustration and text is the
result of a systematic and comprehensive study, carried on during
a period of thirty months, with the sole purpose of mapping out an
ideal project for the physical development of this city.   Perfection
of detail is not claimed, but the design as a whole is placed before
the public in the confident belief that it points the way to realize
civic conditions of unusual economy, convenience, and beauty.

It is fully realized that a plan calling for improvements on
a scale larger and more inclusive than any heretofore proposed
seems, on first consideration, beyond the financial ability of the
community.   If, however, the plan meets public approval, it can be executed without seriously
increasing present burdens.   The very growth of the city, creating as it does wealth greater than
mines can produce, gives a basis of bond issues in excess of the utmost cost involved in carrying
out this plan.   The increase in the assessed value of real estate in the city of Chicago for the past
ten years exceeds the expense required to put the plan into execution; and at the same time
the very character of the proposed changes is such as to stimulate the increase in wealth.   The
public, therefore, has the power to put the plan into effect if it shall determine to do so.

It is quite possible that some revision of existing laws may be necessary in order to enable
the people to carry out this project; but this is clearly within the power of the people themselves.
The realization of the plan, therefore, depends entirely on the strength of the public sentiment
in its favor.   And what hope is there that the people will desire to make Chicago an ideal city?
A brief survey of the past will help to form an opinion on this subject.

Sixty years ago, when Chicago was scarcely more than a village, it became apparent that in order to secure proper drainage the street levels must be raised to a considerable extent throughout what we know as the old city, from the main river to Twelfth Street, and also for a distance on the West and North Sides. This project, albeit a very formidable one for that time, was promptly entered upon and duly carried out, although it involved raising all the streets and most of the buildings throughout that large territory. For that day and generation the undertaking was much more serious than the reconstruction of the city thoroughfares now proposed.

Again, some fifty years ago, when the idea of creating great metropolitan park areas was new, Chicago undertook to acquire and improve a chain of parks surrounding the city on three sides. This scheme, which has well supplied the needs of Chicago until recent times, was carried out in such a manner that it never was burdensome. The creation of a park system for Chicago was not undertaken from motives of utility, but purely because of a desire to make the city attractive; and the success was magnificent.

Later, in the Eighties, the purification of the water of Lake Michigan by the diversion of the sewage became a public issue. Once again the people of Chicago rose to the occasion; and after years of hard work the Drainage Canal, built at a cost of $60,000,000, has been completed.

Next came the World's Fair, in the early Nineties, and here also a result was accomplished which has never been surpassed either in scope or in architectural beauty. The cost of the Fair (over $20,000,000 for grounds and buildings alone) was very large for that day. The fact that the Fair came into being here indicated that this people, generally regarded as a commercial community, were deeply appreciative of the higher forms of good order and municipal beauty.

The Chicago World's Fair, like the raising of the grades of the city, the creation of a complete system of parks and boulevards, and the building of the Drainage Canal, went far beyond anything of the same kind ever before undertaken by a city. These four works are the greatest ones which have been achieved by Chicago. They have proved the readiness of the people to take up large schemes of public improvement which at the time of their inception required great foresight and great faith in the future. Two of them were demanded by considerations exclusively practical, while the other two were not so regarded, but on the other hand were the expression of the deeper sense in man of the value of delightful surroundings. If an accurate statement of the costs of the four improvements could be made, it would probably show that about equal sums have been spent on the practical and on the æsthetic side.

Besides the public enterprises mentioned, the people of Chicago, either collectively or as individuals, have established many agencies for the improvement of the intellectual, social, moral, and æsthetic conditions. The Chicago Orchestra occupies land and buildings on Michigan Avenue which have a present value of over a million and a quarter of dollars; and during the past twenty years private subscriptions have amounted to at least another million, all expended for an organization purely artistic. The Art Institute building in Grant Park cost $700,000, and since its completion, in 1893, it has never been closed for a day. Besides its large and excellent art school, there is a good collection of the works of old and modern masters, which is constantly receiving additions. The Crerar Library has an endowment fund of three and a half millions, besides a substantial building fund; and the Newberry Library and the Armour Institute of Technology are other worthy public benefactions.

Especially notable are the educational foundations which contribute so largely to the intellectual life of the city, and exert an influence throughout the Middle West,— Lake Forest University, Northwestern University, and the University of Chicago. The last-named institution, established in 1892, has already taken its place among the foremost universities in this country, not only by reason of its endowment and property (representing more than $23,000,000), but also because of wise administration along a well-considered plan.

Quite in accord with the plan of Chicago is the Benjamin Franklin Ferguson Monument Fund of a million dollars, the income of which is available for defraying the cost of statuary commemorating worthy men and women of America, or important events in American history, to be erected in the parks and boulevards of the city, under the direction of the trustees of the Art Institute. The Field Museum, representing gifts aggregating $9,000,000, is a further instance of loyalty to the city and a desire for its improvement.

Such enterprises and such gifts as those enumerated show what may be expected from individual benefactions as wealth increases and the idea of public service is encouraged. When opportunities for enriching the city are provided, individual citizens rise to the occasion, and find true satisfaction in leaving memorials useful or agreeable to the people.

Mere increase in numbers does not warrant the belief that public sentiment in favor of extensive public works will grow in proportion to the population; but the history of the past does prove that the people of Chicago are always ready and anxious to follow when the way to great benefits is plainly open. We believe that the tendency which the community has shown by its acts points hopefully to the adoption of a great scheme of public improvement. In other words, Chicago having already carried out large projects strictly on the lines of this report, may we not, therefore, confidently expect this people to go on doing as they have done?

There is a still stronger reason for the belief that the public will favor such a plan as is herein presented. It lies in the growing love of good order, due to the advance in education. Every one knows that the civic conditions which prevailed fifty years ago would not now be tolerated anywhere; and every one believes that conditions of to-day will not be tolerated by the men who shall follow us. This must be so, unless progress has ceased. The education of a community inevitably brings about a higher appreciation of the value of systematic improvement, and results in a strong desire on the part of the people to be surrounded by conditions in harmony with the growth of good taste; and as fast as the people can be brought to see the advantage to them of more orderly arrangement of the streets, transportation lines, and parks, it is well-nigh certain that they will bring about such desirable ends. Thus do the dreams of to-day become the commonplaces of to-morrow; and what we now deem fanciful will become mere matter-of-fact to the man of the future.

If the plan as a whole be approved by the majority of our citizens because it is found to be both practical and beautiful, the next question is as to what it commits us. In answering this query a general review of the principal elements composing the plan will be of value. The following list comprises the main items:

First. The improvement of the Lake front.

Second. The creation of a system of highways outside the city.

Third. The improvement of railway terminals, and the development of a complete traction system for both freight and passengers.

Fourth. The acquisition of an outer park system, and of parkway circuits.

Fifth. The systematic arrangement of the streets and avenues within the city, in order to facilitate the movement to and from the business district.

Sixth. The development of centers of intellectual life and of civic administration, so related as to give coherence and unity to the city.

The improvement of the Lake front from Winnetka to the Indiana line is an economic necessity. As has been stated, the aggregate of the waste material seeking dumping ground on the
Lake shore because that is the cheapest place to deposit it, is not less than one million cubic
yards per annum. This material is sufficient to produce annually from twenty-seven to thirty
acres of land if used to build the Lake parkways and park-strips herein recommended. The park
authorities would only have to furnish breakwaters and bridges and to finish the grounds. The
utilization of this material in thirty years would produce all the Lake front land recommended
in the report for the region between Grant and Jackson parks. But long before the expiration
of the thirty years the amount of filling urgently seeking the Lake front dump will be enormously
increased. This dirt should be utilized for the public benefit, instead of being wasted as at
present in the open Lake, where it becomes detrimental to health and an interference to navigation. The dirt to be disposed of in building new traction tunnels under the principal streets of
the city will go far toward the completion of the new Lake shore parks. It is evident, therefore,
that this improvement, involving the redemption of the entire Lake front from Winnetka to the
Indiana state line, and the creation of an extremely beautiful and useful public recreation ground,
will involve very little public expense. There can be no doubt that this part of the plan of
Chicago will be carried through; and in fact much is already being accomplished along these lines.

The interurban highway system can be realized very cheaply. Ninety-five per cent of the
necessary roads now exist as public highways, and the cost of acquiring the other five per cent
will be merely nominal. The diagram (Plate XL) is laid out with a radius of approximately sixty
miles from the city hall. The cost of widening that comparatively small portion of the roadways
which require to be widened; the straightening of the few which need such treatment; the planting of trees along the highways; and the macadamizing of the roads are improvements that may
be hastened by concerted intelligent action. The expense involved is comparatively small, but
the economy and convenience to the public are very large. Is it not evident that this portion of
the plan can be realized at no distant day provided a strong organization of active men shall be
formed for the purpose of carrying it into effect?

The suggestions in regard to trunk lines, their rights-of-way, stations, and general conditions,
are many and serious. The suggestions have been made for the purpose of bringing about the
greatest economy of money and time, both in freight and passenger handling. If the recommendations herein contained will produce conditions really beneficial to the individual shipper and
passenger, undoubtedly they will be found best for the railroads themselves. The direct object
in view is to free a large portion of the South Side from tracks and stations and restore it to business use; to double the capacity of the streets of the whole city by opening circulation to the
north, west, and south, and by connecting the outlying parts in the best possible manner with the
heart of the city. Over and above all these considerations, highly important as they all are,
is economy in the freight handling of Chicago as a shipping center. The object here has been to
find that general principle which, if applied, will give to the merchants, manufacturers, and jobbers
of this city all the advantages that should naturally be theirs throughout the great territory dom-
inated by Chicago. If the general scheme herein proposed shall not be adopted by the public and
the railroads, some other inevitably must be, because the very life of the community is involved in
the solution of this problem. The commercial prosperity of the community is represented by the
cost per ton of handling freight into and out of this territory as a shipping center. General changes
in railroad conditions take years to accomplish. That will be the case if such a scheme as we

recommend is carried out; but the public should remember that they will not be taxed to pay for it. When these improvements come they will be railroad enterprises, undertaken by the railroads and carried out by the railroads.

The traction recommendations contained in this report are already in progress, and no question need be raised as to whether or not this portion of work will be carried out. It has practically been decided upon, and no doubt will be accomplished. The cost will be borne in part by the traction lines themselves, and partly by the public.

The additional parks and parkways recommended are extensive, as should be the case. Although it is true that the men of forty years ago did devise a scheme which has been sufficient almost up to the present moment, it is also true that the number, location, and arrangement of the parks and parkways of Chicago to-day are entirely inadequate for its future development; and nothing is suggested in this report except what has seemed to be absolutely required. Fifty years ago, before population had become dense in certain portions of the city, people could live without parks; but we of to-day cannot. We now regard the promotion of robust health of body and mind as necessary public duties, in order that the individual may be benefited, and that the community at large may possess a higher average degree of good citizenship. And after all has been said, good citizenship is the prime object of good city planning. In some locations parks and parkways are sufficient to accommodate the people in the immediate neighborhoods; other sections of this city, and suburbs which will soon become parts of this city, should be equally well provided. "Nature," says President Charles W. Eliot, "is the greatest factor in the continuous education of man and woman." The extensive woodlands proposed are an addition not usually designed for American cities, although almost invariably used in Europe. The cost of these added parks and woodlands will be considerable, and it must be borne by the public; but it is a sane proposition that the people of Chicago and its suburbs should have the sixty thousand acres of wooded territory as well as the great Bow, (Plate CIII) which will occupy from six to eight hundred additional acres. The acquisition and completion of an outer park system may easily be carried through in ten years; and if the cost shall be distributed over that period of time, it will not prove burdensome. The returns will come in the shape of increase of health and joy of living for all the people; and incidentally the value of every real estate holding in the city will be enhanced.

The land necessary for the civic center should be secured at once, while values at the point proposed are reasonable. For the time being this land may be treated as park space; but the sites and the general scheme of grouping for the buildings should be approved, so that as the city, the county, and the general government outgrow their present structures, the new ones may take their appointed places, each one contributing its part to an orderly and convenient scheme. The adoption of such a scheme would save a very large amount of money in the purchase of public building sites; and would create stability in real estate values. To the West Side especially the development of a civic center along the lines indicated is a matter of prime importance; for it will give to that portion of the city the needed impetus towards higher standards than now prevail there. At the same time it will benefit all other parts of the city, since it is for the advantage of Chicago as a whole that each portion shall be developed equally with every other portion. The cost of the civic center should be paid by the whole community.

The street plan as laid out involves a very considerable amount of money; but it will be found that in Chicago as in other cities, the opening of new thoroughfares, although involving large initial expense, creates an increase in values, due to increase in convenience and the provision for adequate sites for the increasing retail traffic of the city. The cost will amount to many millions of dollars, but the result will be continuous prosperity for all who dwell here; and such prosperity the city cannot have unless it becomes a convenient and pleasant place in which to live.

Finally, it seems probable that the schemes of outer highways and of all the Lake front improvements may come about quite naturally and with very little expense to the city; that the railways will pay most of the expense of their changes and improvements, thus leaving a portion of the cost of the traction system and all of the cost of the civic center, of the parks and parkways, and of the street development for the general public to meet. The community has ample financial ability to do its part without placing undue burdens upon the people. Paris had not much more than half a million people, and her commercial prospects were far less than are ours to-day, when that municipality adopted a street improvement scheme involving over two hundred and sixty million dollars, and carried it to completion in thirty-five years. The motive of the French people in undertaking this enterprise was to create a great attraction for all men: a city so delightful as to insure continuous prosperity to the inhabitants. The success of the undertaking has amply justified the pains and the expense. People from all over the world visit and linger in Paris. No matter where they make their money, they go there to spend it; and every proprietor and workman in Paris benefits by reason of that fact. Conditions in Chicago are such as to repel outsiders and drive away those who are free to go. The cream of our own earnings should be spent here, while the city should become a magnet, drawing to us those who wish to enjoy life. The change would mean prosperity, effective, certain, and forever continuous.

If, therefore, the plan is a good one, its adoption and realization will produce for us conditions in which business enterprises can be carried on with the utmost economy, and with the certainty of successful issue, while we and our children can enjoy and improve life as we cannot now do. Then our own people will become home-keepers, and the stranger will seek our gates.

CXLII. THE GREAT LAKES.
From the group by Lorado Taft.

THE following opinion, prepared by WALTER L. FISHER, as counsel for the Plan Committee of the Commercial Club, has been submitted to EDWARD J. BRUNDAGE, Corporation Counsel for the City of Chicago, HARRY A. LEWIS, County Attorney of Cook County, BENJAMIN F. RICHOLSON, Attorney for the West Chicago Park Commissioners, CHARLES A. CHURAN, Attorney for the Commissioners of Lincoln Park, ROBERT REDFIELD, Attorney for the South Park Commissioners, to EDGAR B. TOLMAN, FRANK L. SHEPARD, HARRY S. MECARTNEY, FRANK HAMLIN, and R. P. HOLLETT, who have been counsel for these official bodies, respectively, and to MILTON J. FOREMAN, Member of the City Council of Chicago, and GEORGE A. MASON, Special Assessment Attorney for the City, all of whom concur in the conclusions and recommendations stated. WILLIAM W. CASE assisted in the preparation of the opinion.

LEGAL ASPECTS OF THE PLAN OF CHICAGO

By WALTER L. FISHER, of the Chicago Bar

INTRODUCTORY

The purpose of an inquiry into the legal aspects of the Plan of Chicago is to ascertain to what extent and in what manner the Plan can be carried out under the existing laws, to suggest such additional legislation as may be necessary or desirable, and to consider how far such legislation is controlled or prevented by existing constitutional provisions. It is gratifying to be able to state at the outset that the main structure of the Plan of Chicago is framed with due regard to the limitations imposed by law upon public enterprises, although important details cannot be carried into effect without some aid from the legislature.

In considering the legal aspects of city planning in the United States, the first inquiry naturally relates to the limitations contained in the state and federal constitutions. Governmental powers in the United States, unlike those of many European countries, are defined by written constitutions, which would undoubtedly prevent the imitation here of some of the sweeping undertakings and arbitrary though effective methods of European city planning. European governments have carried to a successful issue many wide-reaching reforms which could be undertaken in this country only with important modifications. It is these modifications with which we are chiefly concerned. A Prussian statute enacted in 1902 empowered the police authorities to prohibit advertising which was calculated to disfigure the landscape;[1] and a provision of the Prussian Code declares that no building shall be so erected as to disfigure cities and public places.[2] Regulations intended to maintain the suburban character of certain localities have been upheld in Prussia, in the absence of statute, as sanitary measures within the jurisdiction of the police authorities, and in other German cities they are authorized by law.[3] The State of Illinois, in attempting to follow such examples, would be obliged to reckon not only with that provision of her own constitution which forbids the taking of private property for public use without just compensation, but also with that other provision, found both in her own constitution and in that of the United States, which declares that no person shall be deprived of property without due process of law. In England, as long ago as 1862, the Metropolitan Local Management Act authorized the Board of Public Works to fix building lines to which all new buildings must conform, and to prohibit the erection of any house beyond the general line of buildings in any street in which the same is situated.[4] Compensation is allowed to any owner of property who can show himself to be injured by such restrictions upon the use of his land, but the parliamentary fiat determines forever that he must submit to the regulations thus imposed upon him. In this country the owner,

[1] Freund on Police Power, sec. 182, note 5.
[2] Freund on Police Power, sec. 181, note 50.
[3] Freund on Police Power, sec. 181, note 50.
[4] Statutes at Large, vol. 102, p. 730; see also subsequent Acts shown in Chitty's Statutes, vol. 8, "Metropolis" p. 253, and vol. 10, "Public Health" p. 53.

even if compensation were provided, could demand the judgment of a court whether the use for which his property was taken was a "public use," within the judicial definition of that phrase as found in our constitutions. In Illinois he could insist upon his further constitutional privilege of having his compensation fixed by a jury before the restriction became operative. The public authorities of Paris, when condemning land for municipal purposes, were authorized to and did take more extensive areas than were actually needed, seeking by this means to recoup the cost of the improvements by selling the adjacent premises at the enhanced values produced by these improvements. Indeed, the contractors for these public works were themselves authorized, in some cases, to acquire considerable areas outside the lines of the actual improvement, so that the prospective profits thus to be realized might be deducted from the cost of the improvement to the public.[1] Governments in this country are forbidden by constitutional principles thus to take private property against the will of the owner merely for pecuniary profit. Many cities in Great Britain and on the continent have removed the entire population of insanitary districts and have constructed new dwellings, at public expense, in the renovated area. Such features figure largely in the town-planning schemes of Europe, but have been considered inexpedient or unnecessary here. The town-planning bill introduced in Parliament last year by John Burns not only confers power upon municipal authorities to impose a town-planning scheme on any land within or near their boundaries, but enables the authorities to take judgment against the owners of neighboring property for the amount by which its value is enhanced through the operation of the plan. Such methods of procedure, however justifiable from an economic point of view, would be contrary to established public policy in this country. The constitution of Illinois requires uniformity of taxation with respect to both persons and property, and while it permits the cost of local improvements to be assessed by the authorities of cities, towns and villages upon property specially benefited thereby, it not only limits the aggregate amount of such special assessments to the cost of the improvement, but requires the distribution of that aggregate over all property similarly benefited.

While, therefore, in every civilized country the makers of laws strive to protect private property and private rights from spoliation and abuse, it remains true that extensive municipal and governmental works are more quickly and easily executed in those parts of the world where the legislative authorities have a free hand than they can be under a system of rigid constitutional restraints. Those vast projects which have created the modern city of Paris and are transforming London and many continental cities would necessarily follow different channels in this country; yet there is every reason to believe that the constitutional limitations which here determine the form of public improvements do not really prohibit any measures that in this country would be considered wise. It will be found that the restraints of the fundamental law under which we live do not forbid any of the steps recommended in the proposed Plan of Chicago, although in many important respects they do fix and control the manner in which, and the means by which, these steps can be taken. The state, and its agent, the municipal corporation, are fully empowered to protect and to promote the public welfare, and for that purpose have been vested with the three great functions of government known as the police power, the power of eminent domain, and the power of taxation, in one or another of which will be found adequate authority for the accomplishment of the Plan.

The police power has been characterized by the Supreme Court of Illinois as "that inherent plenary power in the state which permits it to prohibit all things hurtful to the comfort, welfare

---

[1] House Document No. 288, Commonwealth of Massachusetts, Dec. 29, 1903, pp. 62 and 63, and citations there made from *L'Economiste Français.*

and safety of society."[1] Avoiding too rigid an exactness of definition, the courts have described it in terms which are said to be summed up in the statement that "the police power, in its broadest acceptation, means the general power of a government to preserve and promote the public welfare by prohibiting all things hurtful to the comfort, safety and welfare of society, and establishing such rules and regulations for the conduct of all persons, and the use and management of all property, as may be conducive to the public interest."[2] It is only under the police power that men can be required to submit to the destruction or appropriation of their property without monetary recompense for the loss.[3]

In the exercise of the power of eminent domain, the state may take private property, but only for a "public use" and only upon payment of just compensation. No man can, in this country, be required to surrender his property, even for full value, unless the use for which it is taken is public. The right assumed by some European governments to condemn large areas of land in order, by selling part of it, to defray the cost of improving the rest, would be subject in this country to the inquiry whether such a purpose is "public," within the meaning of that term as expounded by the courts. No judge grounded in the principles of American jurisprudence would countenance the argument that mere pecuniary advantage to a municipality could, without other pretext, justify the taking of private property against the will of the owner. It is quite another question, however, whether the condemnation of more land than is directly involved may not be justified as an incident of a public improvement, when it could not be defended as an independent speculation.

The last of the three governmental powers mentioned is the power of taxation. Like the power of eminent domain, it is inherent in every sovereign state, but no taxes can be levied for other than public purposes. They may be general, representing the tribute due from every person to the government which protects him; or special, measured or limited by the particular benefit accruing to his property from a local improvement. The cost of public works may be paid for outright from the proceeds of a single levy or assessment, or may be defrayed from the proceeds of bonds to be liquidated by annual contributions distributed over a term of years. The constitution of Illinois requires provision to be made for paying all municipal bonds within twenty years, and limits the amount of indebtedness which any municipal body may incur to five per cent of the assessed value of taxable property therein; but does not impose any general limitation upon the amount or rate of taxes which municipal bodies may be authorized to levy.

Such is a brief characterization of the three functions of government upon which chiefly depends the execution of public enterprises in this country. The Plan of Chicago, now under consideration, embraces as its leading features the acquisition, maintenance, and control of parks, boulevards and arteries of communication throughout the metropolitan territory tributary to Chicago; the establishment and control of similar parks, circuits and avenues within the city itself, and incidentally the reclamation of slums and congested areas; the embellishment of the shore of Lake

---

[1] *City of Belleville* v. *Turnpike Co.*, 234 Ill. 428, 437; *City of Chicago* v. *Gunning System*, 214 Ill. 628, 635.

[2] 22 Amer. & Eng. Encyc. of Law, 916.

[3] In the case of *Chicago, Burlington & Quincy Railway Co.* v. *People*, 212 Ill. 103, 116, the Supreme Court quotes with approval the following language from the American and English Encyclopædia of Law:

"The police power is to be clearly distinguished from the right of eminent domain; and the distinction lies in this: that in the exercise of the latter right, private property is taken for public use and the owner is invariably entitled to compensation therefor, while the police power is usually exerted merely to regulate the use and enjoyment of property by the owner, or, if he is deprived of his property outright, it is not taken for public use, but rather destroyed in order to promote the general welfare of the public, and in neither case is the owner entitled to any compensation for any injury which he may sustain in consequence thereof, for the law considers that either the injury is *damnum absque injuria* or the owner is sufficiently compensated by sharing in the general benefits resulting from the exercise of the police power."

This decision was affirmed by the Supreme Court of the United States, 200 U. S. 561.

Michigan; the consolidation and rearrangement of freight and passenger terminals; and the creation of a Civic Center connected with other parts of the city by convenient avenues, and in or about which shall be grouped important public buildings which may hereafter be erected.

OUTER PARKS, BOULEVARDS, AND CIRCUITS

The outer belt of parks and forest preserves, the boulevards and highways connecting country towns with each other and with the city, and the extension of a driveway around the shore of Lake Michigan, involve relations with counties outside of Cook, and even with states beyond the borders of Illinois. It may safely be assumed, without specific inquiry, that the laws of Wisconsin and Indiana, if not already adequate to the performance of their share in the project, can easily be made so by the people of those states.

In Illinois the existing laws are in the main sufficient for the needs of local communities which desire, by the exercise of their present taxing powers or the organization of park districts, to bear their part in a general scheme of improvement. The Act of June 19, 1893,[1] provides for the incorporation of park districts to connect two or more cities or villages by means of boulevards or parks. A more comprehensive measure is the Act of June 24, 1895,[2] under which several park districts in Cook County, such as those at Winnetka, Kenilworth, Wilmette and Rogers Park, have been organized by vote of the people of those communities. A district formed under this act may acquire land for parks or boulevards by purchase or condemnation, and the board of park commissioners may accept from any municipality in the district the control of any park or boulevard therein. Bonds may be issued up to three per cent of the assessed valuation of property in the district, and, in addition to taxes for the payment thereof, a general tax of four mills on the dollar may be collected. Special assessments for local improvements may be levied through the township authorities. Districts bordering upon navigable bodies of water are empowered to reclaim submerged lands, and the title of the state is granted for that purpose to the park district to which such submerged land is adjacent. The park authorities could construct islands or driveways beyond the present water line. They would be required to recompense the owners of the shore for any loss or diminution of their riparian rights; but the benefits to the shore lands would doubtless in many, if not most, instances more than offset the cost of the property and property rights that would be taken or damaged for the improvement.

Among local agencies which might co-operate in suburban development may be mentioned the townships. These have long exercised jurisdiction over country roads, and they were authorized by two Acts of March 2, 1907,[3] to secure small parks by purchase or condemnation and upon vote of the people to issue bonds and levy taxes for that purpose. No park so established can be more than ten acres in extent.

Such limited local authorities may prove serviceable auxiliaries to the main plan, but their powers are inadequate to the execution of the more general features of metropolitan development; nor would it be just to impose on local tax-payers the entire burden of such improvements as the acquisition of extensive areas of park or woodland chiefly for the resort and recreation of the people

[1] Hurd's Statutes of Illinois, edition of 1908, p. 1532.
[2] Hurd's Statutes of Illinois, edition of 1908, p. 1546.
[3] Hurd's Statutes of Illinois, edition of 1908, p. 1574-5.

of the city. These enterprises require the co-operation of a central body of more extensive powers and larger resources.

In looking for instrumentalities through which such plans might be executed, the park legislation of Massachusetts claims first attention. The Metropolitan Park Commission, under whose auspices the city and suburban park system of Boston has been developed, was created by an act of the legislature of Massachusetts, approved June 3, 1893.[1] It consists of five members, appointed by the governor, and exercises jurisdiction over Boston and various other cities and towns which constitute the Metropolitan Parks District. The board has power to acquire and maintain open spaces, taking in fee or otherwise any land necessary for that purpose, and acting so far as may be in consultation with local boards. Any open space in a city or town may be turned over to the board by the local authorities. Subsequent acts empower the commission to construct roadways and boulevards, to purchase or condemn land for that purpose, and to assess property specially benefited thereby. The commissioners are authorized to abandon land which they have acquired, thereby revesting title in the original owner and reducing the damages which he might otherwise justly claim. Authority is also given to sell, at public or private sale, any lands or rights acquired and paid for. Property taken by the commission vests in the Commonwealth of Massachusetts, and is to be paid for by state bonds extending over a term of not more than forty years. Taxes to meet the bonds are, however, apportioned among the cities and towns within the district, and a reapportionment is to be made once in five years. By an Act of March 17, 1903, the commission and the park officers in any city or town were empowered to make reasonable rules and regulations respecting the display of signs or advertisements visible from public parks and parkways; but the Supreme Court, in the case of *Commonwealth* v. *Boston Advertising Co.*, 188 Mass. 348, held that this statute did not and could not confer upon the public authorities any power to prohibit the owners of land from leasing it for advertising purposes, unless just compensation were provided.

The Metropolitan Park Commission is a creature of the state — not of the particular communities directly affected — and over its fortunes the legislature has maintained a constant fostering care, extending and defining its jurisdiction by successive acts, and granting fresh financial powers as occasion arose. Local home rule is a political principle not so firmly established there as in Illinois. Here it would not be feasible to create a similar body by legislative fiat without the concurring vote of the people of the district over which its jurisdiction extended. Legislation designed for similar ends is more likely, in this state, to take the general form of enlargement of the powers and functions of the city and the county; or, especially if more than one county is involved, of the creation of a special commission endowed with extraordinary powers and similar in many of its features to the forest-preserve districts contemplated by the Act approved May 18, 1905.[2]

This measure, which is entitled "An Act to provide for the creation of forest-preserve districts," authorizes the incorporation as a forest-preserve district of any area of contiguous territory containing one or more cities, towns, or villages within the same or adjoining counties. Such a district can only be organized by the affirmative vote of the inhabitants; and if it embraces parts of two counties, there must be a favorable vote in each. The affairs of the district are to be managed by a president and six commissioners, appointed by the governor and drawn from different political parties. The president alone receives a salary. The board is authorized to accept control of streets in any city, town, or village on request of the local authorities, and to designate existing streets and roads as pleasure driveways, and lay out and establish others for that purpose; but

---

[1] Acts of 1893, chap. 407.   [2] Hurd's Statutes of Illinois, edition of 1908, p. 1129.

none of these is to be within any public park district. Power is given to acquire, by gift, purchase, or condemnation, any land not already in a park district for driveways and forest preserves. Bonds may be issued to the amount of one per cent of the assessed value of all property in the district, and this amount may be increased by a vote of the people to three per cent. Authority is given to levy taxes for the payment of bonds and interest thereon, and also to levy for general purposes an additional tax not exceeding one mill on the dollar.

An attempt was made under this act to organize as a forest-preserve district all of Cook County, except a few towns in the extreme north and south ends thereof. It received a majority of the votes cast on the proposition, but not a majority of those cast at the regular election held on the same day. This has left some doubt as to the legal effect of the vote. The result was largely due to indifference and to the creation of a new taxing body with what were regarded by many as unnecessarily extensive powers. A committee of the legislature was appointed to report a revised act more consonant with the wishes of the people. Among the changes which have been suggested are that each district shall be confined to a single county; that the members of the commission shall be appointed by the president of the county board; and that taxes for the purposes contemplated by the act shall not be levied by the district authorities themselves but by the board of county commissioners. The proposed forest-preserve districts are essentially park districts, though called by a different name; and the main objects of this act might be accomplished by creating a forest-preserve commission as a department of the county government, under appropriate legislation — a method certainly less open to attack from a legal point of view than the one embodied in the Forest-Preserve Act of 1905.[1]

Counties in Illinois have under existing law no general powers which would enable them to take a prominent part in plans for the development of the metropolitan district of Chicago; but it would be competent for the legislature to invest them with more extensive functions. There is in the constitution no limit upon the amount of county taxes which may be voted by the people; and county bonds, when authorized by popular vote, may be issued for any authorized county purpose up to the constitutional limit of five per cent of the assessed value of taxable property in the county.

In an inventory of the agencies which might be capable of sharing in the creation of outer parks and boulevards, mention should not be omitted of a Greater City of Chicago, which might be invested by the legislature with power to purchase or condemn land far beyond its own corporate limits in order to establish a system of parks and boulevards commensurate with the needs of its inhabitants.[2] Some doubt has been suggested as to the constitutionality of such a grant of power if attempted under the so-called Chicago charter amendment to the state constitution,[3] which authorizes "a special charter of local municipal government for the territory now or hereafter embraced within the limits of the city of Chicago." The effective policing by the city of parks and boulevards outside the city limits would present practical difficulties, and the plan would impose upon the city the entire cost of improvements in the advantages of which the suburban districts in which these improvements were located would share. If all of the people and property benefited are to bear their proportionate share of the expense, the proposed system of

[1] See *Russell* v. *High School Board*, 212 Ill., 327.

[2] House bill No. 350, introduced in the Illinois legislature, March 23, 1909, provides (Art. IV, Sec. 9) that "the city shall have power to acquire, by dedication, gift, purchase, or condemnation, lands or easements inside or outside of the city limits, for park purposes, and for ways connecting parks with the city or with each other."

[3] Constitution of Illinois, Art. IV, Sec. 34.

outer parks and boulevards should be acquired and controlled by the county or by a new municipal body.

CITY PARKS, SQUARES, BOULEVARDS, AND AVENUES

The existing municipal corporations that might be authorized to bear a part in realizing the Plan within the city limits are the city of Chicago, the county of Cook, and the several park boards. Any participation by the Sanitary District, as by bridging its canals or improving the appearance of their banks, would be incidental.

City councils are empowered by Article V of the City and Village Act of 1872 to lay out, establish, open, widen, pave, and otherwise improve streets, alleys, avenues, parks, and public grounds, and to plant trees upon and regulate the use of the same.[1] In the case of *Thompson v. Highland Park*, 187 Ill. 265, the court sustained the power of the city to include parkways and grass plots in the improvement of a street to be paid for by special assessment. The special Act of May 18, 1905,[2] relating to the city of Chicago only, confers upon the council power to acquire, by purchase or otherwise, municipal parks and playgrounds, and declares that the city may exercise the right of eminent domain for the acquirement of property useful, advantageous, or desirable for municipal purposes; and that the procedure in such cases shall be, as nearly as may be, like that provided for in the Act of June 14, 1897, concerning local improvements as amended or to be amended. Land taken for a park is "property useful, advantageous, or desirable for municipal purposes," and a public park is a "local improvement," the cost of which may be assessed upon contiguous property to the extent of the special benefits when the legislature authorizes that course to be pursued.[3] The "Act concerning local improvements"[4] directs the city council to provide, in any ordinance for a local improvement, whether it shall be made by special assessment or special taxation, or by general taxation, or otherwise; and, in sections 13 to 33, inclusive, defines the procedure for ascertaining the compensation to be paid for private property taken or damaged, and for assessing the cost on other property to the extent to which it is specially benefited. The city, therefore, already possesses power to acquire public parks within the city limits and to assess the cost, or the greater part thereof, against property in the neighborhood of the improvement. Under the present law all ordinances for local improvements in the city, to be paid for wholly or in part by special assessment or special taxation, must originate with the board of local improvements; but if the park boards were merged in the city government, it might be feasible to grant to an administrative department of parks the initiative with respect to local improvements within their special jurisdiction.[5] The city authorities have now ample power, to the extent of their financial resources, to improve and widen existing streets and to open new streets, parks and public grounds. The city council has adequate discretion to determine how wide any street shall be, and whether it shall be devoted entirely to travel or given up partly to lawns, trees, and parkways.

[1] Hurd's Statutes of Illinois, edition of 1908, p. 316.
[2] Hurd's Statutes of Illinois, edition of 1908, p. 336.
[3] *Shoemaker v. United States*, 147 U. S. 282; *Dunham v. People*, 96 Ill. 331; *People v. Brislin*, 80 Ill. 423.
[4] Hurd's Statutes of Illinois, edition of 1908, p. 421.
[5] House bill No. 350, Illinois, 1909, already mentioned, which contemplates the merger of the park boards in the city government, provides (Art. IV, Sec. 19) as follows: "The provision of the statutes governing the making of local improvements in the city shall be as nearly as possible applied to the proceedings for the taking of lands and the meeting of the expenses in connection with such improvements, except that the board of park commissioners shall act in place of the board of local improvements."

It is highly important that the city should be able effectively to control the traffic on streets and boulevards, and especially to keep designated residence streets free from heavy teaming or particular kinds of traffic (such as through teaming, not going to or from property fronting on the particular street), without formally turning such streets over to park authorities as boulevards. This power may be given by the 96th paragraph of Section 1 of Article V of the statute in relation to cities, villages, and towns,[1] which authorizes the city council to "direct, license, and control all wagons and other vehicles conveying loads within the city, or any particular class of such wagons or other vehicles." If more specific authority is required, it should be obtained from the legislature. The streets are held by the city in trust for the general public and cannot be diverted from that purpose by the city without special authority.[2] The legislature, however, as representative of the public, has control over them, and may limit the public right to make free use of streets; as it actually has done in the statute authorizing the wheel tax.[3] It may authorize municipal authorities to designate certain streets as pleasure driveways, to the exclusion of heavy traffic,[4] or to turn over any of its streets to park boards for boulevard and driveway purposes;[5] but the city cannot, without legislative authority, divest itself of the control of a street nor restrict the public in the reasonable use and enjoyment thereof.[6] General authority has been conferred upon city councils to regulate the use of streets, but this provision of the statute cannot safely be relied upon as an unqualified delegation of power to set aside some streets for exclusive use as pleasure driveways, since the Act of March 27, 1889,[7] expressly empowers the municipal authorities of a city or village to select for that purpose *not more than two streets* within the corporate limits. This doubt the legislature should be asked to set at rest.

The narrow scope of the powers of Cook County has already been commented upon. While counties could not, under the present constitution, be authorized to pay for improvements by special assessment, the general assembly might empower the county board to purchase or condemn land within or without the city limits for parks or other public uses, the cost to be paid from the proceeds of any bond issues which the people might see fit to vote within the five per cent limit of indebtedness. A park commission or forest-preserve commission, established as an administrative department of the county government, would be an appropriate agency for carrying out these objects.

The only park authorities now exercising any considerable jurisdiction within the city limits are the South Park Commissioners, the West Chicago Park Commissioners and the Commissioners of Lincoln Park, all of which were incorporated by the legislature in the year 1869 for the purpose of acquiring certain specific parks and boulevards. They have received additional powers from time to time. The West Chicago Park Commissioners, within whose jurisdiction the proposed Civic Center would lie, were authorized by the Act of 1869 to purchase or condemn the land described therein, and to levy special assessments for that purpose. The Act of April 9, 1879,[8] as amended, gives every board of park commissioners power to connect its parks or boulevards with any part of a city, town, or village by taking any appropriate street

[1] Hurd's Statutes of Illinois, edition of 1908, p. 321.
[2] *Kreigh* v. *Chicago*, 86 Ill. 407.
[3] *Harder's Storage Co.* v. *Chicago*, 235 Ill. 58.
[4] *Cicero Lumber Co.* v. *Cicero*, 176 Ill. 9; *Brodbine* v. *Revere*, 182 Mass. 598.
[5] *People* v. *Walsh*, 96 Ill. 232.
[6] *Ligare* v. *City of Chicago*, 139 Ill. 46; *Smith* v. *McDowell*, 148 Ill. 51.
[7] Hurd's Statutes of Illinois, edition of 1908, p. 408.
[8] Hurd's Statutes of Illinois, edition of 1908, p. 1518.

with the consent of the corporate authorities and of the owners of a majority of the frontage. In 1885 park boards were authorized to accept from municipal authorities any parks under their control.[1] The Act of May 10, 1901,[2] empowers every park board to acquire, by purchase or condemnation, as many small parks, not exceeding ten acres each, as it desires and can pay for.

By the Act of March 4, 1907,[3] even more extensive powers are conferred upon the commissioners of every public park district appointed or selected pursuant to any act which has been or may be submitted to the legal voters of such park district and by them adopted. Full power is given to purchase or condemn any land for the establishment of new parks or the extension of old parks, and, by vote of the people, to issue bonds to any desired amount within the constitutional limit. This act materially increases the powers of the boards to which it applies. The West Park board is within its terms; and may, upon favorable vote of the people of the district, bond itself up to the constitutional limit; and it can probably also levy special assessments under authority of the Act of June 24, 1895,[4] to pay for property condemned for park purposes.

Land for the proposed Civic Center might be acquired through any one of several agencies. The city of Chicago, if financially able, could purchase the necessary area, or condemn it and assess back part of the expense on real estate in the vicinity. Any portion of the cost not raised by special assessment would have to be defrayed from the proceeds of bonds, which, under the constitution, must be redeemable within twenty years, and must not increase the indebtedness of the city beyond five per cent of the assessed value of property therein. Additional borrowing powers may be conferred upon the city through consolidation of various local authorities with the city under the so-called charter amendment to the state constitution, or through a change in the statutory method of fixing the assessed valuation of property. Appropriate legislation should be enacted at once in order to make land thus acquired available not only for city buildings or park purposes, but for the location of the buildings of other public bodies, upon financial and other terms to be fixed by negotiation with the city.[5]

The county of Cook, though now lacking the necessary powers, might be authorized by the legislature to acquire, with the proceeds of a bond issue, the requisite area for the Civic Center, and to make appropriate arrangements for the location therein of federal and city buildings and other public edifices.

The West Park board might well be asked to treat the Civic Center as a legitimate object for the exercise of its functions, and with that end in view it should be invested by the legislature with powers adequate to the immediate acquisition of the land embraced in the proposed Civic Center, and should be authorized to arrange appropriate terms for the future occupation of part of the area by the buildings of other governmental and public bodies; among which terms might be the reimbursement of part of the original cost.

[1] Hurd's Statutes of Illinois, edition of 1908, p. 1521.
[2] Hurd's Statutes of Illinois, edition of 1890, p. 1560.
[3] Hurd's Statutes of Illinois, edition of 1908, p. 1569.
[4] Hurd's Statutes of Illinois, edition of 1908, p. 1544.
[5] House Bill No. 350, Illinois, 1909, already mentioned, contains the following provision: "Art. IV, Sec. 14. The city shall have authority to acquire and hold lands for the erection and maintenance thereon of public buildings of the city and for public grounds surrounding such buildings or connected therewith, and shall have the right to permit buildings of the County of Cook, the State of Illinois, the United States of America or other governmental or public bodies to be erected and maintained on such lands and grounds upon such terms and conditions as the city council may prescribe. Subject to such use, the board of park commissioners shall, when directed by the city council, have the same power to manage and control, improve, maintain, and beautify such lands and grounds, as is in this Act conferred upon said board with respect to parks; and for any of the purposes hereinbefore in this section specified, the city may acquire or dispose of the title to or rights in lands or rights or easements in or over lands abutting on or in the vicinity of such lands or public grounds in like manner and to like extent as in this Act provided with respect to parks."

Among the agencies which might be created to carry out this and other features of the Plan should, perhaps, be mentioned a municipal corporation organized along the lines indicated by the forest-preserve legislation already alluded to. The Act of 1905 [1] permitted cities and villages to be included in a forest-preserve district, and the city of Chicago was included within the boundaries of the proposed district the creation of which was submitted to popular vote. Section 6 of that act, providing for the designation of streets as pleasure driveways, specified that none of them should fall within any park district, and that no preserves should be within the limits of a park district. The legislature may have power to eliminate such restrictions, and to sanction the incorporation of a metropolitan board capable of exercising all the powers of a park commission within and without the city limits.

With reference to the proposed boulevard link on Michigan Avenue, connecting the north and south sides, it is to be borne in mind that the city under its general powers can enlarge Michigan Avenue to any desired width and can alter the grade of the whole or any portion of the street. There were, however, passed by the legislature May 25, 1907, four acts which were designed to facilitate the construction of this boulevard link. It was in contemplation at that time that the South Park and Lincoln Park boards would do part of the work and defray part of the expense, and that the city would meet the balance of the cost by annual appropriations extending over a series of years.

The first of these four acts [2] was designed to enable the South Park board to contribute such part of the expense as to it might seem best. This bill provides that the corporate authorities of any public park district having control of any park in a city wherein other park districts and parks are situated, but not connected therewith by any boulevard or driveway or other park thoroughfare, may from time to time in their discretion issue and sell additional bonds, not exceeding the five per cent limitation, in order to defray the expense of connecting any park under their control with any other public park or parks by means of a boulevard and driveway in the city, and altering and improving any connection or connections between such parks. Such bonds must, however, be authorized by the voters of the park district at an election.

By the second act, [3] the Lincoln Park board is authorized to issue, upon a favorable vote of the electors of the district, bonds not exceeding $1,000,000 for the purpose of constructing surface and elevated boulevards and the approaches thereto over or along streets and alleys, when authorized to do so by any city having control thereof.

The other two acts referred to were passed in order to dispel any doubt about the power of municipalities to erect an elevated structure in a public street. One [4] empowers any city to grant, by ordinance, to any board having jurisdiction over parks and boulevards the right to take and improve, by means of surface or elevated ways, a street not more than one mile in length, with all convenient or necessary approaches, inclines, and superstructures; while the other [5] confers power upon any city to construct and maintain an elevated way in any street, with all necessary approaches, inclines, and superstructures, and to authorize any commission or board having jurisdiction of a public park to take over, maintain, and control, upon terms fixed by ordinance, any street and any incline, approach, or superstructure therein.

[1] Hurd's Statutes of Illinois, edition of 1908, p. 1129.
[2] Hurd's Statutes, edition of 1908, p. 1570.
[3] Hurd's Statutes, edition of 1908, p. 1572.
[4] Hurd's Statutes, edition of 1908, p. 1577.
[5] Hurd's Statutes, edition of 1908, p. 1578.

An alternative method of constructing a surface or elevated boulevard link would be found in a proceeding by the city under the Local Improvement Act. The city has ample power to condemn property for widening the street and to assess the land damages against all property specially benefited thereby. Having thus added contiguous property to the street as a part thereof, the city could, under the enabling act already alluded to, if not under its general powers, construct the proposed improvement. It must be borne in mind, however, that even if the method of special assessment were resorted to in order to defray the cost, a substantial percentage of that cost would, no doubt, be designated by the court to be paid by the city as public benefits.

LAKE SHORE DEVELOPMENT

The treatment of the shore of Lake Michigan within the city limits involves comparatively little difficulty from a legal point of view. Ample legislation has been provided under which the Lincoln Park and South Park boards can extend their driveways and parks over the bed of Lake Michigan, subject to the consent of the Secretary of War. An Act of May 14, 1903,[1] expressly confers upon every board of park commissioners having control of any park, boulevard, or driveway bordering upon any public waters in the state the power to extend the same over the bed of such waters, and to connect two parks under their control by a boulevard or driveway over the bed of the water. Private riparian rights or titles may for such purpose be acquired by contract with or deeds from the owners, and may be paid for out of the general revenues of the park board. By Section 4, the title of the state to the submerged lands between the shore and the boulevard or parkway — in other words, the bed of the intervening lagoon — is granted to the board of park commissioners. Several other statutes on this subject were enacted on the same date. One authorizes the South Park Commissioners to extend any park under their control out into the lake over the adjacent submerged lands;[2] another conveys to the South Park Commissioners Grant Park from Randolph Street to Park Row, together with the submerged lands lying between those streets extended east to the harbor line established by the Secretary of War;[3] another grants to the South Park Commissioners title to all submerged and artificial lands between the south boundary of Jackson Park and the south line of Seventy-ninth Street extended one thousand feet into Lake Michigan, and to the land included within a triangle formed by the shore of Lake Michigan, the extension of Ninety-fifth Street and the extension of the state boundary line.[4]

This legislation did not authorize the condemnation of riparian rights, but only the acquisition of such rights by negotiation. To facilitate settlement, an Act passed May 2, 1907,[5] empowered the park commissioners, with the approval of the Circuit Court, to agree with the riparian owners upon a boundary line between the public park and the private shore lands, and to convey to the riparian owners all submerged land lying inside of the boundary line thus fixed by agreement; in other words, the park board, having received from the state a grant of its title to the bed of the lake, is authorized to sell and convey to the shore owners so much thereof as may be necessary to induce them to release their riparian rights. If any shore land is owned by persons who are incompetent to contract or who are unknown, the power is given to condemn their riparian rights,

[1] Hurd's Statutes, edition of 1908, p. 1562.
[2] Hurd's Statutes, edition of 1908, p. 1563.
[3] Hurd's Statutes, edition of 1908, p. 1564.
[4] Hurd's Statutes, edition of 1908, p. 1565.
[5] Hurd's Statutes, edition of 1908, p. 1570.

pursuant to the provisions of the statute of eminent domain.   That power should not be limited to the lands of unknown or legally incompetent owners.   Under this legislation, the park board has power to build a boulevard far out into the lake and to settle with the riparian owners by conveying to them as wide a strip of the submerged lands as may be deemed expedient; and the shore owners will then have the right to fill in such submerged strip, thus adding extensive areas of valuable shore land to their present holdings.   The constitutionality of this legislation is virtually settled by the case of *People* v. *Kirk*, 162 Ill. 138, sustaining a similar arrangement between the Lincoln Park board and the proprietors of the shore south of Oak Street.   The Lincoln Park board has been given power to condemn shore lands and riparian rights under an amendment of Section 2 of an act passed June 15, 1895, and court proceedings are authorized for the establishment of the boundary line between the park lands and the lands of private owners.[1]

The right of the state to authorize structures which might interfere with navigation is subordinate to the paramount control of the War Department of the United States; and the improvements contemplated by the legislation last described cannot be carried out without the consent of the Secretary of War.   Proceedings looking to a grant of such consent were temporarily stayed by the remonstrance of Mayor Busse, and the appointment by him, under authority of the city council, of the Chicago Harbor Commission, which has made a comprehensive study and detailed report on the harbors of the city, together with recommendations as to harbor, railway terminal, and park plans along that part of the shore of Lake Michigan between Twelfth Street and Jackson Park.   The report is entirely favorable to the essential features of the plan for park and boulevard development on the Lake Front, but with appropriate reservations for future harbor development.   It strongly favors the accomplishment of such plans at the earliest possible moment. stating that "there is no real conflict between the harbor and the park interests of Chicago and no artificial or unnecessary discord should be permitted to retard the complete and prompt execution of the plans necessary for the development of both sides of the city's life,"   It recommends that " a detailed plan carrying out this idea should be worked out jointly by the experts of the park authorities and an expert engineer appointed by the city, subject to the approval of the city council and the South Park Commissioners," and urges immediate action by these authorities. As soon as such a plan can be worked out and the consent of the War Department be secured, there is nothing but the question of ways and means to delay the execution of this plan.   The legislature has already authorized the South Park board, upon obtaining authority from the people at an election, to issue bonds up to the constitutional limit for the construction of the Lake Front Park.[2]

[1] Hurd's Statutes, edition of 1908, p. 1540.

[2] House Bill No. 352, introduced in the Illinois legislature on March 23, 1909, proposes to confer on the city complete legal power to create harbors and provides as follows: "Sec. 14.   For the purpose of acquiring or constructing wharves, docks, levees, or in connection with such wharves, docks, or levees, elevators, warehouses, vaults or necessary or appropriate tracks or terminal facilities, the city may reclaim the submerged lands under any public waters within the jurisdiction of or bordering upon the City of Chicago, and shall thereupon be vested with the absolute title, in fee simple, to the lands so reclaimed; and for any of the purposes aforesaid the city may acquire, by purchase, condemnation or otherwise, the title of the private or public owners, if any there be, to lands lying beneath such public waters and to any lands penetrating into or abutting on such public waters, and also the riparian or other rights, if any there be, of the owners of the shore lands abutting on such public waters in or over such public waters or the submerged lands under such waters.   The city or owners of any such abutting lands or riparian or other rights are hereby authorized to agree upon a division of the said submerged lands between the said city and the said owners, and upon a boundary line dividing the submerged lands acquired or to be acquired by said city, and the submerged lands to be taken, owned and used by said owners in lieu of and as compensation for the release or transfer of such riparian or other rights to said city; subject, however, to the requirement that in all cases in which said city shall have agreed upon any such division, the said city shall file a petition or petitions in chancery and obtain a decree of court thereon, in like manner as is provided with respect to boards of park commissioners in and by a statute of the State of Illinois entitled, 'An Act authorizing park commissioners to acquire and improve submerged and shore lands for park purposes, providing for the payment therefor, and granting unto such commissioners certain rights and powers and to riparian owners certain rights and titles,' approved May 2, 1907."

TRANSPORTATION PROBLEMS

The readjustment of freight and passenger traffic and the relocation of railroad terminals is a subject which requires little comment from a legal point of view. When railway companies are brought to the point of hearty co-operation with the Chicago Plan, the powers which they already enjoy will be found adequate to the execution of their part. The state has placed at their service all necessary powers of eminent domain, and those portions of streets and alleys required for railway terminals may be vacated by the city. Although the action of the city council in vacating streets to make room for a railway station has been attacked, it has been sustained by the lower courts.

It may be that the legislature should be asked to confer upon the city additional powers that would enable it to acquire property for railway terminals and appropriate connections to be used by the various transportation lines on just terms. A city cannot condemn land for the purpose of turning it over to a railway corporation, but there can be little doubt of the power of the legislature to authorize a city to condemn land in order to create a central clearing place for traffic. Chapter 247 of the Acts of the legislature of Wisconsin for the year 1907 is an example of a law designed for that end. This statute authorizes cities of the first class to acquire, establish, own and operate railway terminals, and to condemn land for that purpose. Having established such a terminal, the city may permit any railroad corporation to use it upon agreed terms, or, if the parties cannot agree, then upon terms to be fixed by the state railroad commission. To meet the first cost, the city is authorized to issue "railway terminal certificates," payable only out of the revenues derived from the terminals for the acquisition of which they are issued. These certificates may be secured by trust deed, and there are provisions for foreclosure similar in many respects to those contained in the so-called "Mueller Law" enacted by the legislature of Illinois, authorizing municipal ownership of street railways. Under the decision of the Supreme Court of Illinois,[1] such certificates would constitute "indebtedness" of the city, and the amount which could be issued at any time would be controlled by the constitutional limitation of municipal indebtedness. That municipal certificates or bonds secured by revenue-producing utilities and not made a charge upon the other property or general credit of the city should be exempted from the general constitutional debt limit is advocated by men of widely different opinions upon the public-utility question,[2] and is provided in various state constitutions.[3] Constitutional amendments to this effect are being proposed in New York and elsewhere.

CONTROL OF LANDS ADJACENT TO PUBLIC IMPROVEMENTS

In order to secure the full benefit of a park, boulevard, avenue or other place of public recreation or resort, some control of the immediate surroundings is indispensable. The municipal authorities which establish parks, boulevards, and other public places need some power to regulate the use of premises within immediate view of the public grounds, so as to prevent offensive

---

[1] *Lobdell* v. *Chicago*, 227 Ill. 218

[2] See Report of National Civic Federation Commission on Public Ownership and Operation, Part 1, Vol. 1, p. 25.

[3] Digest of City Charters, prepared for Chicago Charter Convention, pp. 25, 26.

advertising, restrict the kinds of business, if any, to be conducted thereon, and make appropriate regulation of the height, manner of construction, and location of the surrounding buildings.   To that end, resort must be had either to the police power or to the power of eminent domain.

The police power of the state is not available for merely æsthetic purposes, and is quite inadequate to the solution of this special problem.   Owners of land, under existing constitutional limitations, can with impunity lease to advertising companies the right to erect safely constructed billboards and paint the sides and roofs of barns with any advertisements not injurious to morals or contrary to public decency; nor can vulgarities which merely offend the sight and shock temperamental susceptibilities be construed as breaches of decency.   "It is believed," says a writer in the Harvard Law Review,[1] "that both on theoretical and practical grounds the law must be taken as settled that, although public æsthetic ends may be effectuated by statute or ordinance through the exercise of eminent domain, the same object may not be accomplished by legislation under the police power without compensation."

In the case of *Chicago* v. *Gunning System*, 214 Ill. 628, the Supreme Court of Illinois declared that the legislature, by conferring authority upon the city council to abate nuisances and enforce police ordinances, had given that body ample power to regulate, within reasonable limits, the construction of billboards upon private property; but the court nevertheless condemned a particular ordinance for the reason, among others, that the purpose of certain sections seemed "to be mainly sentimental and to prevent sights which may be offensive to the æsthetic sensibilities of certain individuals residing in or passing through the vicinity of the billboards."

A broader control may, however, be exerted under the power of eminent domain. It is possibly within the capacity of the legislature to authorize park boards or other governmental bodies to acquire by condemnation proceedings, upon payment of compensation, the right, even in country districts, to restrict the use of all land within view of a driveway or park; but the exercise of that power with respect to property which does not actually front on the park or driveway scarcely falls within the domain of practical consideration in connection with the present Plan.

Nearer the center of urban population, where the billboard nuisance is even more aggravated, the city is now the only effective repository of the police power.   The county is not at present a factor in the problem; and park boards, while they have adequate police jurisdiction in their own territory, have none outside.   It is competent for the city council, in the exercise of the police power, to regulate the construction of advertising signs for the protection of public decency or public safety by reasonable ordinances, but not to prohibit them altogether, nor restrict their size, construction, or location more than is reasonably necessary to keep them within the limit of safety; nor could land abutting upon parks and boulevards be subjected to substantially different regulations in this respect from those imposed upon property fronting on business streets.   In the case of *Chicago* v. *Gunning System*, already adverted to, a provision forbidding the erection of billboards on residence streets without the consent of residents in the block was condemned by the court as "an arbitrary restriction on the part of the city, depriving an individual property owner of the use of his property as he may choose, without any showing that such use would be injurious to others in the same vicinity."   The city council cannot condemn as a nuisance what the law adjudges not to be a nuisance.   In order, therefore, to control offensive advertising by such regulations as the city ought to have power to impose, resort must be had to some other function of government than the police power.

[1] Vol. xx, p. 43

The construction of buildings is also subject to some regulation under the police power. The city is vested with authority to prescribe the strength and manner of constructing buildings, to define fire limits, and to pass and enforce all necessary police ordinances; and the power conferred upon it to pass "all necessary police ordinances" is construed as delegating to the city all the appropriate police power of the state.[1] No question is made but that the city council has power to regulate the height of buildings with a view to health and public safety; but it may be doubted whether the police power would justify the municipal authorities in imposing more rigorous restrictions upon the character of buildings to be constructed along boulevards and around parks than in other parts of the city. The Supreme Judicial Court of Massachusetts has sustained the right of the legislature to delegate to a city the power to regulate the height of buildings, to prescribe different regulations for different districts, and to invest a commission with the right to determine the boundaries between such districts,[2] and has expressed the opinion that certain special regulations of the height of buildings around a public square might be imposed under the police power without making compensation.[3] It is doubtful whether local distinctions of this character would be sustained in Chicago under existing legislation, except in so far as they might be justified by the power to establish fire limits. The legislature might delegate to city councils the power to district the city and prescribe different building limits in different districts; but any distinctions of this sort would have to rest upon real differences, and it remains doubtful whether the police power could be invoked to justify making a special district of the area surrounding a public square or avenue. The council could not be invested with authority to establish building lines without awarding compensation to the owner;[4] nor could the legislature confer the right to regulate arbitrarily the character of the business to be conducted in premises abutting on a boulevard.[5] A business which is an actual nuisance may be prohibited altogether; and the legal machinery exists for excluding saloons and some other kinds of business from limited areas. Such exercise of the police power must, however, bear some reasonable relation to the public health, safety, or morals, and could not, under existing constitutional restraints, be extended to business in general.

Such being the limits of the police power, it is evident that, in order to secure any effective control of the environs of a public place, resort must be had to some authority of wider scope, and the only available power is that of eminent domain, under which the state and its agencies have the right to take any private property for a public use, upon providing just compensation. The areas adjacent to a public place could probably be controlled under this power, either by condemning them outright as a part of the improvement, or by condemning merely a qualified right to regulate and control them. If they were taken outright, the question would arise whether they could be resold subject to the necessary restrictions upon their future use; thus reducing the cost of the improvement to the extent of the increase in the value of this land caused by the improvement.

The right to appropriate private property for public use is an attribute of sovereignty, existing in the state independently of written constitutions, and vested in the general assembly by those provisions of the constitution which confer upon that body the legislative power of the state. In Illinois, as in all of the states, the power of the legislature to take private property for the use of

---

[1] *McPherson v. Village of Chebanse.* 114 Ill. 46.
[2] *Welch v. Swasey*, 193 Mass. 364.
[3] *Attorney General v. Williams*, 174 Mass. 476.
[4] *City of St. Louis v. Hill*, 116 Mo. 527; *Chicago v. Gunning System*, 214, Ill. 628.
[5] *City of St. Louis v. Dorr*, 145 Mo. 466.

the community is subject to two constitutional limitations: one, that just compensation must be provided for all property so taken; the other, that private property cannot be taken, even upon payment of its full value, for any except a public use. These two restrictions are also imposed by the fourteenth amendment of the federal constitution, which declares that no state shall deprive any person of property without due process of law. Subject to these qualifications, the state has unlimited power to appropriate through its legislature any property within its borders which has become the subject of private ownership; and this power of eminent domain the legislature may delegate, with or without restrictions, to any subordinate agency. The expediency of the exercise of that power in any given case is a subject over which the courts have no control, unless they can say that the proposed use is not public. On these general principles all the authorities are agreed.

The United States Supreme Court has frequently stated the principles of the law of eminent domain. In *Boom Company* v. *Patterson*, 98 U. S. 403, Mr. Justice Field, in delivering the opinion of the court, said:

"The right of eminent domain, that is, the right to take private property for public uses, appertains to every independent government. It requires no constitutional recognition: it is an attribute of sovereignty. The clause found in the constitutions of the several states providing for just compensation for property taken is a mere limitation upon the exercise of the right. When the use is public, the necessity or expediency of appropriating any particular property is not a subject of judicial cognizance. The property may be appropriated by an act of the legislature, or the power of appropriating it may be delegated to private corporations, to be exercised by them in the execution of works in which the public is interested."

Parks, boulevards, and places of recreation are now universally recognized as legitimate objects of public concern, for which the power of eminent domain may appropriately be exercised; and it seems clear that if private property can be taken to create such utilities, it may also be taken for the purpose of realizing the full benefit of these works by adequate control of the surroundings. The legislature might at least authorize a city, park district, or other subordinate agency to exercise the power of eminent domain by imposing upon property in the neighborhood of a public place restrictions upon the location or character of the buildings to be erected, or the kinds of business, if any, to be conducted upon such adjacent land. It could not be successfully argued that such a use was not public.

The conception of a public use must alter and expand with the development of civilization, and especially with the growth of cities. In sustaining an act of Congress providing for the condemnation of land for a public park in the District of Columbia, and assessing part of the cost upon the property specially benefited, the Supreme Court, in the case of *Shoemaker* v. *United States*, 147 U. S. 282, 297, speaking through Mr. Justice Shiras, said:

"In the memory of men now living, a proposition to take private property, without the consent of its owner, for a public park, and to assess a proportionate part of the cost upon real estate benefited thereby, would have been regarded as a novel exercise of legislative power. It is true that, in the case of many of the older cities and towns, there were common or public grounds, but the purpose of these was not to provide places for exercise and recreation, but places on which the owners of domestic animals might pasture them in common, and they were generally laid out as part of the original plan of the town or city. It is said, in Johnson's Cyclopedia, that the Central Park of New York was the first place deliberately provided for the inhabitants of any city or town in the United States for exclusive use as a pleasure ground for rest and exercise in the open air. However that may be, there is now scarcely a city of any considerable size in the entire country that does not have, or has not projected, such parks. The validity of the legislative acts erecting such parks, and providing for their cost, has been uniformly upheld."

Again, in the case of *Attorney General* v. *Williams*, 174 Mass. 476, the Supreme Judicial Court of Massachusetts used the following language:

"The uses which should be deemed public in reference to the right of the legislature to compel an individual to part with his property for a compensation, and to authorize or direct taxation to pay for it, are being enlarged and extended with the progress of the people in education and refinement. Many things which a century ago were luxuries, or were altogether unknown, have now become necessaries. It is only within a few years that lands have been taken in this country for public parks. Now the right to take land for this purpose is generally recognized and frequently exercised. . . . . The grounds on which public parks are desired are various. They are to be enjoyed by the people who use them. They are expected to minister not only to the grosser senses, but also to the love of the beautiful in nature, in the varied forms which the changing seasons bring. Their value is enhanced by such touches of art as help to produce pleasing and satisfactory effects on the emotional and spiritual side of our nature. Their influence should be uplifting, and, in the highest sense, educational. If wisely planned and properly cared for, they promote the mental as well as the physical health of the people. For this reason it has always been deemed proper to expend money in the care and adornment of them, to make them beautiful and enjoyable. Their æsthetic effect never has been thought unworthy of careful consideration by those best qualified to appreciate it. It hardly would be contended that the same reasons which justify the taking of land for a public park do not also justify the expenditure of money to make the park attractive and educational to those whose tastes are being formed, and whose love of beauty is being cultivated."

When once it is conceded that a use is public, the courts have no control over the character of the estate or easement to be taken for the purpose. The constitution of Illinois provides, indeed, that when a railroad company condemns a right-of-way the fee shall remain in the former owner; but, subject to that restriction as to these particular corporations, the legislature has unlimited power to specify the nature, extent, and duration of the estate that shall be taken for any public use. Having the right to authorize the taking of an absolute title, it could direct the appropriation of any lesser interest; and could confer upon public bodies power to condemn the right to restrict the use and improvement of property contiguous to public grounds.

It does not appear, however, that the present statutes of Illinois do confer upon municipalities any express power to condemn such easements over lands contiguous to a street, boulevard, park or other public place. In the legislation under which the West Chicago Park Commissioners were incorporated and organized, there were sections expressly directing the park commissioners to impose building lines upon property adjacent to the parks and boulevards authorized thereby, and in the condemnation proceedings compensation was to be included for this burden. The West Park board, however, never undertook to avail itself of these extensive powers, which were limited to the acquisition of the original parks and boulevards authorized by the act. It might be argued that the city, under its present authority to establish and enlarge parks, boulevards, and streets, could condemn such easements directly, or that it could condemn a wide strip for a new street or land contiguous to an old street, and, by the familiar device of a stipulation entered of record in the condemnation suit, limit the appropriation to a restricted control of the use of the property. The latter method, if lawful, would be clumsy and inadequate, and additional legislation would be desirable to enable public authorities effectively to acquire, under the power of eminent domain, a qualified jurisdiction or control over property of which the exclusive use is not taken.

Even such a law, however, would fall short of the public need. To give the city or other agency a free hand in controlling the environs of a public place, the authorities should be invested with power to acquire the actual title, and then to dispose of it subject to such restrictions as might be deemed expedient. This course offers the double advantage of giving the public agency absolute control of the future use and improvement of the surrounding property, and of enabling it, if the price of acquisition is not too great, to recoup in some measure the cost of the improvement by selling the residual title. A lot abutting on a park or boulevard might be worth much more after it had become part of a larger area subject to uniform building lines and restrictions than it was in its unencumbered condition; and the public authorities, by treating the whole improvement and its environment as a unit, might reap a pecuniary advantage which they could not have conferred upon individual owners even if they had desired to do so. An examination of the power of municipalities to take land in excess of physical requirements involves two questions: first, whether extra land can be taken merely for the purpose of selling it and defraying the cost of the improvement; and, second, whether, even if that right is denied, such land can be condemned and resold for the purpose of imposing upon it building or sanitary restrictions and limitations of use.

As already stated, it may be accepted as elementary that neither the state, through its legislative department, nor any subordinate agency of the state can take a man's property against his will, under the power of eminent domain, merely for the purpose of giving it or selling it to another man. Such a taking would not be for public use and would violate the state and federal constitutions. It by no means follows, however, that a state agency, exercising the power of eminent domain, is always forbidden to derive profit from the sale of property not found to be actually needed. The activities of the Sanitary District of Chicago suffice to show how an area larger than is demanded by the ultimate needs of the public work may be acquired and converted into a source of revenue. A municipal corporation enjoys a large discretion in determining for itself how much land it needs for its public works, and courts will not ordinarily curb its freedom of action unless the exercise of the power of eminent domain is clearly excessive. If the city council saw fit to condemn a strip of land five hundred feet wide for an avenue or boulevard, the courts would have no right to question its decision unless, in the particular instance, there was some "manifest injustice, oppression or gross abuse of power";[1] nevertheless, if it did clearly appear as a fact that the ultimate object was to lay out an avenue only one hundred feet in width, the question would be squarely presented whether the margins on each side could be taken outright in order to govern their future use and development.

In an early New York case, a legislative attempt to authorize the taking of more land than was actually needed was condemned by the court in the following language:

"This power has been supposed to be convenient when the greater part of a lot is taken, and only a small part left not required for public use, and that small part of but little value in the hands of the owner. In such case the corporation has been supposed best qualified to take and dispose of such parcels, or gores, as they have sometimes been called; and probably this assumption of power has been acquiesced in by the proprietors. I know of no case where the power has been questioned and where it has received the deliberate sanction of this court. Suppose a case where only a few feet or even inches are wanted from one end of a lot to widen a street, and a valuable building stands upon the other end of such lot, would the power be conceded to exist to take the whole lot, whether the owner consented or not? Or suppose the commissioners had deemed it expedient and proper in this case, in the language of the statute, to take the whole of the churchyard, the act would have been equally within the letter of the statute with their act in the present case; and yet no one would suppose that the legislature ever intended to confer such a power. The quantity of the residue of any lot cannot vary the principle. The owner may be very unwilling to part with only a few feet; and I hold it equally incompetent for the legislature thus to dispose of private property, whether feet or acres are the subject of this assumed power. I am clearly of opinion that the commissioners have no right to take the strip of land in question against the consent of the corporation of Trinity Church."[2]

[1] *Dunham v. Hyde Park*, 75 Ill. 371.
[2] *Matter of Albany Street*, 11 Wend. 148.

While there is a dearth of modern authority on this subject, it is believed that the courts would still accept the reasoning of this Albany Street case, and would sustain the position of an owner who refused to surrender his property in order merely to diminish the cost of a public improvement. Such enactments, however, though void as to an unwilling property owner, are valid in so far as they confer authority on the city to take and pay for the whole parcel with the owner's consent, and to spend the people's money for that purpose.[1] A plan for acquiring a large area by private purchase could not be successfully carried out if one or two of the proprietors could refuse to part with their property, and such a scheme must therefore be confined within the limits of the power of eminent domain.

In order to justify the appropriation of a zone outside of the actual lines of the public space, it must appear that the property is to be made, in some sort, a part of the improvement; and that fact does appear when the control of the debatable zone is sought in order to save the environment of the public place from disfigurement or objectionable use. That end suffices to justify the condemnation of some interest in the zone; and it is well established by the authorities that when the public good requires the appropriation of some interest, the legislature is sole judge of the particular nature of the interest that shall be taken, and may, without being answerable to any court, declare that the interest to be taken shall be a fee simple absolute. A railway company does not require the title, or even the exclusive use, of its entire right-of-way; yet it is not doubted that, in the absence of a constitutional restriction, the legislature might authorize a railway company to take the entire title. In most states, the fee of a street remains in the owner of the property over which the street is laid out under the power of eminent domain; yet there is no question but that the legislature has power to vest the fee in the city. The Supreme Court of Minnesota, in the case of *Fairchild* v. *St. Paul*, 46 Minn. 540, where the question was raised whether the city acquired through condemnation proceedings the actual title to the street or only an easement, stated the established principles of the law in the following language:

"There is nothing better settled than that, the power of eminent domain being an incident of sovereignty, the time, manner and occasion of its exercise are wholly in the control and discretion of the legislature, except as restrained by the constitution. It rests in the wisdom of the legislature to determine when and in what manner the public necessities require its exercise; and with the reasonableness of the exercise of that discretion the courts will not interfere. As the legislature is the sole judge of the public necessity which requires or renders expedient the exercise of the power of eminent domain, so it is the exclusive judge of the amount of land, and of the estate in land, which the public end to be subserved requires to be taken. * * *

"When the use is public, the necessity or expediency of appropriating any particular property is not a subject of judicial cognizance. Consequently, if in the legislative judgment it is expedient to do so, it has the power expressly to authorize a municipal corporation compulsorily to acquire the absolute fee simple to lands of private persons condemned for street or any other public purpose. The authorities are so numerous and uniform to this effect that an extended citation of them is unnecessary. * * * It is often laid down as the law that the taking of property must always be limited to the necessity of the case, and, consequently, no more can be appropriated in any instance than is needed for the particular use for which the appropriation is made. But it will be found that this is almost invariably said, not in discussing the extent of the power of the legislature, but with reference to the construction of statutes granting authority to exercise the right of eminent domain, and where the authority to take a certain quantity of land or a particular estate therein depended, not upon an express grant of power to do so, but upon the existence of an alleged necessity, from which the disputed power is to be implied."

The city of Brooklyn acquired land for public parks under a statute authorizing the acquisi-

[1] *Embury* v. *Conner*, 3 N. Y. 511; *Dorgan* v. *Boston*, 12 Allen, 223.

tion of the title, and the court, in sustaining the validity of a subsequent act of the legislature authorizing the sale of portions of the land no longer needed, said:

"Doubtless, in most cases, when land is condemned for a special purpose on the score of public utility, the sequestration is limited to that particular use. But this is where the property is not taken, but the use only. Then, the right of the public being limited to the use, when the use ceases the right ceases. Where the property is taken, the owner paid its true value, and the title vested in the public, it owns the whole property, and not merely the use; and though the particular use may be abandoned, the right to the property remains."[1]

Land acquired for canal purposes has often been held to have vested absolutely in the state, so that upon abandonment of the canal the premises could be devoted to a different use or sold to a private purchaser.[2]

Some courts have intimated that land condemned for park purposes is presumptively dedicated to that use forever; and, hence, that authority to condemn for such a use implies authority to take the absolute title. Moreover, if a statute provided that land acquired for a public purpose could be sold when no longer needed, the implication would seem to be unavoidable that the title acquired under the statute was absolute. No general authority, however, has as yet been conferred upon municipalities in this state to take under the power of eminent domain a title that would survive the public use.

Under appropriate legislation, then, a city could take the absolute fee to any property in which it required an interest for the public use. It is equally well settled that the legislature can authorize the sale of any such land when it is no longer needed for the purpose for which it was acquired. The property, it is true, is held in trust for the public, but that trust could be relinquished by authority of the legislature, which represents the public, and the property could then be sold; and the authority to sell such surplus when no longer needed could be contained in the act authorizing the original condemnation. Of such a statute it was said in *Matter of City of Rochester* 137 N. Y. 243:

"It is claimed that this provision is in conflict with the provisions of the constitution respecting the taking of private property for public use, as it in fact authorizes the city to take it for a purpose not public. We think the objection is without merit or substance. Of course, the city could not take private property for the purpose of selling it or dealing in it; but, having once acquired it for a park, and it becoming, in the course of time, unnecessary or useless for that purpose, by the growth of the city or other changes in the situation, a sale in the manner prescribed by the statute would be within the legitimate functions of the city as a municipal corporation, and power to that end, conferred by the legislature at any time, or in the act authorizing the taking, cannot invalidate the delegated right to exercise the power of eminent domain."

The power of the municipality to sell superfluous land under the authority of such a statute could not be challenged at the time of sale. If the title had been acquired, it could be sold. The only question that could be raised would be one in the original condemnation proceeding as to the power to take the land at all. That question would be merely the question of good faith. The petitioner could be made to file plans showing some reasonable need for the property sought to be condemned; and the courts would not permit an obvious abuse of the power of eminent domain either by the state legislature or by any of its agencies. It is believed, however, that no question of abuse or bad faith could arise when the legislature was shown to have authorized, in its sovereign discretion, the taking of the whole title as the most direct and convenient method of controlling the use.

[1] *Brooklyn Park Comm'rs.* v. *Armstrong*, 45 N. Y. 234, 243.
[2] *Heyward* v. *New York*, 7 N. Y. 314; *Rexford* v. *Knight*, 11 N. Y. 308; *Malone* v. *Toledo*, 34 Ohio, 541.

An instructive case bearing upon this argument is that of *Dingley* v. *Boston*, 100 Mass. 544. For the purpose of draining and grading up a part of the Back Bay district, the Massachusetts legislature authorized the city of Boston to take land within a certain area, and provided that the title should vest in the city. The contemplated use, although extensive, was merely temporary; when the land was filled and the surface raised to a higher grade, the purpose for which it was taken would have been accomplished. The Supreme Court, nevertheless, holds that it was the object of the statute to authorize the taking of a fee simple absolute, and that after the filling had been completed the title remained in the city, subject to such use or disposition as the authorities might deem expedient. The use being public, it could not be said that the taking of a fee simple was any the less for public use than the taking of a smaller estate would have been; the legislature was sole judge of the expediency of taking one or the other. The court speaks as follows:

"The act provides that the city government may first take the land, and thereby transfer to the city a title in fee simple, without the consent of the owners. It is contended that, as the only object of the act is to abate a nuisance, the act ought only to have granted the power to occupy the land temporarily until the object of the act should be effected, and it should then be restored to the owners, with a provision that the benefit done to the land should be applied in offset to the damages. It is true that the raising of the grade does not require an occupation of the land for a great length of time. When this work is completed the nuisance will be abated, and the land will be in a condition to be occupied by private persons. But its condition will be greatly changed; almost as much so as raising flats into upland. The former surface will be deeply buried under the earth that will have been brought upon it, and the changed condition is to be perpetual. If the old property is restored, the new property which has been annexed to it must go with it. This would be very unjust to the city, who have been compelled to incur the great expense of destroying the nuisance, unless the owner were required to make a reasonable compensation, which might be far beyond the amount of the damages to which he would be entitled.

"It would be difficult to adjust the matter; and in many cases it might operate harshly upon the owner to compel him to take and pay for the improvements. On the whole, therefore, the plan of compelling the city to take the land in fee simple, and the owner to part with his whole title for a just compensation, would seem to be the most simple and equitable that could be adopted; unless there is some objection on the ground that a fee simple is more sacred than an estate for life or years, or than an easement of greater or less duration. We can see no ground for regarding one of these titles as more sacred than another, or for regarding land as more sacred than personal property. * * *

"Whether land be taken under the clause authorizing the making of wholesome and reasonable laws, or by virtue of the clause authorizing the appropriation of private property to public uses, it must in either case be left to the legislature to decide what quantity of estate ought to be taken in order to accomplish its purpose, and do the most complete justice to all parties."

If a municipality were justified in taking an area in order to control the surroundings of a park or boulevard, the proceeding would not be rendered illegal by the fact, if fact it was, that the hope of pecuniary profit was a strong, or even the controlling, motive. If there is a sound basis which justifies the action of public officials, the motive by which those officials are actuated is not open to judicial inquiry.[1]

If, then, it be a legitimate part of a public improvement — as few would question that it is — to impose appropriate restrictions upon the use and improvement of adjacent property, and if, as seems probable, the condemnation of the entire title can be authorized for that purpose, a municipal body could be empowered by the legislature to acquire title to land outside of the physical area of improvement; and if the municipality had also been authorized by the legislature to sell any interest no longer needed in any of its land, it could sell the land subject to all necessary conditions or restrictions; nor would it lie in the mouth of any court to question the

---

[1] *Meyer* v. *Teutopolis*, 131 Ill. 552; *People* v. *Wieboldt*, 233 Ill. 572; *Wisconsin River Improvement Co.* v. *Pier*, 118 N. W. Rep. 857.

proceeding or brand it as illegal because the real, efficient motive may have been to get the bene-fit of the enhancement in the value of the property.

There is probably no constitutional obstacle to legislation investing a city, park board, county, or other appropriate agency with power to condemn as part of or supplementary to a public im-provement such contiguous area as the reasonable needs of the improvement itself might require to be subjected to proper restrictions; nor could such a law be condemned by reason of its also authorizing the sale of the land subject to such conditions or restrictions as the public author-ities saw fit to impose upon it.[1]

If any local legislation authorizing the condemnation and sale of surplus lands were brought to the test, the question for the courts would be whether the use for which the property was taken was a public one; and it must be borne in mind that upon this point the judgment of the Supreme Court of a state would not be final. By the Fourteenth Amendment to the Constitution of the United States it is provided that no state shall deprive any person of property without due process of law; and it is now settled that this clause prohibits the taking of private property for any use that is not public. The United States Supreme Court, however, has always paid the greatest deference to the opinions of state legislatures and the state judiciary as to what uses are public. The power of the United States Supreme Court to review a state decision in this particular, and also the extreme respect which will be paid to local decisions, are both well illustrated in the case of *Clark* v. *Nash*, 198 U. S. 361, sustaining a statute of the state of Utah, by the terms of which an individual land owner was empowered to condemn the right of conveying water in a ditch across his neighbor's land for the purpose of irrigating his own farm. Mr. Justice Peckham, delivering the opinion of the court, said:

"In some states, probably in most of them, the proposition contended for by the plaintiffs in error would be sound. But whether a statute of a state permitting condemnation by an individual for the pur-pose of obtaining water for his land or for mining should be held to be a condemnation for a public use, and therefore a valid enactment, may depend upon a number of considerations relating to the situation of the state and its possibilities for land cultivation, or the successful prosecution of its mining or other in-dustries. Where the use is asserted to be public, and the right of the individual to condemn land for the purpose of exercising such use is founded upon or is the result of some peculiar condition of the soil or climate, or other peculiarity of the state, where the right of condemnation is asserted under a state statute, we are always, where it can fairly be done, strongly inclined to hold with the state courts, when they uphold a state statute providing for such condemnation. * * *

[1] House Bill No. 350, Illinois, 1909, already mentioned, contains the following provisions, the legality of which is based upon the conclusions above stated.

Art. IV, Sec. 10. "The city council, on recommendation of the board of park commissioners, shall have power to extend the park system of the City of Chicago, both within and outside of the city limits, by adding to or otherwise enlarging any parks, and by opening and establishing new parks, and by extinguishing or acquiring such title to, or such easements and rights in or over, any lands abutting on or in the vicinity of any existing or projected park as may be necessary or appropriate to control the surroundings of such park so as to increase the advantage thereof to the public, or secure to the public the full benefit, use and enjoyment thereof. For any such purpose the city may extinguish easements or rights in land, and may acquire lands and easements and rights in or over land, by gift, devise, dedication, purchase or condemnation, and may in its discretion, take under the power of eminent domain or otherwise the title in fee simple absolute to any land which the city is authorized to acquire, or in or over which it is authorized to acquire easements and rights as aforesaid, and such title shall not terminate or be defeated by cessation or abandonment of the use for which it was acquired. The declaration of the city council that any such lands or easements or rights in or over land are necessary or appropriate for any such purpose shall constitute sufficient prima facie evidence of such necessity or appropriateness. The city council may vacate streets and alleys within the limits of or adjacent to any lands acquired for the purpose of this section."

Art. IV., Sec. 13. "The provisions in this Act contained authorizing the city to acquire the absolute title in fee simple to lands in or over which the city is authorized to acquire easements or rights, shall be subject to the provision that any lands so taken for such purpose shall, unless appropriated to some public use within ten (10) years after acquisition of the title thereto, be sold and disposed of by the city in the manner now or hereafter provided by statute for the sale and conveyance of property no longer required for the use of the city, subject, however, to such easements or rights in said lands, and to such conditions, covenants and restrictions respecting the use or improvement thereof as the city, upon recommendation of the board of park commissioners, shall, in the deed of conveyance, impose or reserve, and subject further to the power (which is hereby granted) of the city council, with the consent of the board of park com-missioners, to release, waive or (by or with the consent of the grantee or owner of the conveyed premises) alter any such easements rights, conditions, covenants or restrictions."

"We do not desire to be understood by this decision as approving of the broad proposition that private property may be taken in all cases where the taking may promote the public interest and tend to develop the natural resources of the state. We simply say that in this particular case, and upon the facts stated in the findings of the court, and having reference to the conditions already stated, we are of the opinion that the use is a public one, although the taking of the right of way is for the purpose simply of thereby obtaining the water for an individual, where it is absolutely necessary to enable him to make any use whatever of his land, and which will be valuable and fertile only if water can be obtained."

Again, in the very recent case of *Hairston* v. *Danville & Western Railway Co.*, 208 U. S. 598, the facts were that the Supreme Court of Virginia had sustained a proceeding by which a railroad condemned land for a spur track to a tobacco factory, the owner of which agreed to reimburse the company for the cost of acquiring the land. The decision of the federal court sustaining the judgment of the state court was delivered by Mr. Justice Moody, who said:

"When we come to inquire what are public uses for which the right of compulsory taking may be employed, and what are private uses for which the right is forbidden, we find no agreement, either in reasoning or conclusion. The one and only principle in which all courts seem to agree is that the nature of the uses, whether public or private, is ultimately a judicial question. The determination of this question by the courts has been influenced in the different states by considerations touching the resources, the capacity of the soil, the relative importance of industries to the general public welfare, and the long-established methods and habits of the people. In all these respects, conditions vary so much in the states and territories of the Union that different results might well be expected. . . . . No case is recalled where this court has condemned as a violation of the Fourteenth Amendment a taking upheld by the state court as a taking for public uses in conformity with its laws. . . . . We must not be understood as saying that cases may not arise where this court would decline to follow the state courts in their determination of the uses for which land could be taken by the right of eminent domain. The cases cited, however, show how greatly we have deferred to the opinions of the state courts on this subject, which so closely concerns the welfare of their people. We have found nothing in the Federal Constitution which prevents the condemnation by one person for his individual use of a right of way over the land of another for the construction of an irrigation ditch; of a right of way over the land of another for an aerial bucket line; or of the right to flow the land of another by the erection of a dam. It remains for the future to disclose what cases, if any, of taking for uses which the state constitution, law and court approve will be held to be forbidden by the Fourteenth Amendment to the Constitution of the United States."

It thus appears that it would require an extreme case of manifest abuse of the power of eminent domain to lead the Supreme Court of the United States to condemn as private a use which a state legislature had recognized as public, and which had been sustained by the Supreme Court of the state. If the abuse of power were manifest, the United States courts would not hesitate to condemn the proceeding, even though expressly sanctioned by the constitution of a state; but there is every reason to believe that any method of taking and selling land justified by the reasonable purpose of controlling the environs of a public place would withstand the scrutiny of the United States Supreme Court if sanctioned by the legislative and judicial departments of the state government.

In concluding this topic, some experiments made in other states towards taking more property than was demanded by the physical requirements of an improvement, either to control the environs or for mere pecuniary considerations, may be passed briefly in review. The experience of foreign countries need not be recounted here, since some governments, unlimited by constitutional restrictions, have conducted real estate transactions of a wide range, far beyond anything that could reasonably be contemplated in America. The State of New York had upon its statute books early in the last century an act already adverted to, purporting to authorize municipalities to take all of a connected tract of land when only part was needed and to sell the surplus.

This statute was adjudged by the courts to be unconstitutional, in so far as it sought to author-ize the taking, against the owners' consent, of land not actually needed. A resolution, however, has, after many years, been introduced (January 27, 1909), in the senate of the State of New York for the submission of a constitutional amendment in the following language:

"When private property shall be taken for public use by a municipal corporation, additional adjoining or neighboring property may be taken, under conditions to be prescribed by the legislature by general law. Property thus taken shall be deemed to be taken for public use."

In Massachusetts, Section 4 of Chapter 50 of the revised laws provides that the owner of abutting land liable to assessment may at a certain stage of the proceedings give notice that he elects to surrender his land; in which event the board may, if it thinks expedient, take the whole parcel at its estimated value, and any part not required may be sold. A somewhat similar statute, authorizing an owner to convey to the city his entire property at its appraised value when part of it was taken for widening a street, was involved, and by implication sustained, in the case of *Dorgan* v. *Boston*, 12 Allen, 223.

Chapter 443 of the Massachusetts laws of 1904 sanctions the taking of remnants of parcels part of which are condemned for public improvement, and authorizes the city to sell any of such remnants subject to any building or other restrictions which the proper authorities may see fit to impose. The power to take the whole of a tract when part only is needed is limited to the case where the remnant after such taking would, from its size or shape, be unsuited for the erec-tion of suitable and appropriate buildings, and where also the public convenience and necessity require such taking. There are provisions authorizing such remnants to be sold and united with adjacent property if the owner thereof consents; but the legislature refused to adopt the more radical plan, recommended by a committee, of uniting such remnants with the contiguous prop-erty, without the consent of the owner thereof, by condemning his land in order to incorporate the remnant with it and thus effect an advantageous sale. This act has never been tested in the courts, and it may be surmised that, in spite of the very liberal views of the Massachusetts courts, the fate of a proceeding under its provisions would be problematical, unless it could be made to appear that the "public convenience and necessity" actually did require such taking of entire tracts for the purpose of imposing upon the odd remnants some conditions and restrictions ger-mane to the major improvement.

Another statute, framed on somewhat similar lines, but also never submitted to a judicial test, is Section 10 of the Ohio Municipal Code, as amended in 1904. This section provides that all municipal corporations shall have power to appropriate real estate within their corporate limits for certain specific purposes, among which are the following:

"For establishing esplanades, boulevards, parkways, park grounds and public reservations in, around and leading to public buildings, and for the purpose of reselling such land, with reservations in the deeds of such resale as to the future use of said lands so as so protect public buildings and their environs, and to preserve the view, appearance, light, air and usefulness of public grounds occupied by public buildings and esplanades and parkways leading thereto."

Chapter 194 of the Acts of the Virginia General Assembly for the session of the year 1906 provides as follows:

"Any city or town of this Commonwealth may acquire by purchase, gift or condemnation property adjoining its parks, or plats on which its monuments are located, or other property used for public purposes, or in the vicinity of such parks, plats or property, which is used and maintained in such a manner as to im-pair the beauty, usefulness or efficiency of such parks, plats or public property, and may likewise acquire property adjacent to any street, the topography of which, from its proximity thereto, impairs the convenient use of such street, or renders impracticable, without extraordinary expense, the improvement of the same, and the city or town so acquiring any such property may subsequently dispose of the property so acquired, making limitations as to the uses thereof, which will protect the beauty, usefulness, efficiency, or convenience of such parks, plats or property."

CONGESTED AREAS

In considering a model plan for the city of Chicago, attention is naturally called to the example of European cities which have removed the inhabitants from whole areas where the population was congested or the arrangement of the streets unwholesome, and have transplanted them to new territory while the condemned area was being renovated or rebuilt. The Plan of Chicago does not contemplate any imitation of such examples. The police power is adequate to the destruction, without recompense, of single buildings which are insanitary or unsafe; but the legislature of Illinois has not yet undertaken to go further and license the condemnation by municipal authorities of congested or unwholesome areas under the power of eminent domain. Local drainage districts may be organized, with power to reclaim wet agricultural lands and locate ditches over private property, on the payment of proper compensation; and it would also doubtless be competent for the legislature to sanction the taking by eminent domain of a district even within the city which was by nature low or pestilent, as was done with the Back Bay flats in Boston. Different considerations, however, apply to an area where the noxious conditions are due to the arrangement of streets or to the manner of building upon land by individual owners. Each proprietor might with reason demand the right to be dealt with individually; and if his own lot was vacant, or was improved with buildings transgressing no sanitary laws or regulations, he might well oppose any scheme which required him to part with his land on account of the transgression of his neighbors. A tract of land fit to breed pestilence because of the niggardliness of nature might be reclaimed under the power of eminent domain, because the arch offender was not subject to the police jurisdiction of the state; but if a plague spot has been created by the fault of men, an innocent victim of their malfeasance would have some reason and more law on his side if he insisted upon the state proceeding against the culprits singly.

Accordingly, the Chicago Plan deals only incidentally with this subject. The city can, as has been done in some European capitals, open wide thoroughfares and avenues through congested areas, or take the heart of the district for a public park; and the legislature might authorize the condemnation of a zone of reasonable width around these open spaces on the principles already laid down. It may be doubted, however, whether the courts would sustain as constitutional a statute designed to appropriate a whole congested area merely for the purpose of renovating it. If the power to do so in a flagrant case were sustained by the Supreme Court of the state, or if such a project were authorized by constitutional amendment, the measure would probably not be condemned by the federal courts as contravening the Constitution of the United States. To the opening of wide streets, however, through congested districts, as proposed in the Plan, there is no obstacle unless it be the lack of financial resources.

PRESENT BORROWING AND TAXING POWERS

In carrying out so comprehensive a scheme of development as is outlined in the Plan of Chicago, some subsidiary sources of revenue may be found, but the main dependence must be upon the taxing power of the state and its agencies. Current expenses are properly met by current taxes; but it is a main principle of economics that the cost of permanent improvements should be distributed over a series of years commensurate with the probable duration of the benefit. Lest, however, the existing generation should lay inordinate burdens upon posterity, limitations have been set upon the amount and duration of indebtedness which may be incurred by any municipal body. Section 12 of Article IX of the constitution of the State of Illinois declares that no municipal corporation shall become indebted for any purpose to an amount exceeding five per cent of the value of the taxable property therein, as ascertained by the last assessment; and that, at or before the time of incurring such debt, the municipality shall provide for the collection of a direct annual tax sufficient to pay the interest and to discharge the principal within twenty years from the time when the debt was contracted. Under the present revenue laws applicable to Cook County, all taxable property is valued by assessors at its "full value," and one-fifth of that figure is entered in the books as the "assessed value," and, as afterwards equalized, is made the basis on which all tax and debt limitations are computed.[1]

The constitutional limit of municipal indebtedness does not mean that every public corporation has power to incur debts to that amount. Municipalities have no greater powers than the legislature confers upon them. There is no constitutional limit on the amount of taxes that the legislature can authorize municipalities to levy.[2] They may incur only such debts, not exceeding the constitutional limit, and levy such taxes as the general assembly authorizes them to do. Several municipal corporations, however, may be created under legislative authority for different purposes, embracing all or part of the same territory, and each of these overlapping municipalities may be given power to levy taxes and incur debts up to the constitutional limit. To restrain the increasing burden of taxes, the legislature in 1901 passed the so-called Juul law, designed to limit the aggregate taxes which might be levied upon any community in any one year to five per cent of the assessed valuation of property therein; but the constitutionality of this statute has been questioned and the amendments of and numerous exceptions to its provisions made by the legislature have left its operation, if not its continued existence, so doubtful that its repeal has been sought on divers occasions.[3]

The county of Cook is permitted to levy taxes not exceeding seventy-five cents on every one hundred dollars, without popular vote, and to levy any additional taxes voted by the people. County bonds may be voted by the people in any such amount as not to cause the total debt of the county to exceed five per cent of the assessed value of the property therein. The assessed value for the year 1908 was $514,730,186, of which five per cent is $25,736,509. Up to that limit the county might become indebted by vote of the people. The present bonded debt is $9,360,000, and the floating debt averages about $1,600,000. Without aiming at nicety of detail, it may be said that the county has at present a borrowing capacity, in round figures, of $15,000,000. The operation of the Juul law, however, now reduces the tax available for the general expenses of Cook County to sixty-five cents on one hundred dollars; and the increasing demands upon the county would probably necessitate a modification of this law, so as specifically to exclude from its limitations the taxes necessary to care for additional bond issues and provide for future maintenance of county parks or boulevards.

[1] House Bill No. 293, introduced at Springfield, March 11, 1909, seeks to make the assessed value one-third, instead of one-fifth, of the full value.

[2] Schnell v. Rock Island, 232 Ill. 89, 98.

[3] For the Juul law as amended see Hurd's Statutes of Illinois, edition of 1908, p. 1814.

The city of Chicago is practically indebted at all times to the constitutional limit of five per cent of its assessed valuation, and has been given power by the legislature to levy an annual tax for corporate purposes not exceeding two per cent on that valuation, exclusive of taxes levied for the payment of bonds. Under the operation of the Juul law, the maximum rate has been cut down to one and eight-tenths per cent. The assessed valuation of city property for 1908 was $477,190,399. A two per cent tax on that amount is $9,543,808, and a five per cent indebtedness would be $23,859,520. The legislature could authorize a higher annual tax, but could not, under the constitution, increase the limit of indebtedness unless by means of some change in the method of assessing the property on which the limitation was to be computed.[1] One of the chief reasons for asking a new charter was to increase the bond-issuing power of the city by changing the basis of computation of the limit of indebtedness.

The taxing powers of the three park districts in the city of Chicago are contained in a mass of separate laws, which authorize the issuing of bonds for particular purposes and the levying of taxes to pay the interest and retire the principal. The park boards could be authorized by the legislature to incur debts somewhat in excess of their present bonded liability, without infringing the provisions of the constitution; but here also the tax limitations of the Juul law would have to be modified unless maintenance expenditures were scaled. The assessed valuation for the year 1908 of property in the West Park district was $105,614,809, of which five per cent is $5,280,740. The present bonded debt of the West Park board is $3,270,000, leaving a possible margin of about $2,000,000 of additional indebtedness that the legislature could authorize to be incurred by the board.

An entirely new taxing body could, with the consent of the voters, be created by the legislature, having jurisdiction over all or part of Cook County. That body, if properly constituted, could be invested with power to levy such taxes as might be deemed advisable, and with power to issue bonds up to the constitutional limit of five per cent of the assessed valuation. It is also to be borne in mind that by some slight changes in the method of fixing the assessed valuation of property, which is now arbitrarily defined as one-fifth of the full valuation, the legislature could largely increase the borrowing power of all the taxing bodies.

Large improvements need not only extensive borrowing powers, but the distribution of the burden over a long series of years. While twenty years has been heretofore deemed the limit of time which ought to be allowed for paying any debt incurred by the issue of bonds, it may be thought that the radical changes contemplated by the Plan of Chicago are of such unusual magnitude and of such permanent character that justice might demand distribution of the burden over more than one generation. Upon that view, bonds running for a longer period might be thought reasonable. The present constitutional limit of twenty years is, however, absolute, and an amendment to the constitution would be required to enable any municipality to issue bonds for a longer term.

[1] House Bill No. 293, Illinois, 1909, already mentioned, would, if enacted into a law, give the city power to issue bonds for its share of the cost of the north and west connecting boulevards, or for a beginning on the Civic Center. The other necessities of the city would, however, exhaust most of the increased bonding power provided by this bill.

CONCLUSIONS

From the foregoing examination of the legal aspects of the Plan of Chicago it appears

First: That without any additional legislation many of the recommendations of the Plan can be adopted and practical steps be taken to carry them into effect;

Second: That the legislature has ample power to grant either to the city or to other governmental agencies such additional authority as may be necessary to carry out all of the recommendations of the Plan as fully and as rapidly as may be found wise; and

Third: That additional authority, and especially a substantial increase in the local bonding power, is essential to the effective accomplishment of the most important of these recommendations.

It remains for the people of Chicago, through their legally constituted representatives, to decide upon the wisdom of the suggestions and to adopt them in the order of their relative importance and availability. The necessary funds can no doubt be secured as rapidly as it can be clearly shown that their expenditure will result in real advantage to the individual citizens who constitute "the public," and upon whom rests, directly or indirectly, the burden of expense. In the last analysis it must be clear that a community which makes wise expenditure for public works not only imposes no real burden upon private property, but increases the value of all private property within its limits. Such a community should be given adequate authority to levy taxes and incur debt, subject always to such intelligent supervision of expenditures as will effectively guard against extravagance and waste. Certainly, any limitations upon a progressive municipality should be broad enough to make it possible to undertake such public enterprises as are recommended in this Plan.

Fortunately, this is entirely possible in Chicago within the constitutional limitations upon municipal indebtedness. By consolidating the local authorities within the city of Chicago under the provisions of the so-called charter amendment to the state constitution (Article IV, Sec. 34), the present bonding capacity of the city can be multiplied five times, less the aggregate indebtedness of the consolidating bodies, and subject to such limitations as may be imposed in the consolidating act. By merely changing the statutory method of fixing the assessed value of property, the present bonding power will be proportionately increased. By utilizing the county for making such improvements as it may well be authorized to make, we can secure additional bonding capacity even greater than that available through the agency of the city. There would seem to be no valid objection to an act authorizing any county which chose to adopt its provisions by popular vote to acquire, construct, and maintain parks and boulevards, with all the powers (including those of eminent domain) already recommended as to cities and park or forest-preserve districts, and with appropriate increase of taxing and of bonding powers subject to popular approval. For many, if not all, of the purposes now sought under the Forest-Preserve Act, the county of Cook would seem to be the appropriate and available agency. It would be a distinct public gain to enlarge its functions so that membership on its board of commissioners would both demand and permit the highest type of public service. If the Forest-Preserve Act, or an act of this general character, is constitutional, the agency thereby provided is also available for many of the purposes of the Plan, and could be given additional bonding power subject only to the constitutional limitation. It will thus be seen that ample bonding power for all the purposes of the Plan can be conferred by the legislature. Significant precedents are not lacking to justify the expectation that private generosity will co-operate in the accomplishment of some of the recommendations here made for the practical and effective promotion of the public welfare. Some of the conspicuous benefactions of this general nature, already made by public spirited citizens of Chicago, have been mentioned earlier in this volume,[1] and the movement for small parks and playgrounds has already received very substantial assistance from the generosity of private individuals. To other individuals other features, such as outer parks or the improvement of tenement conditions, may make an equal or greater appeal.

Some increase in the bonding power of the city is, however, essential to the effective accomplishment of certain park and street improvements which the city itself should immediately undertake. The two great connecting links — that between the North and South Divisions at Michigan Avenue, and that between the West and South Divisions by means of Twelfth Street — might well proceed immediately; and yet to raise the entire cost of these improvements by special assessment, spread over a wide area, would be to arouse vigorous opposition both in and out of the courts. This contest should, if possible, be confined to the adjustment of damages and benefits to the property directly affected and which abuts on or is in the immediate vicinity of the improvements. Property which is clearly benefited in a special and peculiar manner should be assessed its fair share — and only its fair share — of the cost of these improvements, and the remaining cost should be borne by the city at large as a public benefit. The present machinery of the special assessment law is adequate for all these purposes. What is needed is sufficient bonding power to enable the city to issue bonds for the portion of the cost assessed as "public benefits."

The power to condemn or otherwise acquire easements, and to acquire and thereafter sell the fee simple title to property in the immediate vicinity of public parks and boulevards, subject to such easements as may enhance and protect the public use, would be of great advantage in the practical accomplishment of many improvements, and might aid in overcoming serious financial obstacles. The available space will, however, not permit the discussion of the particular instances to which this suggestion especially applies.

It remains only to consider the official agencies which are most desirable and most available for the effective working out of the Plan. As a matter of theory, the best results could be achieved through a consolidation of the city and county governments, or by placing the entire metropolitan district, which constitutes the real city of Chicago, under a unified municipal administration, endowed with broad powers of local self-government, including the power to levy taxes and incur indebtedness. Practically, however, the enlargement of the powers of these two governing bodies — the city and the county — within the limits permitted by the present constitution, is probably the most available method of attaining desirable results. As a means of co-ordinating the two it is respectfully suggested that a permanent Commission on City and County Plan should be created by joint resolution or ordinance of the city council and the county board. This commission should contain appropriate representation for each body, and it should be charged with the duty of reporting to each its recommendations as to all matters falling within the general scope of a city and county Plan. It might well be ordained by the city council that no public buildings should be hereafter located or erected, and that no parks should be acquired and no streets or boulevards be opened, without a report from the commission or the city members thereof. The commission

[1] See Chapter VIII.

might be composed entirely of city and county officials, or might contain some representation of those who are not public officials but who are particularly interested in and particularly qualified for its work. The city board of local improvements and the present park boards or any future consolidated park board should be directly represented.

Whether the functions of the Commissions on Municipal Art and Small Parks should in the interest of simplification and efficiency be transferred to such a Commission on City and County Plan might be profitably considered. While such an advisory commission would be entirely extra-legal, it would be of distinct service in securing the harmonious development of a single comprehensive Plan for the city of Chicago and its environs.

INDEX

INDEX

A

Advertising, regulation of, 127, 131, 132, 140.
Algonquin, 40.
Alvord, John W., his paper on good roads, 39 (note); his report on Chicago pavements, 83.
American cities, centers of industry and traffic, 4.
Annapolis, Md., laid out on lines similar to those proposed by Wren for London, 29.
Ancient civilization, decay of, 13.
Antwerp, 100; the influence of the Reubens collection on, 116; treatment of the river banks in, 116.
Apartment houses, 33, 34.
Arc de Triomphe de l'Etoile, Paris, begun by Napoleon I, finished by Louis Phillippe, 17.
Arc du Carrousel, Paris, 17.
Architects, present plans for World's Columbian Exposition, 6, (note); should work together in street building, 86.
Architectural Record, quoted, 18.
Armour Institute of Technology, 120.
Arnold, Bion J., estimates increase in the population of Chicago, 33.
Art, a source of wealth and moral influence, 116.
Art Institute, the Lake Front improvements presented at, 6; students at, 109; new building for, 114; cost of, 120, 121.
Art Schools, 34.
Ashland Avenue, 117.
Atlantic Monthly Magazine, quoted, 19.
Athens, works of Pericles in, 11; characteristics of architecture in, 11; the Acropolis, 117.
Athletic Field, proposed location on the lake front, 116.
Aurora, 40.
Austria, finds new strength in union with Hungary, 19.
Automobiles, damage to roads by, 39; promote suburban life; 42, 46.
Avenue, the, the character of, 82; division of traffic on, 84; use of the elipse in, 90.

B

Babylon, the greatest commercial city of ancient times, 10; description of, 10.
Baltic, the, yachtmen of, 52.
Baltimore, improvements in, 28.
Baguio, summer capital of the Philippines, plan for, 29.
Batavia, 40.
Baths, in Rome, accommodations of, 13.
Baumeister, German city-builder, 21, (note).
Baxter, Sylvester, secretary of Metropolitan Improvement Commission, Boston, 20.
Beauty, Greek passion for, 11, commercial advantages of, 110.
Berlin, rapid growth of, 1; physical conditions in, 14; parks of, 49, 80; building restrictions in, 107.
Bill-boards, 41, 131, 140.
Blue Island, 40, 41.
Board of Local Improvements, powers of, 133.
Boating facilities, need of increased, 115.
Bois de Boulogne, 48.

Bois de Vincennes, 48.
Bond issues for improvements, 151.
Boston, defenses of, 9; cost of park system, 27; metropolitan sewage and park commissions, 38; extension of streets, 38; extent of park system, 49; apartment houses in, 88; improvements in Back Bay district, 108, 110.
Boulevard, character of, 82.
Boulevards of Chicago, 84, 93, 120.
British Museum, 110.
Brown, Glenn, Secretary American Institute of Architects, 21, (note).
Brussels, boulevards in, 20, 90.
Budapest, commercial progress of, 19; treatment of the Danube in, 116.
Buildings, regulation of the height of, 141.
Building-lines, 127.
Burnham, Daniel H., 6 (note); plan for San Francisco, 280.
Burns, John, town-planning scheme of, 22, 128.
Bushy Park, London, 48.

C

Chicago, rapid growth of population, 1; realizes that a city plan is necessary, 1; the plan presented the result of experience, 2; justification of the plan, 4; legal aspects of plan, 127-156; Chicago a center of industry and traffic, 4; future greatness, 4; public spirit, 4; understands the necessity of experts, 4; results of the World's Fair, 6; plans for improvement of the Lake front, 6; Merchants Club begins plan, 7; prosperity the result of comprehensive plan, 8; the Spirit of Chicago, 8; a typical example of a palisaded town, 9; surroundings similar to those of Paris, London and Berlin, 14; opportunity for systematic improvement, 15; population greater than that of Paris when Haussmann's work began, 18; nature of the Chicago problem, 30; the metropolis of the Middle West, 31; extent of city's influence, 32, 34; probable growth, 32, 33; size of the city not the first consideration, 32; lack of foresight after the fire of 1871, 32; B. J. Arnold's estimates of growth of population, 33; James J. Hill's prophecy as to growth, 33; circulation of Chicago newspapers, 33; bank reserves, 33; commercial influence, 34; political headquarters, 34; responsibilities of the city, 34; Commission to lay out territory adjoining the city, 34; provision should be made for public buildings and playgrounds, 35; churches, 36; suburbs, 36; need of highways into surrounding country, 38; building of good roads, 39; highways surrounding the city, 40, 41; streets of Chicago, 43; beginnings of park system, 43; park area second to that of Philadelphia, 44; park extension begins, 44; small parks, 44, 54; proposed arrangement of new parks, 44; park area relative to population, 44; park circuits, 45; recommendations of Special Park Commission, 46; development of suburban railway service, 46; need for outlying parks, 47; compared with London, 48; opportunities for large parks, 50; development of Lake front, 50; yachting, 52; Chicago made largely by the railroads, 61; problem of freight traffic, 61; necessity for revising transportation facilities, 62; only goods to be consumed in city should

159

Chicago—*Continued.*
enter therein, 63; a traffic clearing house proposed, 64; railway and water traffic compared, 64; relief from congestion of traffic, 65; harbors, 65; tunnel system, 65; a loop system, 66; excursion piers, 68; circuits for freight and passenger traffic, 68; passenger stations, 70, 71; locations of passenger stations, 72, 112; street-car loop system, 73; extension of business area, 74; suburban passenger traffic, 74; mail service, 76; ideal nature of proposed transportation system, 78; natural features of Chicago, 79; how effective results may be obtained, 80; needs of the growing city, 80; adequate circulation and sufficient park area essential, 80; cost of postponing improvements in circulation system, 81; report on street paving, 83; existing diagonals, 84; location of the city, 89; advantages of rectilinear street system, 89; circular avenues, 90; necessity for platting outlying district, 91; preserving width of existing avenues, 92; circuit arteries suggested, 92; avenues paralleling railways, 94; diversion of traffic from the business center, 95; proposed circuits, 95-96; encroachments on the river, 97; treatment of river banks, 97, 112; widening of streets, 97; requisites for area outside the business center, 98; the heart of Chicago, 99; spread of population, 99; disposition of traffic within the business center, 99; Michigan Avenue the base-line of the city, 100; width of streets, 100; bridge at Michigan Avenue, 105; expenditures for permanent improvements, 107; the improvement of Halsted Street, 107; slums of the city, 108; Berlin an example for housing conditions, 109; opportunity for comprehensive treatment of the central portion of the city, 110; development of Grant Park, 110; economy and effectiveness of group-plan for Grant Park, 111; a yacht harbor, 111; gifts by citizens should be encouraged, 112; Congress Street as the grand axis, 113; reasons for choice of Congress Street for grand axis, 113, 114; the civic center, 115; buildings composing civic center, 115, 116; dome of civic center, 116, 118; Federal group of buildings, 117; increase in real estate values, 119; raising street levels, 120; creation of the park system, 120; purification of Lake Michigan, 120; cost of World's Fair, 120; cultivation of the fine arts, 120; influence of the universities, 120; taxing powers, 153.

City-planning, begins in Paris, 13; in Europe, 19; French and German theories, 20.

Civic Center of Chicago, buildings comprising, 115; location of, 115; architecture of, 117; dome of, 118; cost of, 123; power of park commissioners to acquire land for, 134.

Civil Law, unifying force of, 31.

Cleanliness, a necessity for the city, 82.

Cleveland, Ohio, group plan for, 27, cost of improvements in, 27.

Club houses for the people, 44.

Colbert, one of the Paris planners, 15, 20.

Commerce, governing motive in location of cities, 9; beginning of in Europe, 13; expansion of, 19; makes art creations possible, 22.

Commercial Club, undertakes plan of Chicago, 1; designs for Lake Front improvement presented to, 6; consolidates with Merchants' Club, 7; carries on work for plan of Chicago, 7; meetings of, 7; discussion of good roads, 39 (note).

Condemnation, limitations on the right of, 128; congested areas, power to open, 151.

Congress of the Confederation, 31.

Congress Street, should be developed as central axis of city, 113; width of, 114; its relation to Grant Park, 115.

Cook County, creates outer belt Commission, 44; County building part of the civic center group, 116; attempt to organize a forest-preserve district, 132; limited powers of, 134; taxation in, 152.

Courtland, 40.

Courts, building for, 116.

Crerar, John, endows Crerar Library, 109.

Crerar Library, 108, 114, 120.

Crown Point, 40.

Calumet Feeder, 55.

Calumet River, importance of harbor, 57.

Canal Street, location of railway stations on, 107; widening of, 113;

Cathedral, the, embodied the highest expression of civic art, 13.

Cedar Lake, 40.

Cemeteries, Roman, 12; characteristics of modern, 36.

Century Magazine, quoted, 21, (note.)

Charles River, Mass., improvement of, 49.

Charleston, 9.

Chicago Avenue, traffic on, 116, 117;

Chicago Heights, 40.

Chicago Ridge, 41.

Chicago River, forests along, 56; improvement of, 97; treatment of the banks, 116.

Chicago University, 51, 120, 121.

China, opening of, 33.

Christianity, unifying force of, 31.

Churches, usually not architecturally important, 36.

City, the, formless growth of neither economical nor satisfactory, 1; overcrowding and congestion of traffic paralyzes vital functions of, 1; complicated problems of not beyond control of pubic sentiment, 1; efforts to bring about best conditions of life in, 1; parks the lungs of, 12; strain of life in, 32; opportunities for the ambitious, 33; needs adequate circulation and sufficient park area, 80; needs created by increase in population, 81; reasons for growth of population, 81; general character of, 82. 87.

D

Danube, the, 110, 116.

Darmstadt, 20.

Defense, governing motive in location of cities, 9.

De Kalb, 40, 47.

Department of State, facilitates work on plan of Chicago, 7.

Des Plaines River, scenery along, 40; beauty of, 55, 90,91.

Der Städtebau, magazine, 21, (note).

Dewey, Stoddard, on foreign money spent in Paris, 19.

Diagonals necessity for, 84; function of, 91; those proposed for Chicago, 92.

Diodorus, his description of Babylon, 10.

District of Columbia, L'Enfant plan extended over the entire District, 25; plan of, 91.(See also Washington, D. C.)

Douglas Park, 44.

Drainage Canal, 55; cost of, 120.

Dresden, 20, 110, 116.

Driveways, extent of proposed, 58.

Dundee, 40.

Du Page County, 55.

Du Page River, 40.

E

Eagle Lake, 40.

Education, unifying force of in the Northwest, 32.

Edwards, Percy J., his history of London street improvements, 21, (note).

Egypt, defended by deserts, 10; pyramids and temples of, 10.
Electric railways bind outlying towns to central city, 42; promote neighborliness, 42.
Elgin, 40.
Eliot, President, Charles W., quoted, 123.
Ellis Park, 43.
Elmhurst, 40.
Eminent domain, exercise of power of, 129, 140, 141, 142; right to take more than necessary lands, 144, 151.
England, beginning of national life in, 13; growth of commerce, 19; housing schemes, 21, 128; town planning, 21, 22, 34; holds Northwestern posts after the Revolution, 31; roads, 39; regulation of advertising, 127.
Epping Forest, 48.
Evanston, 40, 50.
Evergreen Park, 56.
Euphrates River, tunnel under, 10.
Europe, national life begins in, 13; changes in cities, 19, 22.

F

Federal Building in Chicago, 117.
Ferguson Monument Fund, 121.
Field, Marshall, gives Field Museum of Natural History to Chicago, 108.
Field Museum, the importance of, 108, 114; new building for, 114; location of, 121.
Fischer, Prof. Theodore, German city-builder, 21, (note).
Flag Creek, 55.
Florence, beauty and power of, 13, 20.
Folleston, 40.
Fontainebleau, Forest of, 48.
Foreign peoples in Chicago, 1.
Forest parks, 53, 131, 136.
Fort Dearborn, 115.
Fortifications, in relation to cities, 9; changed into boulevards, 90.
Fountains, location of, 86.
Fox River, 40.
France, beginning of national life in, 13; leads the world in art and taste, 19; improvement of cities, 19; roads, 39.
Franco-Prussian war, improvements in European cities since, 19.
Frankfort-on-the-Main, 20.
Franklin, Benjamin, his connection with the Northwest, 31.

G

Ganges River, 10.
Garfield Park, 44.
Gary, 40, 58.
Geneva, 40.
Genoa, 40.
German city improvements, nature of, 20; modification of French system, 20; aim of to produce variety and interest, 20; in Frankfort-on-the-Main, 20; advertising regulations, 127.
Germany, beginning of National Life in, 13.
Germany, effect of peace on, 19; magnitude of the city-planning movement in, 21 (note); municipal expositions, 21, (note).
Gibbs Woods, 54.
Gifts by public-spirited citizens, advantage of to a city, 110, 116.
Glencoe, entrance to park system at, 54, 55.
Glenview Golf Club, 55.
Good Roads, economic effects of, 42. (See also highways.)

Governor of Illinois inspects work on plan of Chicago, 7.
Government, enlarged participation of people in, 1.
Grade crossings of railroads, 71.
Grant Park, improvement of, 6, 44, 52; proposed treatment of, 108; grouping of buildings in, 109, 114, 115; intellectual center of Chicago, 116.
Grant, Gen. U. S., embodiment of the spirit of the Middle West, 32.
Great Lakes, 32.
Griffith, 40.
Gurlitt, Cornelius, as to German city-planning, 20, 21.

H

Hainault Forest, London, 48.
Hall of Records, 116.
Halstead Street, longest business street in the world, 106. treatment of, 106; known as the king of streets, 106; 117.
Hamburg, 20.
Hammond, 40.
Hampton Court, England, 48.
Harbors, in Chicago, 65, 68.
Harlem, 55.
Hartford, improvement of, 29.
Harvard Medical School, location of, 115.
Harvey, 40.
Haussmann, George Eugene, becomes prefect of the Seine, 17; his place as a city builder, 18; builds on the foundations laid by Louis XIV., 18; character of his work, 18; cost of his improvements, 19; imitation of, 19.
Heart of Chicago, the, 99, 110 (see also Business Center).
Henley, regattas at, 48.
Highways, necessity for adequate, 38; commercial advantages of, 38; along railways, 41, 94; drainage of, 41; proposed system of, 121; cost of creating, 121 (see also Roads).
Hill, James J., predicts future population of Chicago, 33; on improvement of railway terminals, 62.
Hinsdale, 40.
Hobart, 40.
Holidays, necessity of caring for crowds on, 88.
Housing conditions in England, 21; in Chicago, 113, 141.
Hudson Palisades, improvement of, 38.
Humboldt Park, 44.
Hungary, 19.
Hunt, Richard M., presents plan for Administration building at World's Fair, 6 (note).

I

Illinois, good roads in, 39; park legislation, 44, 127; tendency toward city life in, 47; constitutional limitations on improvements, 128.
Illinois Central Railway, 52.
India, 10.
Indian country of North America, settlement of, 9.
Indiana, coöperation of, 130.
Indians in the Northwest, 31.
Irrigation of western lands, 33.
Italy, 13, 19.

J

Jackson Park, site of World's Columbian Exposition, 6; 44, 53.

Japan, opening of, 33.
Jay, John, pertinacity of on behalf of the Northwest, 31.
Jefferson Park, 43.
Jefferson, Thomas, aids L'Enfant in planning Washington, 23, 25.
Joliet, 40.
Johnson, A. N., Illinois State Highway Commissioner, as to good roads, 39 (note).
Juniper, suitable for lake-shore planting, 38.

K

Kankakee, 40.
Kankakee River, 40.
Kansas City, improvement of, 29.
Kenilworth, 130.
Kenosha, 39, 40, 47.
Kew Gardens, 48.

L

La Crosse, 40.
Lagoons, along Lake Front, 52.
Lake Calumet, 55; park reservations near, 57.
Lake Forest University, 120.
Lake Front, improvement of suggested by World's Columbian Exposition, 6; testimony as to advantages of to Chicago, 6; progress of plan for, 6; favored by press, 7; of right belongs to the people, 50; to be made from city waste, 50, 122; improvement of, 122; legislation for improvements, 137, 138.
Lake Michigan, driveway along shore of, 38; beauty of, 50; boating on, 51; treatment of shores, 53.
Lake Zurich, 40, 60.
Lanciani, L., his description of ancient Rome, 13.
La Porte, 40.
La Salle Street, improvement of, 107, 113.
L'Enfant, Peter Charles, makes plan of Washington, 23, 49, 91.
Le Nôtre, plans of for Paris, 15.
Libertyville, 40.
Lincoln Park, 43, 44, 135, 136.
Lincoln, Abraham, embodiment of the spirit of the Middle West, 34; Saint-Gaudens' statue of, 112.
Little Calumet River, 55.
London, physical conditons in, 14; street changes, 20; cost of delaying improvements in, 21; opportunities offered by the Great Fire of 1666, 21; Sir Christopher Wren's plan of, 21; cost of recent improvements in, 21; cost of proposed new thoroughfares, 21; suburbs, 34; police jurisdiction, 37; rehousing of working people, 37, 107, 128; recreation grounds, 48; monuments, 80; housing conditions, 113; treatment of Thames, 116; influence of National Gallery and British Museum, 116.
London Traffic Commission, plan for diminishing congestion, 21.
Louisburg, Cape Breton, a fortified city, 9.
Louis XIV., of France, plan of Paris, 14; his plan a model in Europe, 19; 22, 87, 91.
Louis Phillippe, finished Arc de Triomphe, 17.
Los Angeles, Cal., expenditure for roads, 39 (note).
Lutetia, original name of Paris, 14.

M

Mackinac, defenses of, 9.
Mail service of Chicago, 76.
Manhattan, 40.
Manilla, improvement of, 29
Manufacturers, buildings for, 86.

Marengo, 40.
Massachusetts, good roads in, 39 (note); metropolitan park commission, 131.
Maysville, 40.
McHenry, 40.
Media, 10.
Merchants' Club, Lake Front Improvements presented to, 7; arranges for complete plan of Chicago, 7; consolidates with Commercial Club, 7.
Metropolitan Art Museum, New York, 115.
Michigan Avenue, the base line of Chicago, 100; traffic on, 100; proposed improvement of, 100; grades of, 102; elevation of, 103; necessity for open spaces, 115, 117; the city has power to improve, 136.
Michigan City, 40, 47.
Middle Ages, conditions prevailing among European cities. 19, 31.
Middle West, limits of, 31; Chicago the metropolis of, 31; its distinct history, 31; extent of, 32; navigable waters of, 32; phenomenal growth of, 32; meaning of term, 33.
Milan, 20, 90.
Miller, John S., on maintenance and repair of Chicago streets, 83.
Millington, 40.
Milwaukee, 38.
Minneapolis, improvement of, 28.
Mississippi Valley, development of, 33.
Mobile, 9.
Momence, 40.
Monee, 40.
Morgan, J. Pierpont, president of the American Scenic and Historic Preservation Society, gift of, 38 (note).
Morris, 40.
Mt. Forest, 55.
Music in Chicago, 34, 120.

N

Nantasket Beach, Boston, bathing at, 38.
Napierville, good roads in, 39.
Napoleon Bonaparte, his belief in and work for Paris, 15, 17; suggests improvements for London, 21.
Napoleon III., transformation of Paris under, 17.
Natural forces applied to industry, effects of, 19.
Natural scenery, desirability of for city workers, 53.
Newberry Library, 120.
New Orleans, 9.
New York, rapid growth of, 1; defenses of, 9; civic improvement in, 27; railway congestion at, 62; Riverside Drive, 116; Metropolitan Museum of Art, 109, 116; sudden expansion of, and waste of money in, 153.
Newspapers of Chicago, 34.
Nile, the, 10.
Niles, 40.
Noises, 74.
North Western University, 51, 120.
Norton, Prof. Charles Eliot, his characterization of Venice, 13.
Nuisances, 141.

O

O'Day, Edward, editor of plan for San Francisco, 28 (note).
Ohio River, 32.
O'Meara, Dr. Barry E., his talks with Napoleon, 21.
Ordinance of 1787, 31.
Orient, rapid growth of cities in the, 1.
Outer belt of parks, scheme for, 7; Commission for, 41, 52; 121; cost of, 123; legislation for, 130, 133.

P

Pacific Coast, commercial development of, 33.
Palisades of the Hudson, commission for, 38.
Pallisades of the Potomac, 49.
Palos, 56.
Panama Canal, influence of on growth of Chicago, 33
Parks, economic effects of 51; character of, 54.
Paris, first modern city, 14; has reached the highest state of civic development, 14; origin of, 14; growth the result of commerce, 14; plans of Louis XIV., 14; new portions of laid out in vacant places, 14; 23; congestion of population, 15; grows according to a well-considered plan, 15; improvements of Napoleon I., 15; a center of commerce, 17; first sidewalks in, 17; the quays, 17; commemorative monuments 17; plans of Napoleon III., 17; transformations wrought by Haussmann, 17; grouping of railway stations, 18; compared with Chicago, 18; cost of Haussmann's improvements, 19; civic pride, 19; amount of foreign money spent in, 19; Wren anticipates features of Paris plan, 21, 54; parks, 48, 54, 87, 90, 91, 94, 108; treatment of Seine, 116; influence of the Louvre, 116; commerical advanages of improvements, 124; condemnation of land in, 128.
Paving, report of Commercial Club Committee on street paving in Chicago, 83.
Peace, results of in Europe since 1872, 19.
Pennsylvania Railroad, improvement of station buildings, 77.
People, increased participation of in government, 1; determination to secure better conditions of life, 2.
Pericles, character of his work, 11.
Perkins, Dwight Heald, compiles report of the Special Park Commission, 44.
Persia, 10.
Peterson Woods, 54.
Philadelphia, improvements in, 28; park system, 44.
Philippine Islands, plans for summer capital in, 29.
Pittsburg, railway congestion at, 62.
Place de la Concorde, Paris, 15.
Place de l'Etoile, Paris, 15.
Place Vendome, Paris, 15, 87.
Plainfield, 40.
Plan of the City, necessity for, 1; impossibility of perfection in, 2; real test of is in its application, 2; not an expense but a measure of economy, 4; insures orderly growth, 4.
Planting, for Lake Shore drive, 38; winter effects should be studied, 78.
Play grounds, need of, 35, 45, on Lake Front, 51.
Pleasant Prairie, 40.
Plutarch, his description of the works of Pericles, 11.
Poles, disfigurement of streets by, 84.
Police Headquarters, part of the civic center group, 116.
Police power, extent of, 128, 140.
Population, density of in Chicago, 48, 115.
Post-office, 68, 76; new building for, 117.
Potomac Park, Washington, 49.
Potomac, treatment of banks of, 110.
President's House, (White House) the, 23.
Providence, R. I., improvement of, 28.
Public Health Department, 116.
Public Libraries, 35.
Public Library, possible location for in Grant Park, 114.
Public Schools, 35.
Public service plans for heating, lighting and power, 76.
Public Works, department of, 115.
Pullman, 58.
Pyramids of Gizeh, 10.

Q

Quebec, a fortified city, 9.

R

Railway stations, treatment of, 36, 42; in Europe, 70; embellishment of, 77; grouping of on Canal and Twelfth Streets, 110, 116.
Railways, dependence of Chicago on, 61; congestion of traffic, 62; necessity for improved terminals, 62; necessity of combination among to secure Chicago terminals, 62, 121; electrification of, 106; cost of scheme for terminals, 122 (see also Transportation).
Real Estate Board of Chicago, report of on Michigan Avenue, 101.
Recreation piers, 68, 115.
Residence streets, 84, 91.
Revere Beach, bathing at, 38, 49.
Richmond Park, near London, 48.
Ringstrasse, the, Vienna, 20.
River Forest, 55.
Riverside, 40, 55.
Riverside Drive, New York, 110.
Rivers, transformation of banks of, 116.
Riviera, the, 51.
Roads, John Alvord's paper on, 39 (note); in Buena Park, 39; from Versailles to Chartier, 39; English and French roads, 39; value of good roads to the community, 39; in Los Angeles, 39; in Illinois, 39; an adjunct of Chicago life, 40.
Roanoke, Va., improvement of, 29.
Robey, 41.
Rogers Park, 130.
Roman Law, unifying force of, 13.
Rome, growth of, 1; possessed elements that characterize the modern city, 11; parks and gardens of, 12; rejuvenation of, 13; baths, 13; the Forum, 13, 117, 20; suburbs, 34; aqueducts, 72; railway stations, 87.
Royal British Institute of Architects, 21 (note).
Rouen, 90.
Rue de la Paix, Paris, 15.
Rue de Rivoli, Paris, opened by Napoleon, 15

S

Sag Valley, 56.
Saint-Gaudens, Augustus, opinion of architect's meeting for the World's Fair, 6 (note); statue of Lincoln, 112.
Salt Creek, 55.
Sandwich, 40.
San Francisco, comprehensive plan for, 28.
Scheldt, the, 110.
Schools, location of on highways, 39; 98.
Seattle, improvement of, 29.
Seine, the, 51, 110.
Senate Park Commission, the, (Daniel H. Burnham, Charles Follin McKim, Augustus Saint-Gaudens, Frederick Law Olmstead, Jr.) makes plan for park system of the District of Columbia, 25; opposition to plan of, 25; members of the commission also planners of World's Columbian Exposition, 25.
Semiramis, queen of Babylon, the first city builder, 10.
Shaw, Albert, as to cost of delays in London planning, 21.
Shade, advantages of in city, 84.
Shelby, 40.
Sherman Farm, 56.
Sheridan Road, 39 (note), 57.

Sidewalks, first in Paris built by Napoleon I., 17.
Sienna, beauty and power of, 13.
Sistine Madonna, 112.
Slavery excluded from the North West territory, 31.
Slums of Chicago, 106, 129.
Smith, Edward R., on the transformation of Paris, 18.
Smoke, 71, 77, 112.
Sorbonne, the, Paris, 114.
South Chicago, 51, 52, 53.
South Park Commissioners suggest improvement of Lake Front, 6; meeting of on Lake Front improvements, 6; arrangement for Grant park, 114; 134.
South Parks, expansion of, 7, 44.
Special Park Commission, plan of Metropolitan Park system, 7, 44; report of, 46.
Spirit of Chicago, the, 8.
Sport Park at Stockholm, 52.
Spring Forest, 55.
Square of the Innocents, Paris, transformation of, 93.
St. Charles, 40.
St. Louis, plan for improvement of, 28.
St. Paul's Cathedral, London, 21.
St. Paul, Minn., improvement of, 28.
St. Peter's Cathredral, Rome, 116.
Statues, location of, 86.
Stĕubben, German city-builder, 21 (note).
Stockholm, yachting at, 52.
Stony Creek, 55.
Street plan of Chicago, cost of, 123.
Streets, the desirable width of, 83; regulation of traffic on, 88.
Submerged lands granted for park purposes, 44.
Suburban highways, commission for, 39.
Suburbs, apt to be ugly and squalid, 35; when attractive, 34; connections among, 38; residents of concerned with city communication, 41; railway stations in, 77.
Summit, 55.
Sweden, yachting of, 52.
Swimming, exhibition of at Stockhom, 52.
Sycamore, 40.

T

Taxation, limitations on power of, 129, 151.
Terminal railway passenger stations in Chicago, 68.
Territory Northwest of the Ohio River, conquered by Virginia troops, 31; retained as first territorial acquisition, 31; diplomacy, 31; endowed with freedom and popular education, 31.
Thames, the, London, the embankment a part of Wren's plan, 21 (note); use of the river on Sunday, 48, 51; treatment of the banks, 110.
Thatchers Park, 55.
Thoroughfares, improvement of, 37.
Tigris River, 10.
Town-planning in England, 21, 34, 128.
Townships, powers of in suburban development, 130.
Trajan's Forum in Rome, cost of, 13.
Transportation system for Chicago, suggested, 61-76; legislation necessary for, 139.
Treaty of 1783, secures the Northwest, 31.
Trees along streets, 84.
Tuileries, gardens of the, 15.
Twelfth Street, widening of, 110, 116, 117.

U

Union Park, 43.
United States, consuls furnish reports on civic improvements, 7; offices in Chicago, 117, constitutional limitations on city planning, 127.

V

Valparaiso, 40.
Venice, a commercial city, 13; canals of, 15; St. Mark's Square, 117.
Vernon Park, 43.
Versailles, 39; fountains, 49.
Vicksburg, 9.
Vienna as a center of activity, 19; follows example of Paris in planning, 20; parks, 49, 80, 90; boulevards, 94; treatment of the Danube, 116.
Virginia troops conquer the Northwest, 31.

W

Walled towns, 9.
Washington, D. C., planned as National Capital, 22; L'Enfant's plan, 23; city regarded as a unit, 23; comprehensive character of the original plan, 23; plan ridiculed, 23; effect of Civil War on the city, 23; extension of L'Enfant's plan, 23; plan of the Senate Park Commission, 23; Union Station, 71, 87; apartment houses, 88; ownership of front yards, 92; Potomac Quay, 116; influence of Library of Congress, 112.
Washington, George, directs L'Enfant in planning the Federal City, 23-25.
Washington Park, 44.
Washington Square, 43.
Waterhouse, Paul, observations on London improvements, 21 (note).
Waukegan, 38, 40.
Wealth, rapid increase of in modern times, 1, 19.
Wellsboro, 40.
West Park Commissioners, project for improvement of Lake Front presented to, 6, 134.
Wheaton, connected with Chicago by good road, 39.
White House, the, 29.
Williamsburg, Va., suggests features of plan of Washington, 29.
Wilmette, 38, 53, 130.
Wilmington, 40.
Wilmot, 40.
Windsor Great Park, 48.
Winnetka, 40, 122, 130.
Winter Sports, 52.
Wisconsin, coöperation of, 130.
Women's Club, Lake Front Improvement presented to, 6; Woodstock, 40.
World's Columbian Exposition of 1893, origin of plan of Chicago traced to, 4; the beginning of orderly arrangements of public buildings and grounds, 4; results of, 6; suggests improvements of Lake Front, 6; spirit in which conceived, 6; architects present plans for, 6 (note); reasons for success of, 6; effect of on Washington plans, 25; impressiveness of Peristyle, 109; cost of, 120; indicated appreciation of good order and municipal beauty, 120.
Working classes, English schemes for housing, 21.
Wren, Sir Christopher, his plan of London anticipates certain features of Paris designs, 21; plan of Annapolis, similar to his plan of London, 29.

Y

Yacht harbor, on lake front, 52, 109, 115.
Yachting on Lake Michigan, 52.

Z

Zoological Park, Washington, 49.

ENGRAVED AND PRINTED FOR THE
COMMERCIAL CLUB OF CHICAGO, IN THE
YEAR NINETEEN HUNDRED AND NINE,
BY R. R. DONNELLEY & SONS COMPANY,
AT THE LAKESIDE PRESS, CHICAGO